AF252011

SETH RANDAL

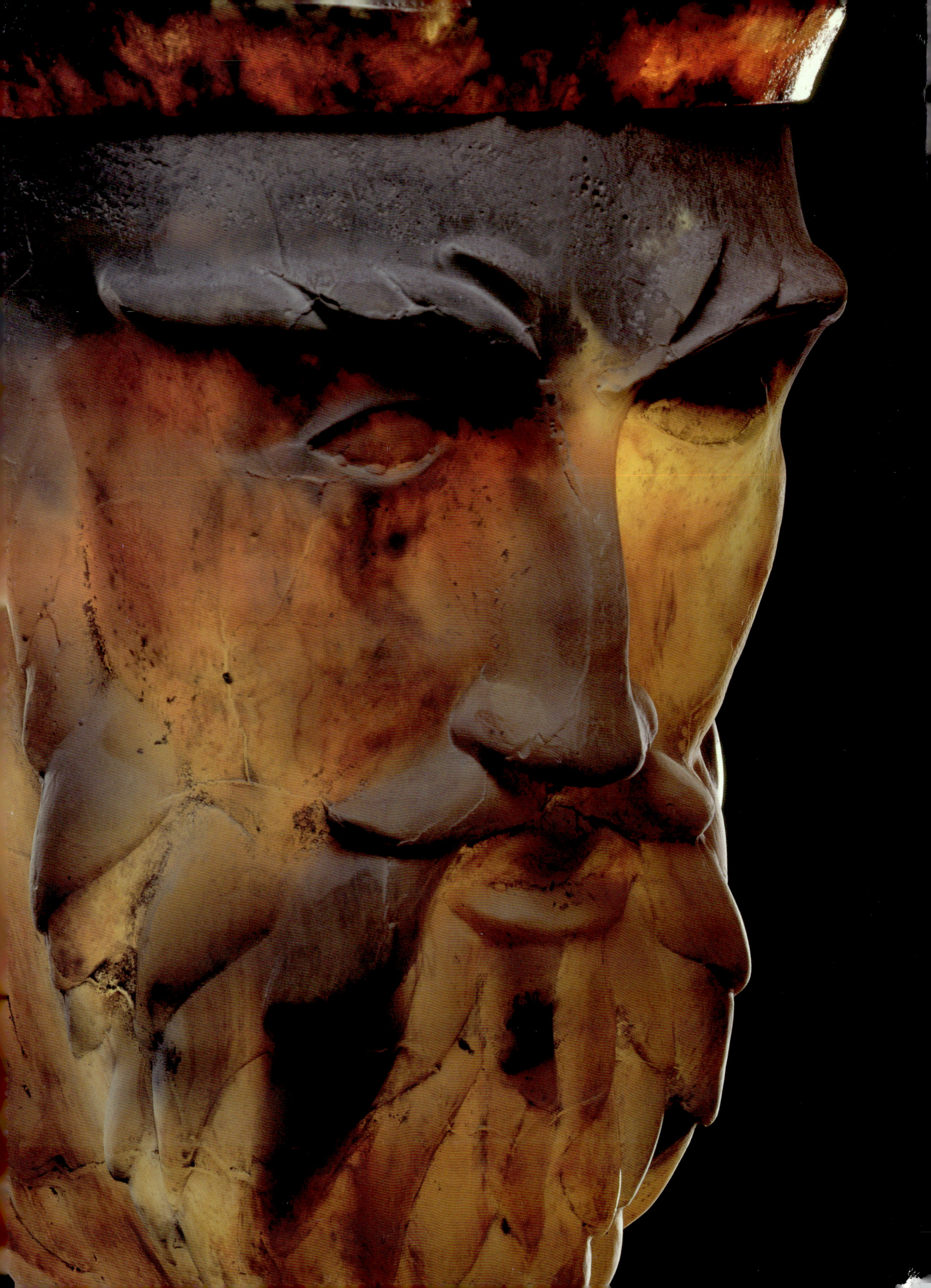

SETH RANDAL
MYTH AND MAJESTY

Jo Lauria

MARQUAND BOOKS, INC., SEATTLE

in association with

UNIVERSITY OF WASHINGTON PRESS

SEATTLE   LONDON

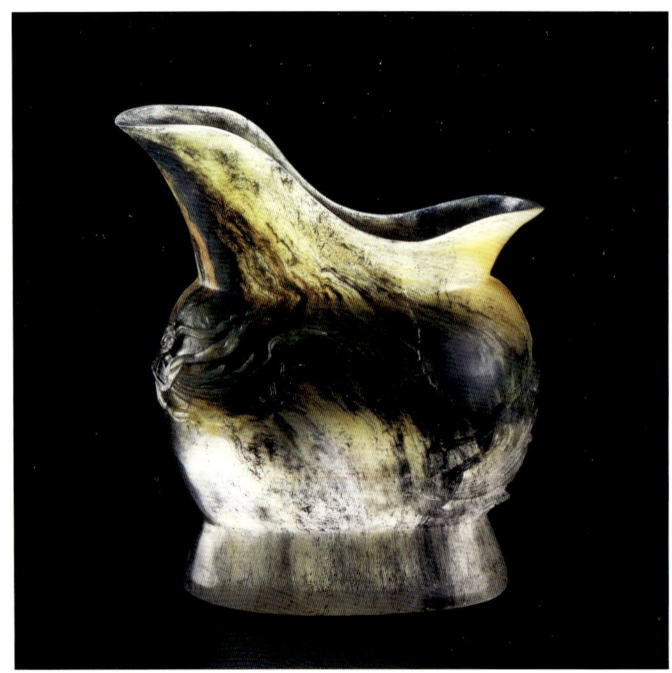

The Spirit of Giving, 1992

Library of Congress Control Number:
   2002104700
ISBN 0-295-98268-3

∞ The paper used in this publication meets
the minimum requirements of the American
National Standard for Information Sciences—
Permanence of Paper for Printed Library
Materials, ANSI z39.48-1984.

Distributed by
University of Washington Press
P.O. Box 50096
Seattle, WA 98145-5096

All artwork by Seth Randal unless otherwise
noted. Dimensions given in inches, in the
order height × diameter × width (unless otherwise noted).

Frontispiece: *Renaissance Man*, 1997 (detail, p. 97)
Pages 113–19: Photography by Seth Randal

Designed by John Hubbard
Edited by Thomas Frick
Color separations by iocolor, Seattle
Printed and bound by CS Graphics Pte., Ltd.,
Singapore

CONTENTS

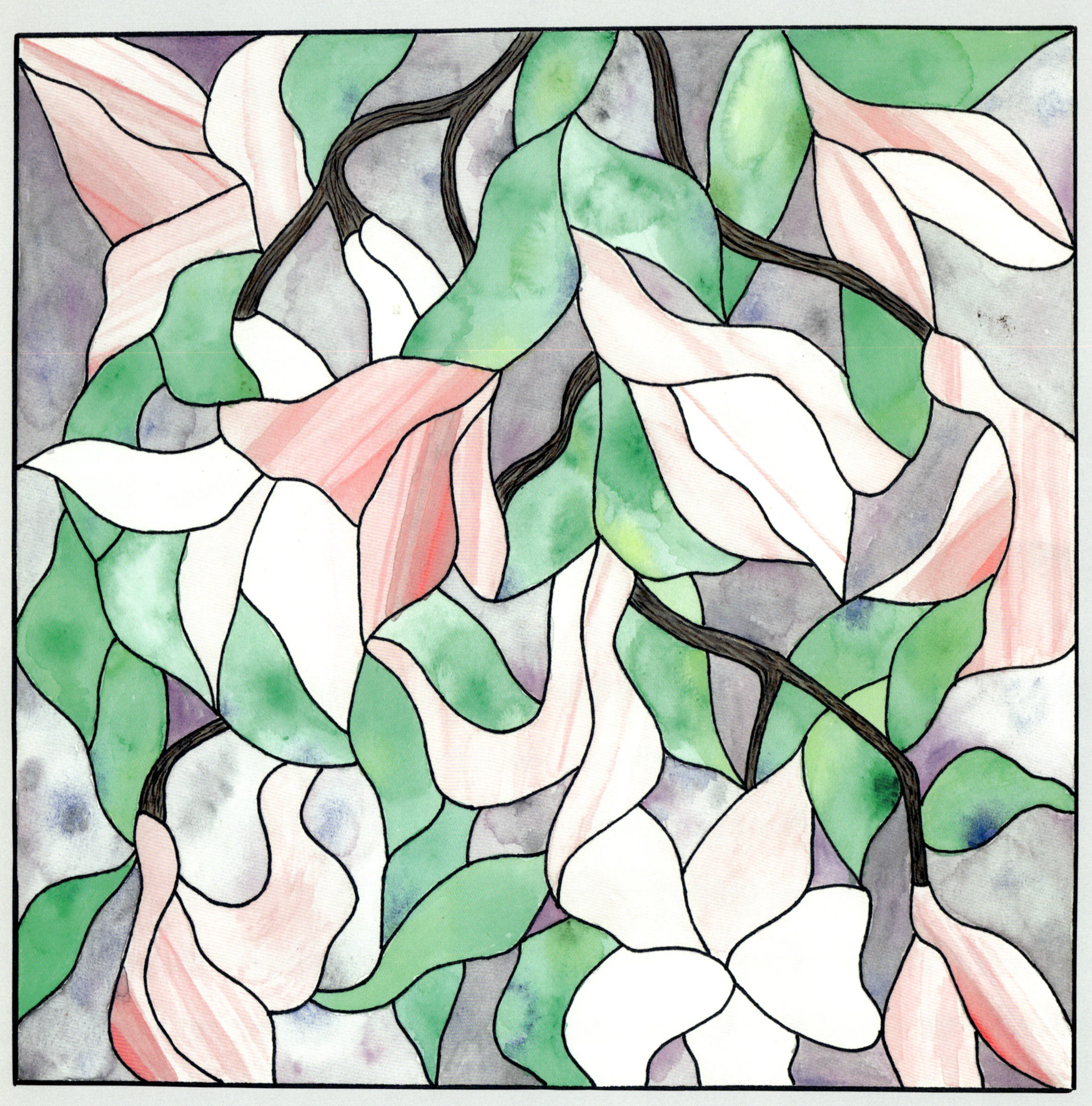

ILLUMINATION AND INSPIRATION

In my beginning is my end.

—T. S. Eliot

Seth Randal has traveled a meandering creative path on the way to discovering his vocation and abiding passion, the fabrication of exquisite sculptural works in glass. His evolution as an artist is a continuing celebration of that mysterious medium, which can be both dazzling and elusive, fragile and impervious, ubiquitous and utterly distinctive.

As an American youth growing up in England in the 1970s, Randal fell under the twin spells of the performing and the visual arts. The metropolis of London provided many opportunities for engagement in both areas. In the mid-1970s, alongside his involvement in the theater world, he entered the Sir John Cass Academy of Art at London Polytechnic. There he studied jewelry, metalsmithing, and the lapidary arts. Subsequently he enrolled in London's Royal College of Art.

Randal's interest in the decorative arts was inspired by an Art Nouveau exhibition at London's Victoria and Albert Museum. He was captivated by the intricate jewelry designs of the French artist René Lalique, especially his extraordinary fusion of material, technique, and form. Lalique's ability to create objects distinctive both for the beauty of their design and for the exactitude of their execution represented for Randal the highest form of accomplishment: the creation of a signature style.

In his classes and studio practice Randal expanded his awareness of the formal aspects of design—the refinement of color and line, the coordination of composition and technique—in order to develop a distinctive visual language. He wanted his designs, like those of Lalique, to embody precisely their individual artistic inspiration.

In 1978 Randal relocated to New York City, and again he was inspired by an art exhibition. This time it was *The Masterworks of Louis Comfort Tiffany*, a survey organized by art historian Alastair Duncan that featured the lighting fixtures and lamps

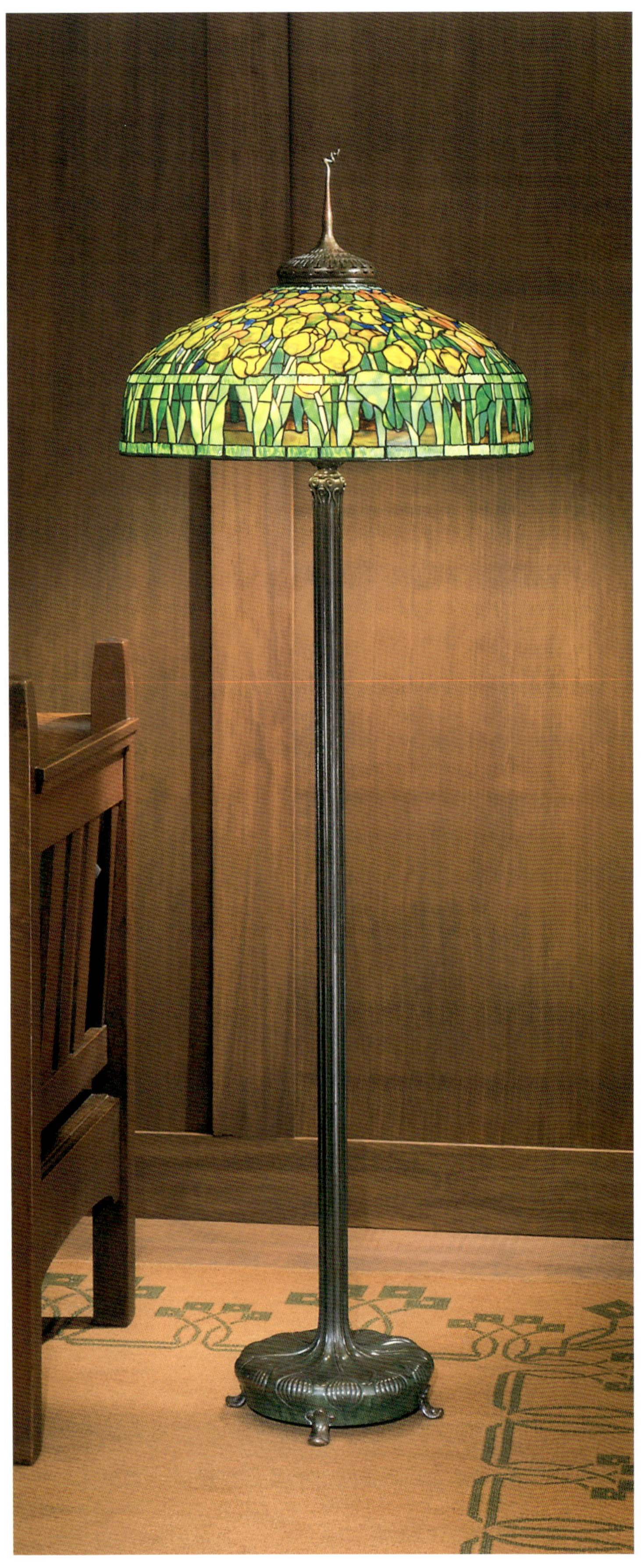

Louis Comfort Tiffany, *Tulip Floor Lamp*, circa 1905

of the renowned American designer. Tiffany's seductive creations fueled Randal's passionate search to find his own avenue of creative expression, and he began intensive research into the history of Tiffany Studios. In the process he acquired hands-on experience in the fabrication of leaded glass windows and lampshades. This quest for knowledge proved intoxicating, and the emulation of Tiffany's genius required his unswerving commitment.

He could not have chosen a better role model. Tiffany was the undisputed master of twentieth-century American art glass. His prodigious output included work in pottery, jewelry, metalwork, furniture, and textiles, but his enduring fame is the result of his innovations in glass-forming techniques and his invention of new types of glass coloration, surface treatments, and textures.

Tiffany was an avid admirer of the ancient and medieval glass he had seen while traveling through Europe and Morocco as a young man. During his journeys he assembled an impressive collection of ancient lustered vessels, especially Roman ones. Drawn to the pearly iridescence of Islamic and Roman glass (resulting from the combination of metallic oxides and decomposition)[1] and the luminous color gradations achieved by medieval stained-glass artists, Tiffany turned his creative energies to reproducing these qualities.

He established the Tiffany Glass and Decorating Company in 1879 to manufacture and market stained-glass windows, polychromatic leaded lamps, and other decorative objects. An integral part of Tiffany's company was an experimental workshop, where chemists tested formulas that would yield new glass colors and

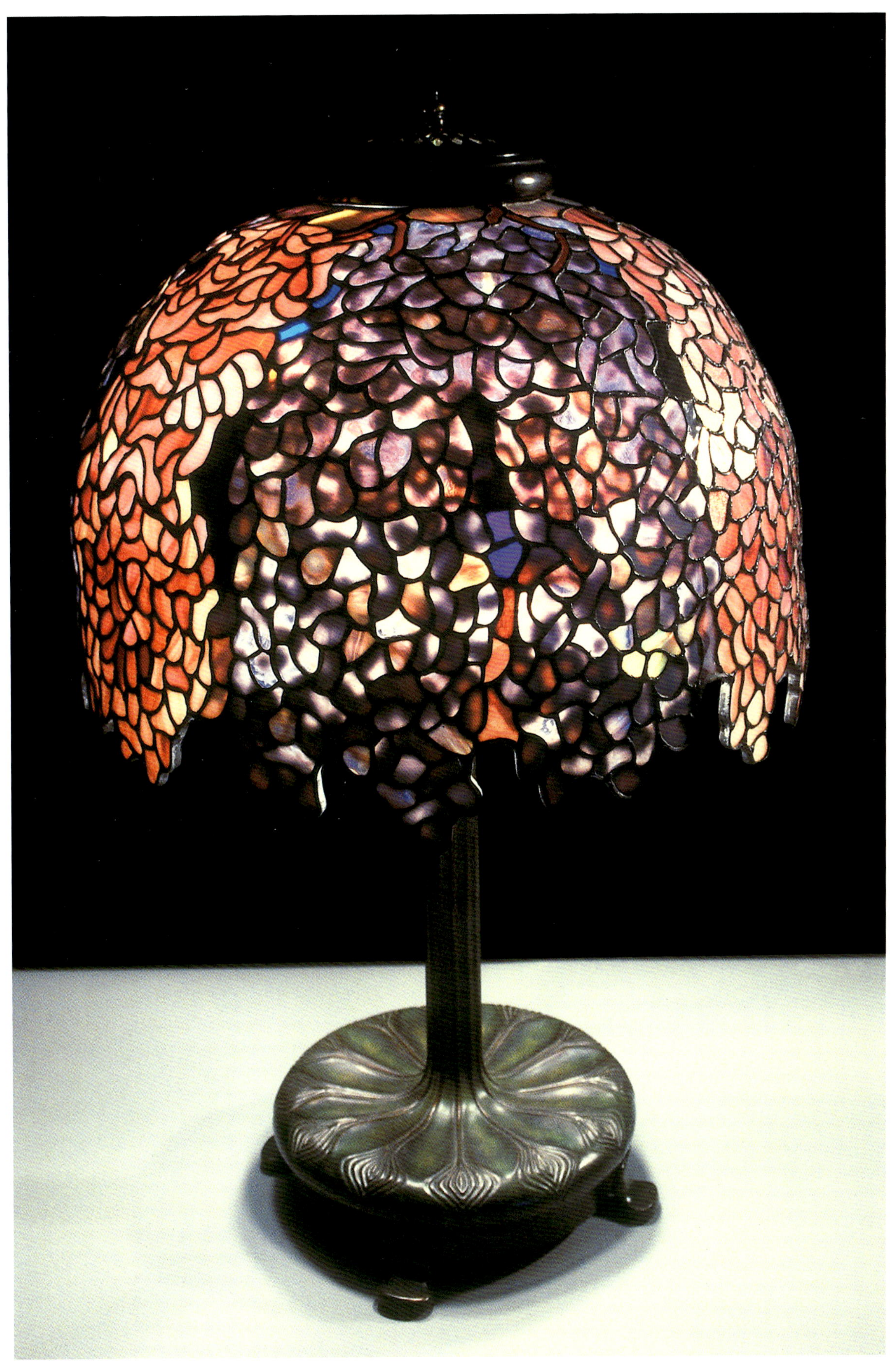

9

exploit the desired effects of iridescence and opalescence.[2] In 1880 Tiffany patented a type of iridescent glass that he called Favrile (a term derived from the word "fabrile," which means "pertaining to a craftsman or his craft").[3] Favrile closely imitated the shimmering glow and burnished surface of ancient glass. Produced in a variety of rich, lustrous colors, it became a Tiffany trademark and was used for all of his art-glass production.[4]

Tiffany's lighting fixtures as well are a testament to his technical achievements. Each leaded glass lampshade was a tour de force, combining elegant design, superb craftsmanship, and opulent materials. The shades exhibit a remarkable range of color schemes, variously incorporating transparent, translucent, semi-opaque, and opaque glass. They employ the modulated textures of fractured, drapery, confetti, and rippled handmade glass to suggest dappled sunlight, folded fabric, billowing clouds, waves, and withered leaves. Tiffany favored organic forms and motifs derived from nature, most notably patterns based on flowers, plants, and insects. Many of his lamps are titled by their identifying design, such as *The Magnolia*, *The Tulip*, and *The Butterfly*.

Having gained an understanding of the work of this protean genius, Randal began the process of translating Tiffany's uncompromising aesthetic vision and pioneering spirit into a personal strategy for working as a studio glass artist. He began humbly, learning the basics of stained and leaded glass fabrication through an adult education course in New York City. "Within weeks I transformed the second bedroom of my New York apartment into a small studio, learning by trial, imitation, and error," he recalls. "It was a challenging but rewarding time." Within two years he had achieved the proficiency necessary to establish his own firm in San Francisco, which undertook commercial and residential commissions for lighting fixtures and etched and leaded glass windows.

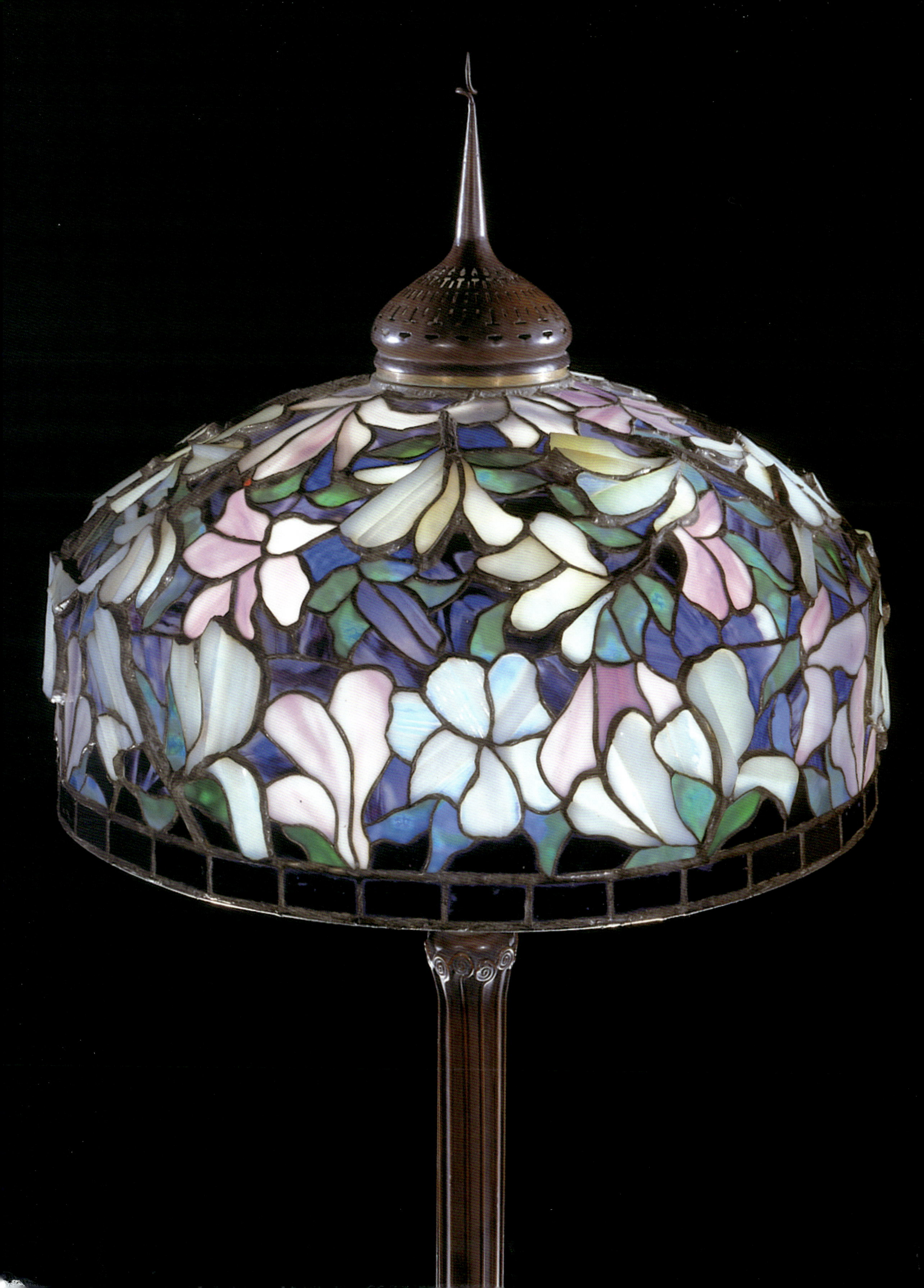

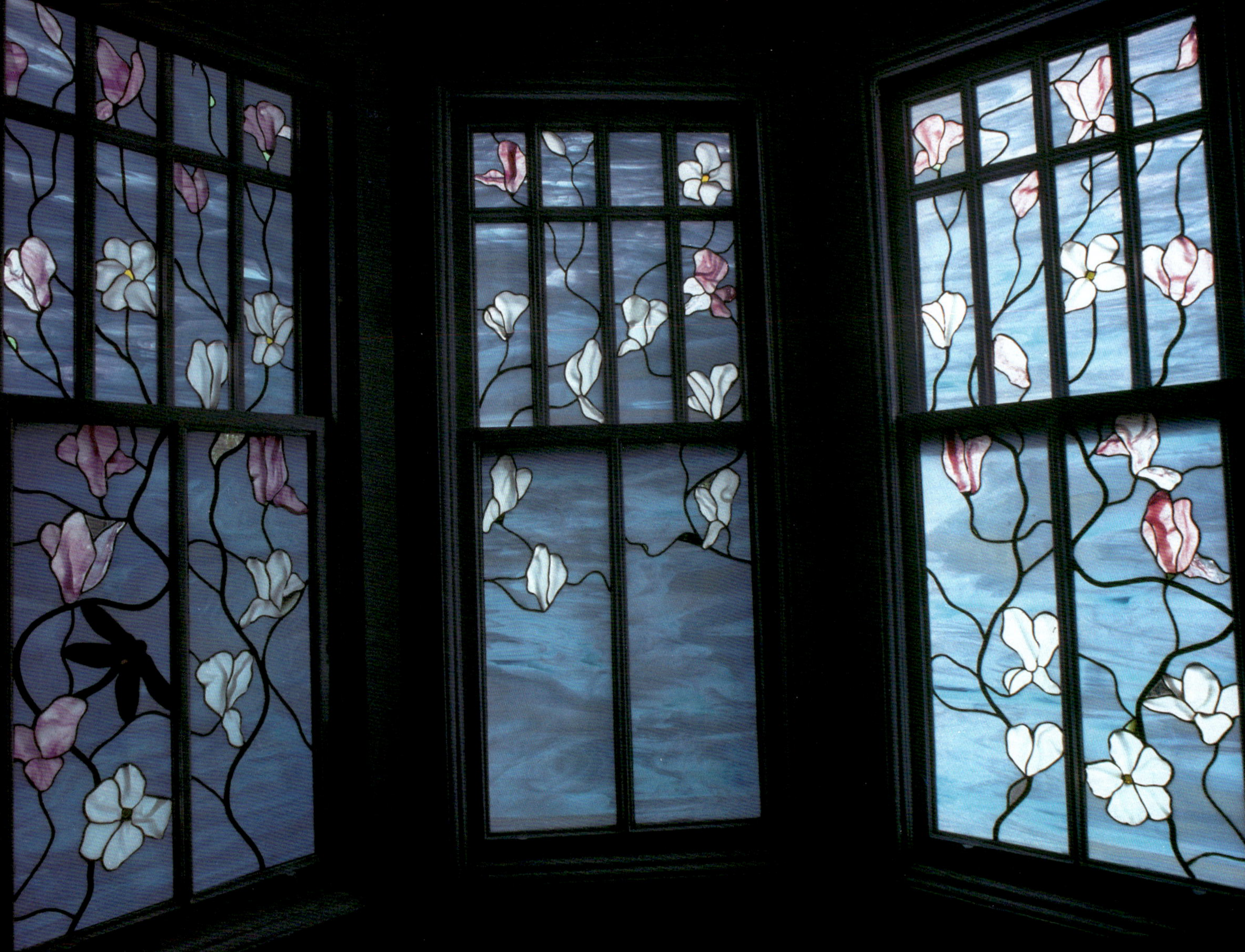

Like Tiffany, Randal was inspired by nature. His most compelling designs of this period were his floral fantasies, as realized in the *Magnolia Bay Windows* and in the schemes for the *Magnolia Floor Lamp* and *Wisteria Table Lamp*. *Magnolia Bay Windows* presented Randal with unique opportunities and challenges: "I was approached by a client who had a beautiful house just off Union Street in San Francisco. The view was south-facing, so the room was flooded with direct sunlight for most of the day. I knew the brilliant, changing light would have an important impact on the colors I chose. It happened to be springtime, and all the magnolia trees were in bloom. My sketches were inspired by the client's front garden, which had the most magnificent pink magnolia tree I'd ever seen.

"The house was quite old, and the windows had to be reinforced to accept the leaded glass. In the individual panels I placed small slivers of clear glass so my client could look onto the street below. The streaky blue background, which at first I thought might be overwhelming, proved just right, as the warm-toned sunlight provided a wonderful color balance."

These works orchestrate an operatic play of color, light, and texture. By using glass of differing densities and varying textures —striated, mottled, iridescent, opalescent, rippled—and strategically applying luminous glass cabochons, Randal created brilliant flowerscapes that float, swirl, and cascade in an ethereal atmosphere. With these objects he achieved the sensual abstraction inherent in Art Nouveau design, creating intensely personal pieces charged with the passion of that early period in his evolution.

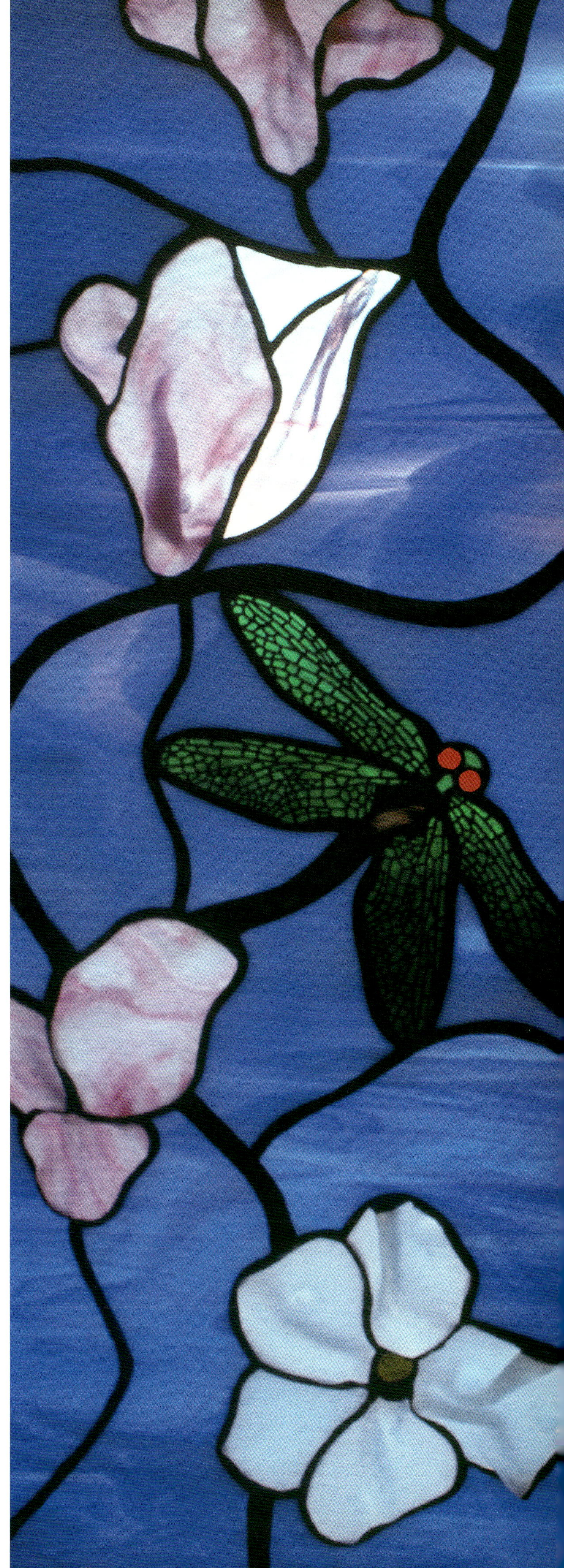

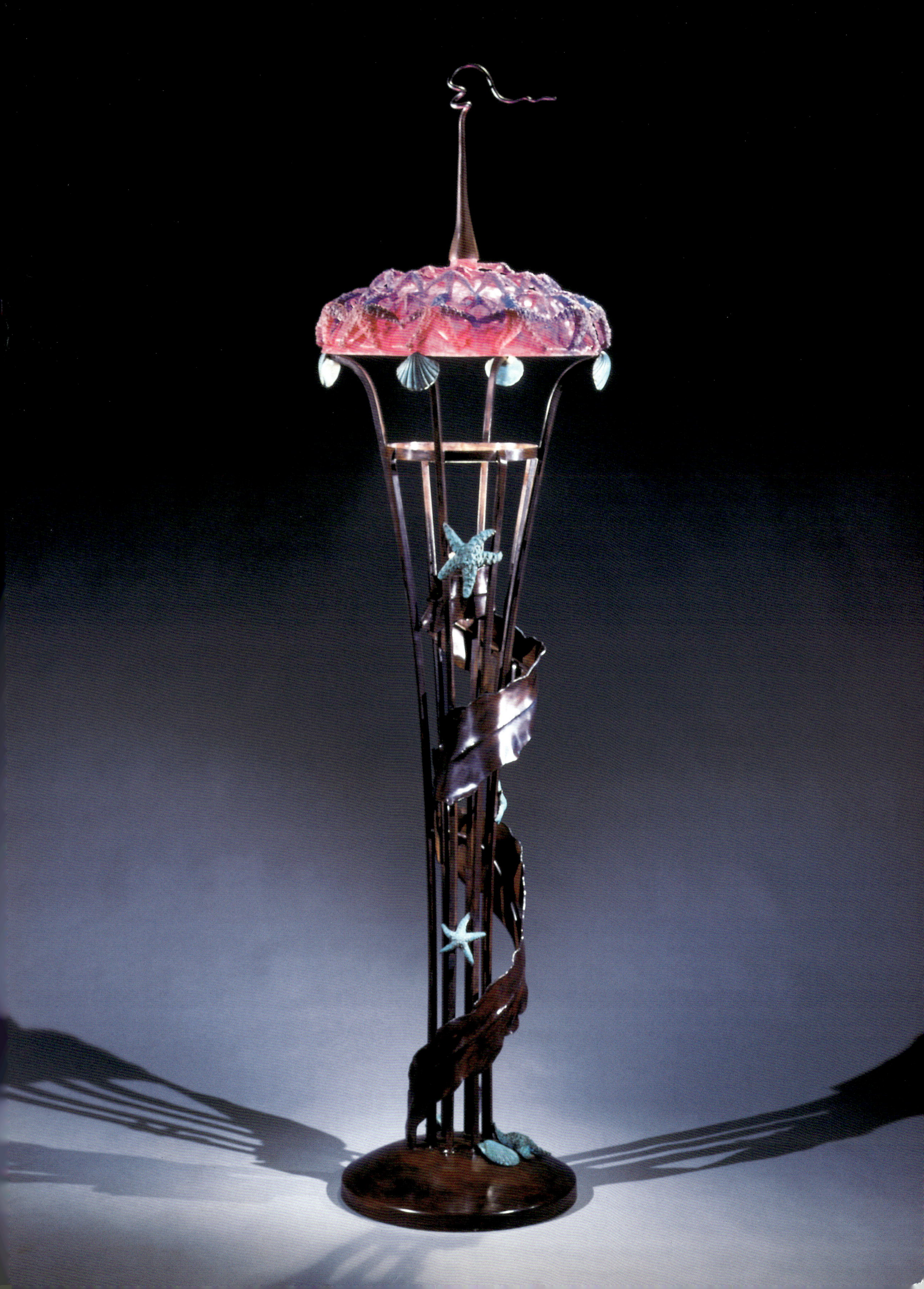

ART NOUVEAU
AND
THE CODEX OF NATURE

It's time to start living the life we've imagined.

—Henry James

Initially drawn to glass simply by its color and light, Randal came, through experience, to recognize that the medium could be a powerful conveyor of creative expression. In making this discovery he realized the limitations imposed by leaded and assembled glass: the entire process relied on predetermined patterns that were intrinsically graphic, not sculptural, and tied to a technique that was static, not spontaneous.

He knew that the colored and textured glass sheets that Tiffany used to execute his designs were handblown by skilled artisans under Tiffany's supervision. Up to this point Randal had worked exclusively with prefabricated sheets of decorative glass and had not engaged in the handcrafting of his materials. Impressed by the skill required to create Tiffany's glass sheets, he decided to expand his artistic repertoire. After three years of running a successful glass studio in San Francisco, he enrolled at the Parsons School of Design in New York City and moved there in 1983.

Characteristically, in his quest to work directly with glass Randal took an indirect route. He spent his first two years at Parsons studying architecture, interior design, and drafting. When pressed to choose, he eventually declared a major in lighting engineering. During the next two years he took courses in mathematics, physics, and design, as well as industrial, residential, and stage lighting techniques. Randal was on the track to becoming a professional lighting engineer, but once again the seduction of glass changed his direction.

It was in his third year at Parsons that Randal finally had the opportunity to pick up a blowpipe and learn the mysteries of molten glass. Elective courses would permit him entry into the Glass Workshop, located in New York City's Little Italy. (The program is currently known as UrbanGlass and is now in Brooklyn.) There,

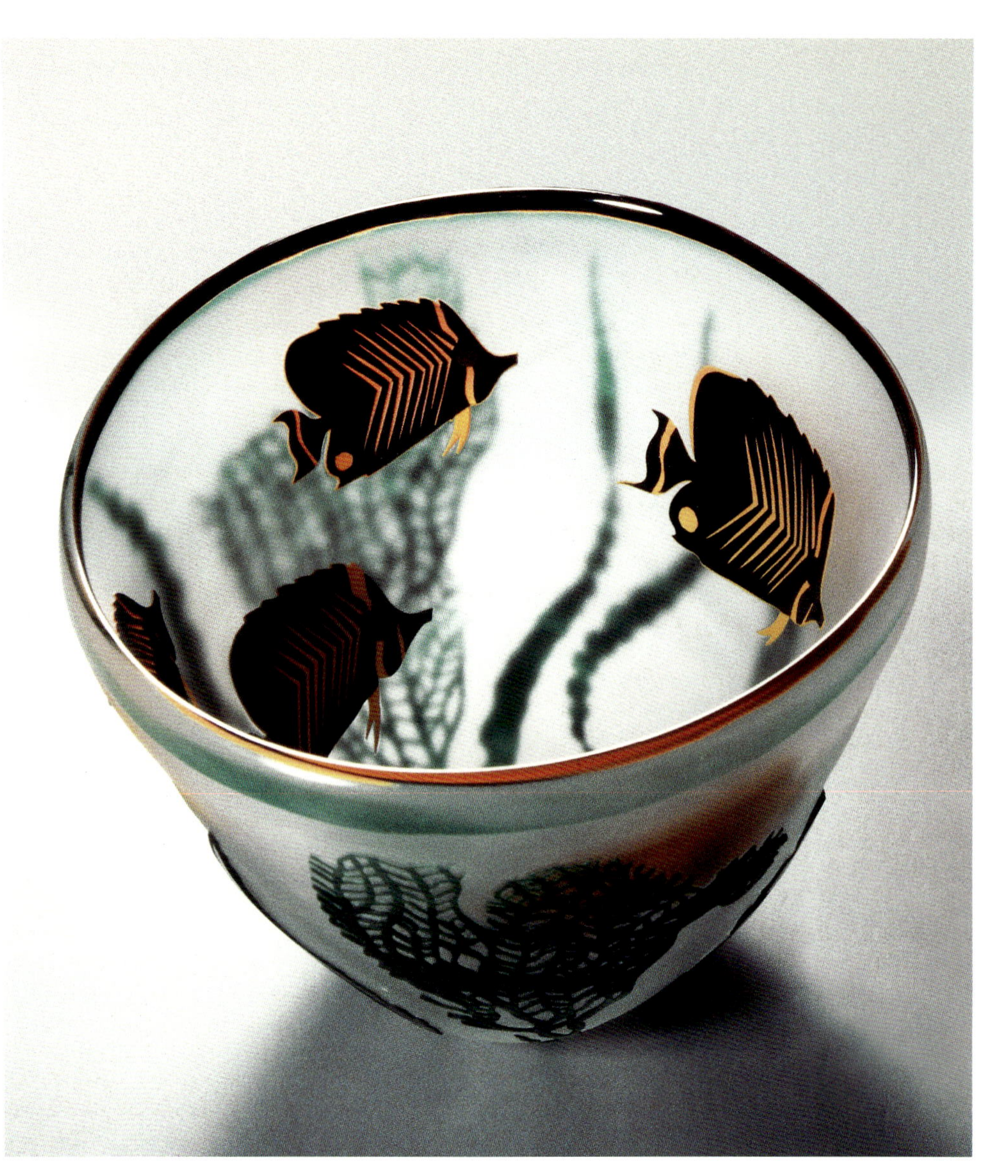

Seabowl #2, 1986

Study for Seabowl #2, 1986

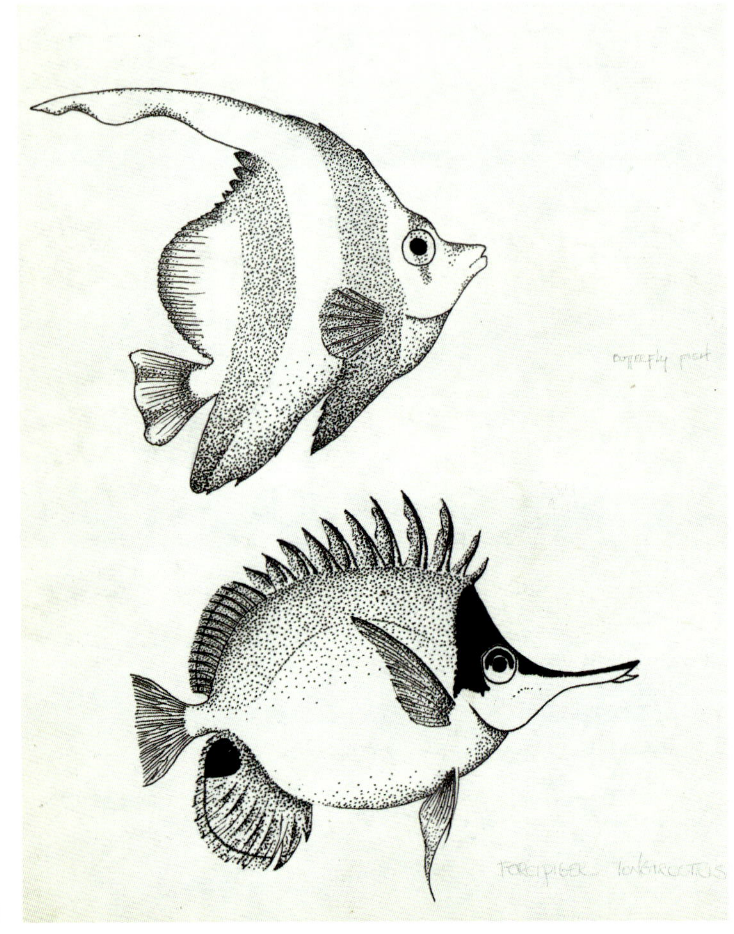

introductory courses were given in all aspects of glassworking. Randal recollects: "My first classes were in basic glassblowing and in simple casting techniques. I remember struggling to blow a small bubble at the end of a pipe and poking holes in boxes of sand to pour in molten glass for casting. And then there was a course in neon fabrication—bending the tubes and pumping in the gas—skills that completely escaped me. But I was *absolutely enraptured* with the processes of glassblowing and casting. I became mesmerized. It was addictive."

At this juncture Randal realized that the sum of his education and practical training thus far provided the driving force that would propel him into the Glass Workshop, a place that he could use as a laboratory of ideas. Happily straddling the glassworker's bench in front of the glowing furnace, he changed his degree program at Parsons to the fine arts. He began to investigate the history of glass and committed himself with fervor to learning advanced glassmaking techniques.

At the Glass Workshop the expert glassblower and adroit teacher John Brekke became his mentor. When Randal had acquired the necessary skill, Brekke taught him to blow glass vessels using the Swedish "graal" technique. This challenging glass-

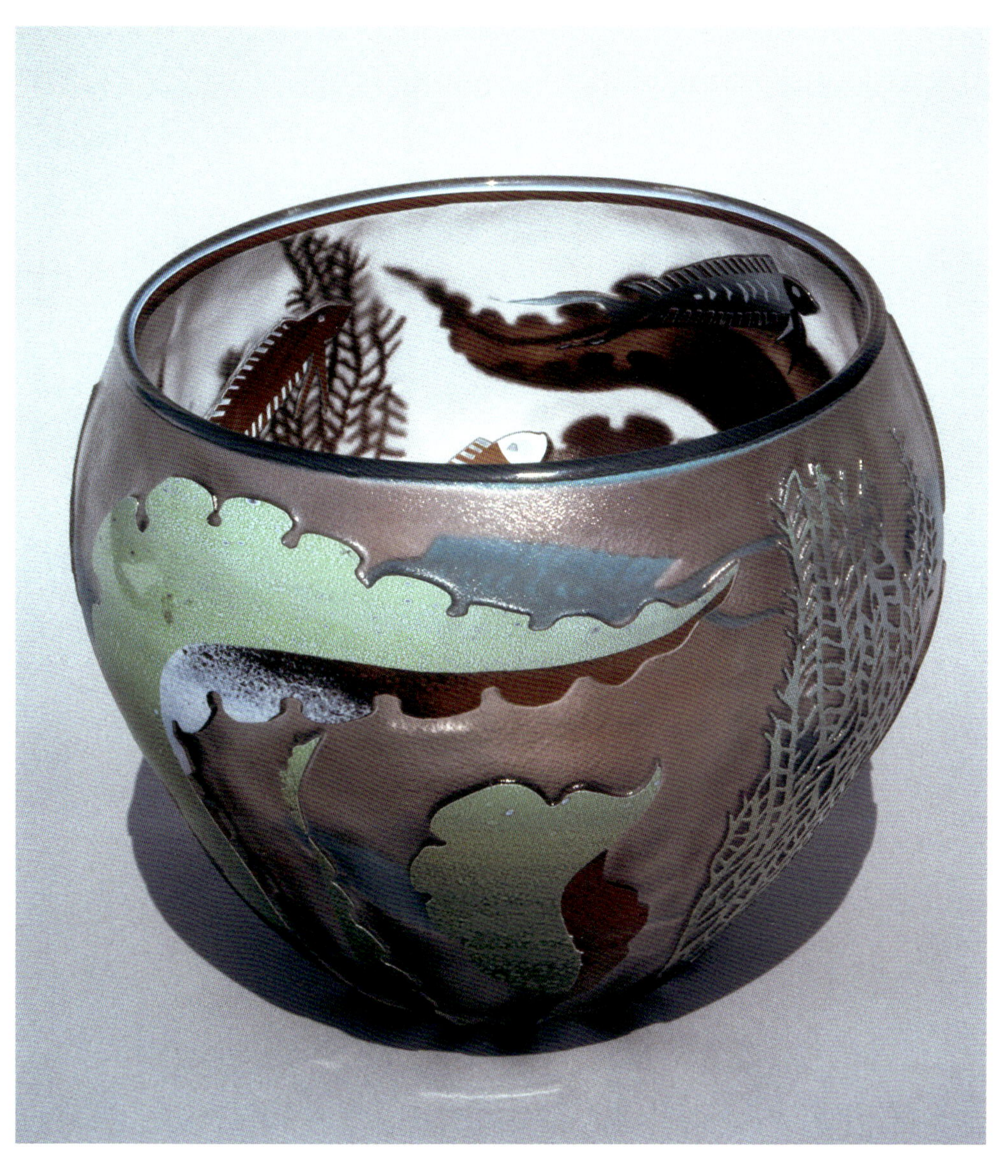

Cristallerie d'Émile Gallé, *Marine Vase,*
circa 1895–1900

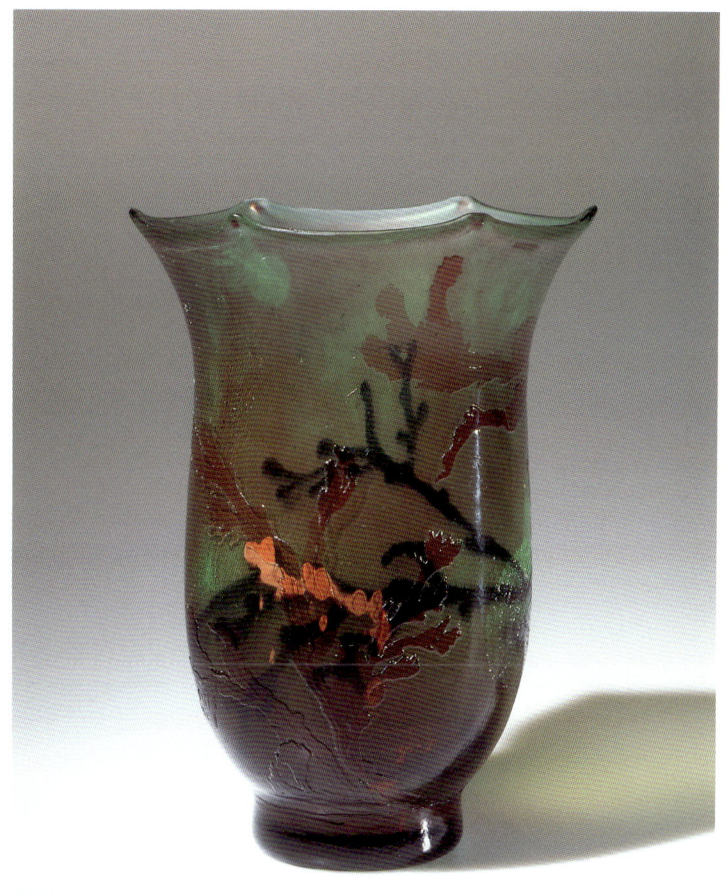

blowing method, named after the Holy Grail,[5] was first developed early in the twentieth century by Swedish designers
working at the Orrefors factory. Essentially it is a procedure
whereby one or more layers of colored glass are applied to the
outside and/or inside of a vessel during the blowing stage. Then
various layers are slowly removed—by cutting, acid etching, or
sandblasting—to reveal the contrasting colors underneath, adding dimensionality to the piece. The graal technique was fre-
quently used by Swedish glassblowers for marine scenes, to
achieve an effect where tropical fish and sea vegetation appear
suspended within an aqueous pool.

Coincidentally, Randal had long been an ardent scuba diver.
While diving along exotic coastlines he had keenly observed the
habitats of tropical fish, crustaceans, corals, sponges, and other
striking marine life. In the way that art often imitates life, he
began to create vessels resplendent with colorful underwater
motifs. Randal's *Seabowl #2* and *Seabowl #3* are deft examples of the
graal technique. Each bowl is blown with multiple overlays of
high-key colors. Etching and sandblasting expose elaborate designs of whirling striped fish, wavy kelp, and undulating sea fans.
This aquatic life appears to float in an ocean of deep stillness, an

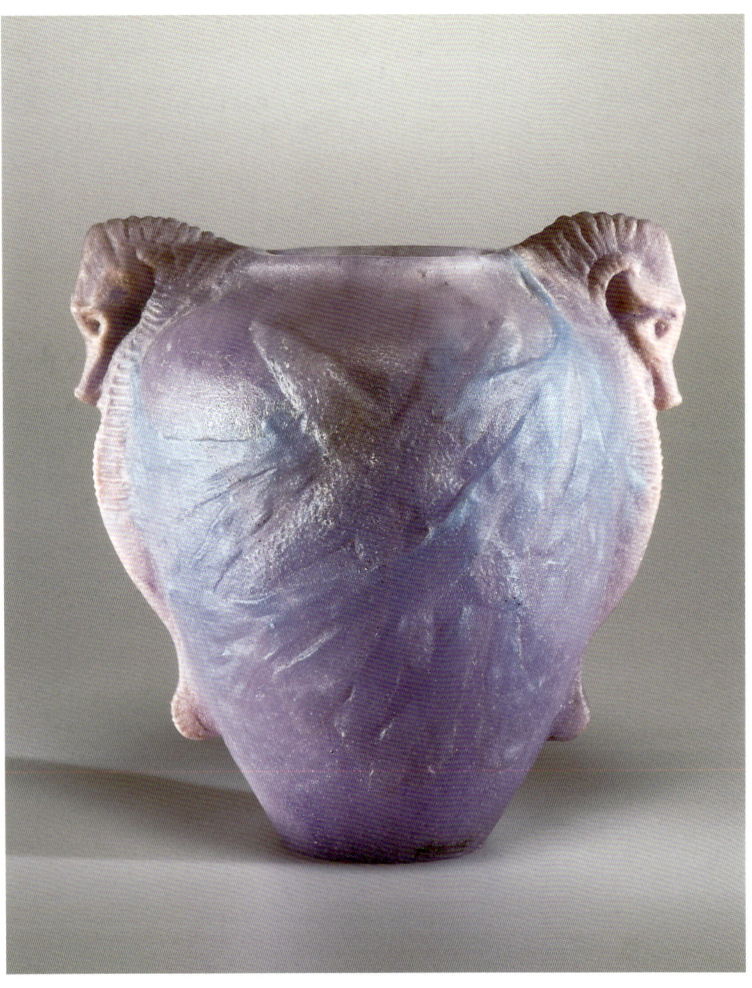

Georges Despret, *Seahorse Vase,*
circa 1906

experience further enhanced by the dimensional layering of color. Randal was learning how to exploit the properties of glass to reflect, refract, and shape light, manipulating the material's innate optical qualities in order to alter perception.

During this period of intense studio work, blowing vessels with naturalistic designs, Randal was also deeply involved in a study of the history of art glass. This led him to an investigation of Art Nouveau, the European decorative movement that began in France in the 1880s, spread across the continent, and found adherents in the United States a decade later.

Randal's work already shared themes with this turn-of-the-century style. Organic forms were favored in Art Nouveau, particularly peacocks, exotic plant life, and marine creatures rendered in languidly swaying, curvilinear lines awash in riotous color. The sinuous, exuberant "whiplash S-curve," or arabesque line, was emblematic in architectural ornament, furniture design, graphics, textiles, ceramics, jewelry, and glass. The Art Nouveau style also drew its inspiration from Asia, appropriating in particular the bold outlines, flat graphical manner, and asymmetry central to Japanese art. The repertoire of rich ornament based on pronounced flowing rhythms made it a style particularly suited to the fluidity of glass.

Researching the major proponents of Art Nouveau, Randal learned of the stunning ornamental glass of Émile Gallé, the fin de siècle French designer. Gallé founded the Alliance Provinciale des Industries d'Art in 1901 (later named the École de Nancy) to promote the applied and industrial arts. He believed that as "painters and ornamental artists, we are one and all priests serving the same religion, worshippers of natural beauty spread through the world."[6]

Gallé himself was a skilled glassmaker, ceramist, and cabinetmaker. But his greatest contribution to the decorative arts was his production of artistic glass—*pièces uniques,*

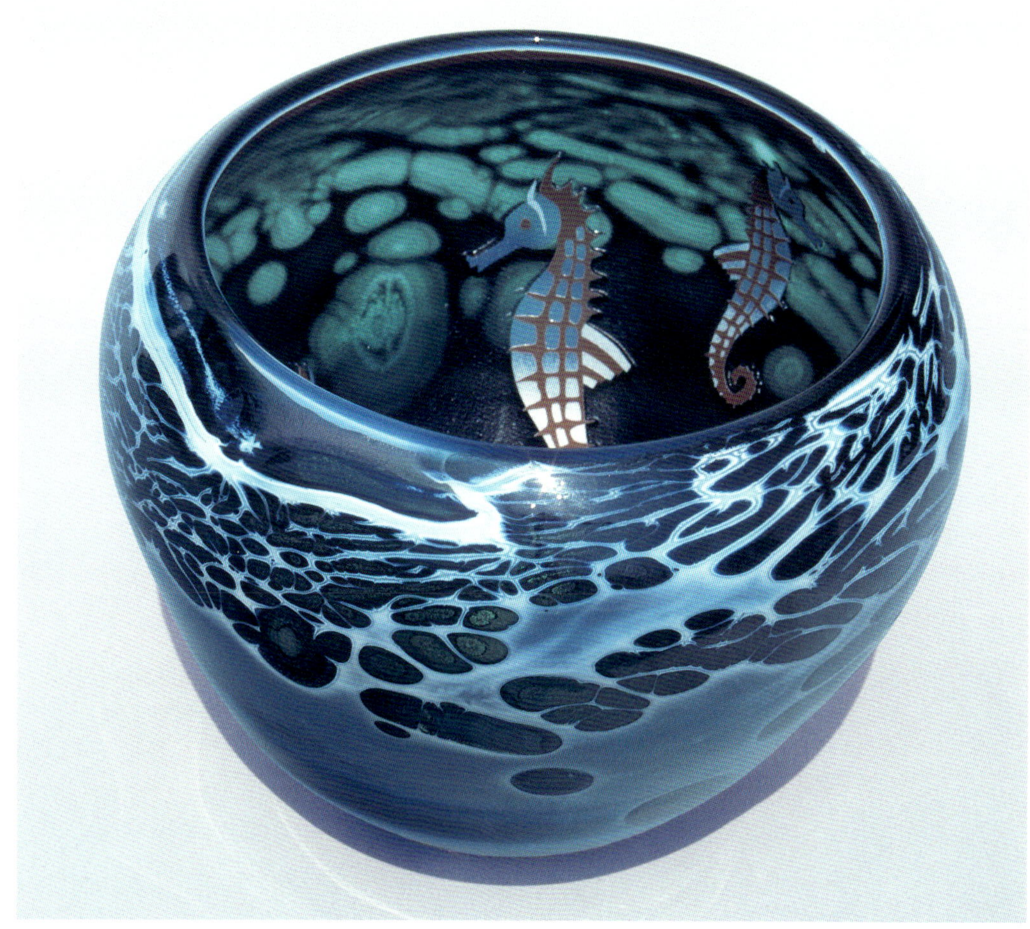

Seahorse Bowl, 1986

individually designed and crafted, some by the hands of the master—alongside the commercial line of mass-produced glass. These opulent original glass objects were marketed by distinguished French glass workshops to their aristocratic clientele as *vases de délectation*. His sensuous, naturalistic designs were executed using his innovative "clair-de-lune" (sapphire colored), cameo (layered, acid-cut, and carved), and *marqueterie de verre* (complex inlaid decoration) techniques. Gallé's brilliant integration of art and technology and his complete command of materials, coupled with his exquisitely rendered representations of nature, made him the avatar of art-glass production.

French art glass now served as Randal's ideal and inspiration. Wanting to produce unique glass pieces that combined rich surface decoration, dynamic forms, and complex glassworking techniques, he searched for new ways to stretch the limits of his chosen medium.

During his research into the history of French art glass Randal had learned of the kiln-casting process known as *pâte de verre*—a term that literally means "paste of glass." *Pâte de verre* refers to the technique of mixing powdered glass with oxides (for color) and water to form a paste. This paste is packed into a mold and then heat-fused by firing in a kiln. During the firing cycle tiny bubbles become trapped in the glass, giving *pâte de verre* its distinctive luminous opacity. After the annealing (gradual cooling) of the glass, the exterior mold is removed and the glass object is revealed.

The technique of *pâte de verre* was known to the ancient Egyptians as early as the 18th Dynasty (1570 BC),[7] and was used by them primarily for small objects such as jewelry and funerary sculptures. The Romans also favored *pâte de verre*; with the addition of various colorants they were able to produce glass objects that simulated marble and gemstones. The skill was subsequently lost for centuries, and the French sculptor Henri Cros is credited with its ultimate revival. In the mid-1880s Cros, then working at the Sèvres porcelain factory, was searching for a casting method to make large-scale molded reliefs. His experiments led to the rediscovery of *pâte de verre* and its application in French art-glass workshops. Soon other prominent Art Nouveau designers were using the technique, most notably Gabriel Argy-Rousseau, François Dècorchemont, Georges Despret (see p. 18), Almaric Walter, and the brothers Auguste and Antonin Daum. In the United States it was adopted by the great Steuben glass designer and technician Frederick Carder.

Entranced by the veiled luminescence of crushed cast glass, Randal decided "to lay down my blowing pipes for good and concentrate on developing the art of kiln casting and of *pâte de verre*." However, he soon discovered that the production of such work was a complex, time-consuming, labor-intensive process that required arcane technical knowledge and rigorous attention to detail. Uncovering the alchemical mysteries of casting glass proved to be a frustrating process. As he recalls, "My teachers at school were never very forthcoming with technical advice and instruction. I used to chase people around with a barrage of questions that were rarely answered. The techniques that I ultimately developed, and use today, were the result of many years of trial and error—and a good share of broken glass."

Randal achieved a technical breakthrough when longtime friend and glass sculptor Clifford Rainey helped him understand many aspects of kiln casting and the lost-wax mold-making process. Through intense experimentation—varying the coloring oxides, the type of glass, the size of the ground-glass particles, the heating temperature, the annealing time, and the materials for moldmaking—he began to master the process.

Randal now labored at a high pitch. He spent his days and most of his nights at the Glass Workshop, "taking classes, working as a teaching assistant, and doing my own work. The Glass Workshop became my home away from home." He experienced his first success in 1987 with *Starfish Bowl*; it emerged from the mold a faultless, precisely formed, and brilliantly colored cast crystal vessel. (For a detailed description of Randal's method of *pâte de verre* and kiln casting with optical crystal, see "The Process of Lost-Wax *Pâte de Verre*," p. 112.)

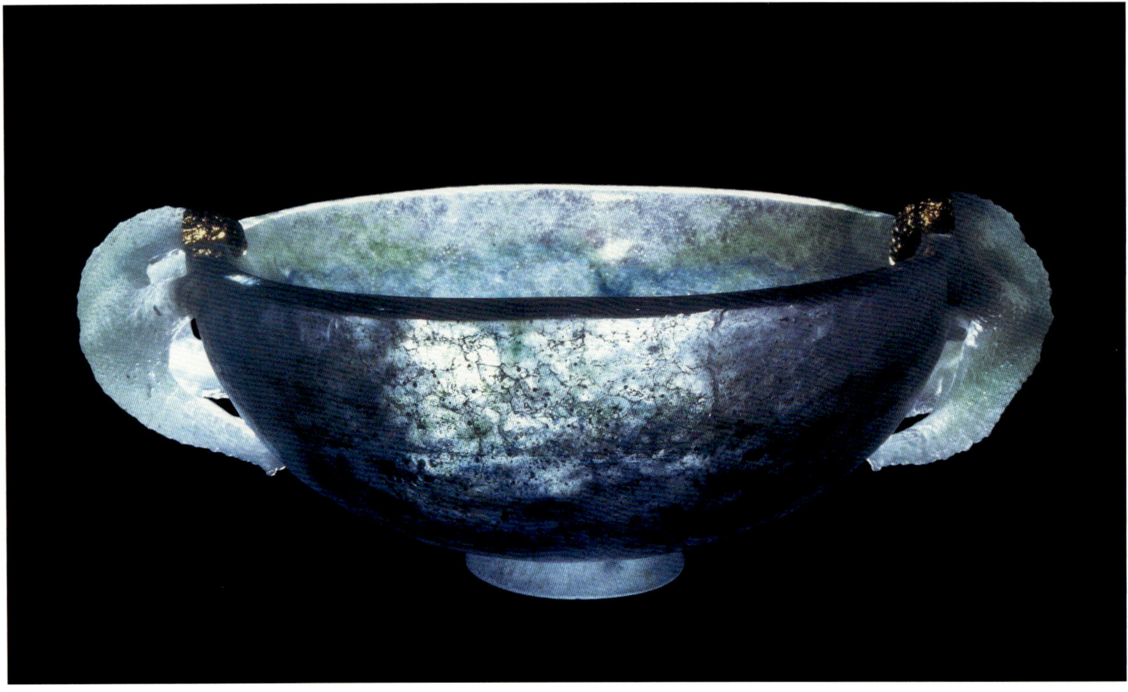

 STARFISH BOWL, 1987

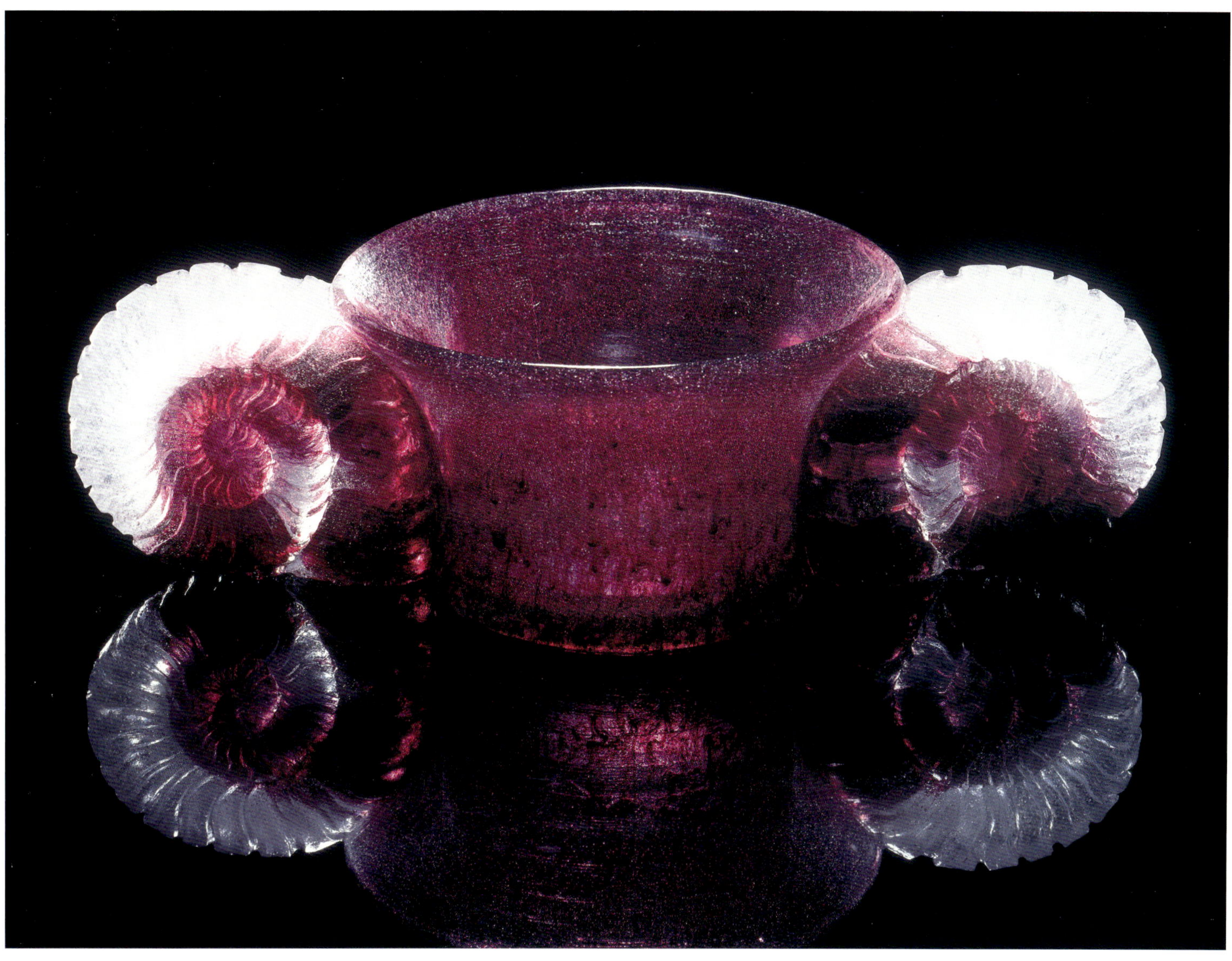

The glass-casting process opened the windows of Randal's imagination, and he saw the way to actualize the vast expressive potential of this art form. He surveyed his repertoire of favored images—the graceful contours of the Art Nouveau line, the fanciful vigor of Nouveau decoration, the dramatic silhouettes and jewel-toned colors of turn-of-the-century art glass—and began to create luxurious pieces that resonated with the sensibilities of this vital period in art history.

The dynamic confluence is readily evident in such inspired pieces as the prototypical *Les Serpents* (p. 22), where slithering snakes create rhythmic curves and a sense of dynamic movement. The translucent glass, colored with intoxicating swirls of peacock green and ruby red, shimmers like a precious jewel. *Les Femmes Dangereuses* (p. 25) features nude sirens drifting in a luscious pool of sea green and cobalt, waiting, as myth would have it, to lure unsuspecting sailors to an untimely watery grave with their irresistible beauty and calls of love. This work owes a debt to Lalique's urbane piece *Coupe Trépied Sirène*. Randal's Nouveau-inspired series contains splendid examples of his ability to draw inspiration from diverse cultural sources, retaining a haunting echo of the original but branding the object with his inimitable personal vision.

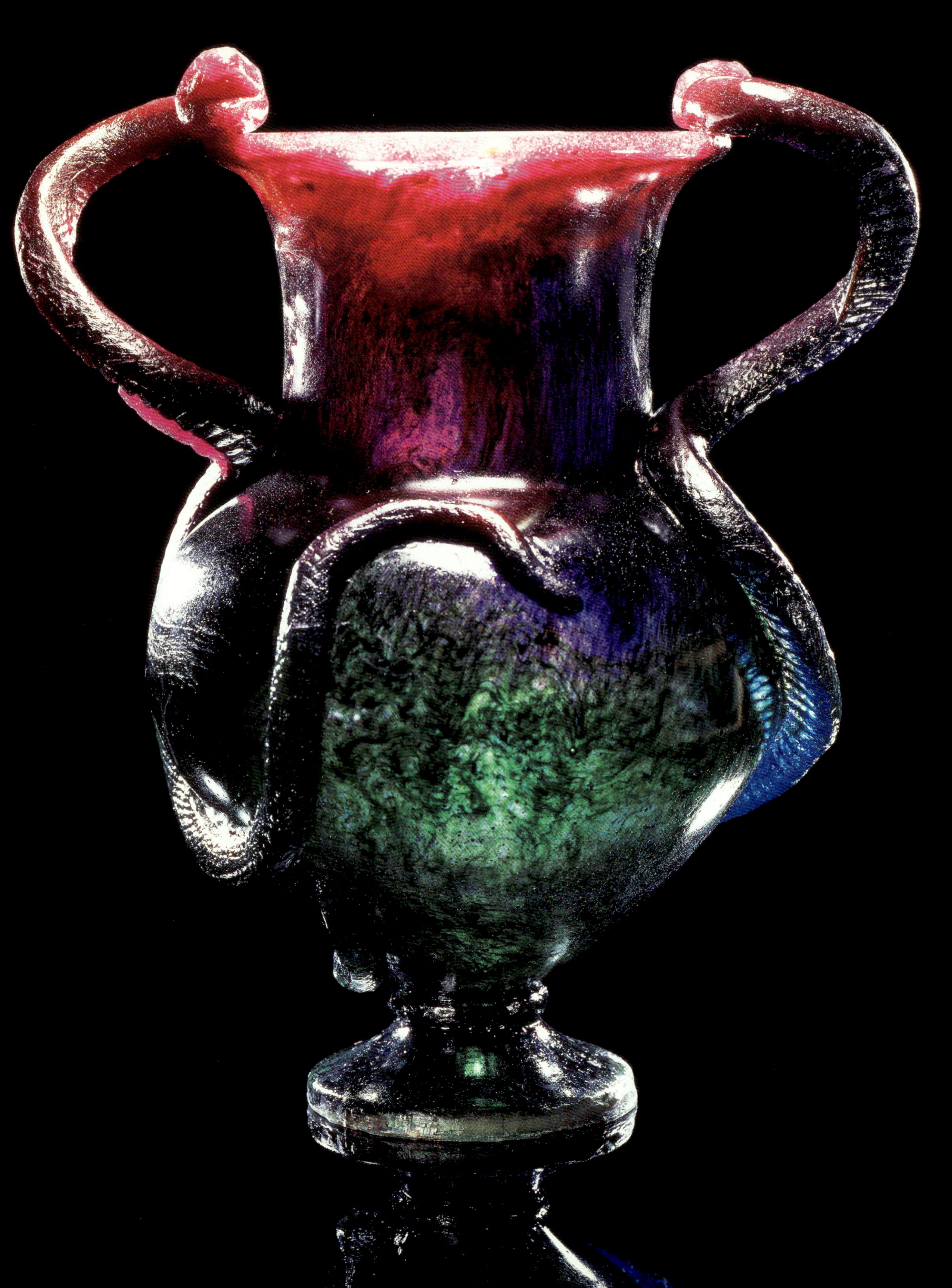

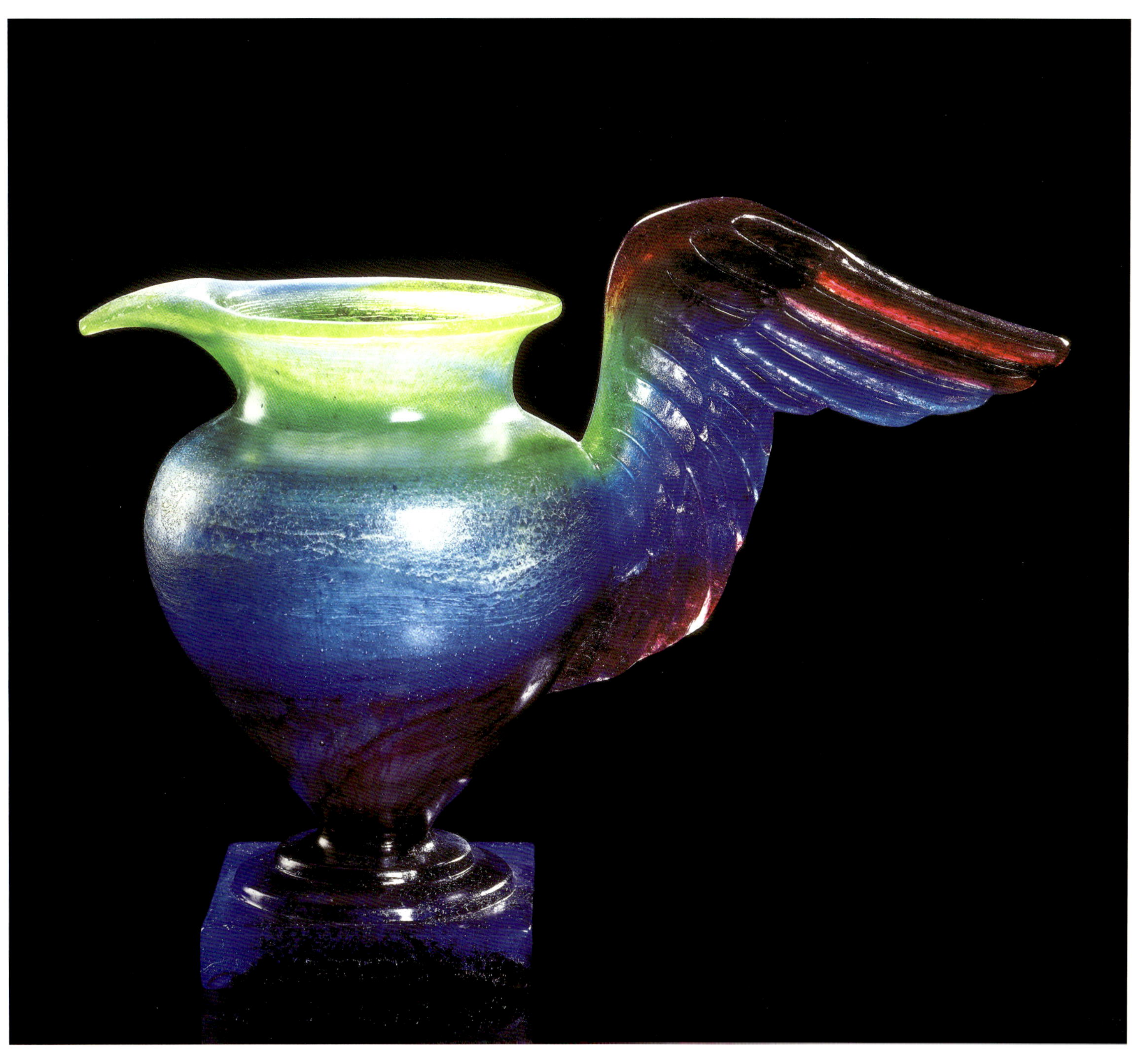

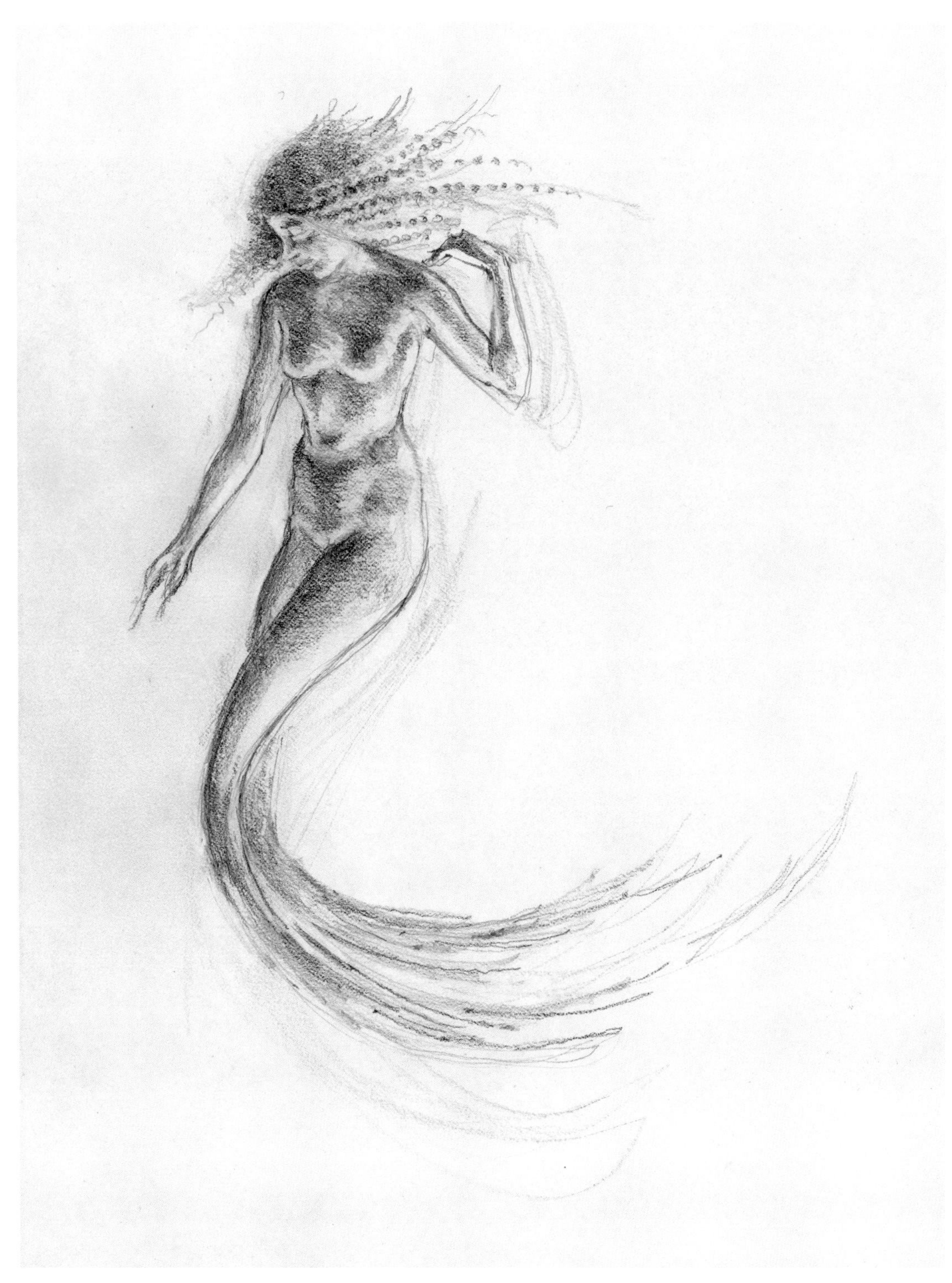

 Study of René Lalique's "Coupe Trépied Sirène," 1992   Les Femmes Dangereuses, 1993

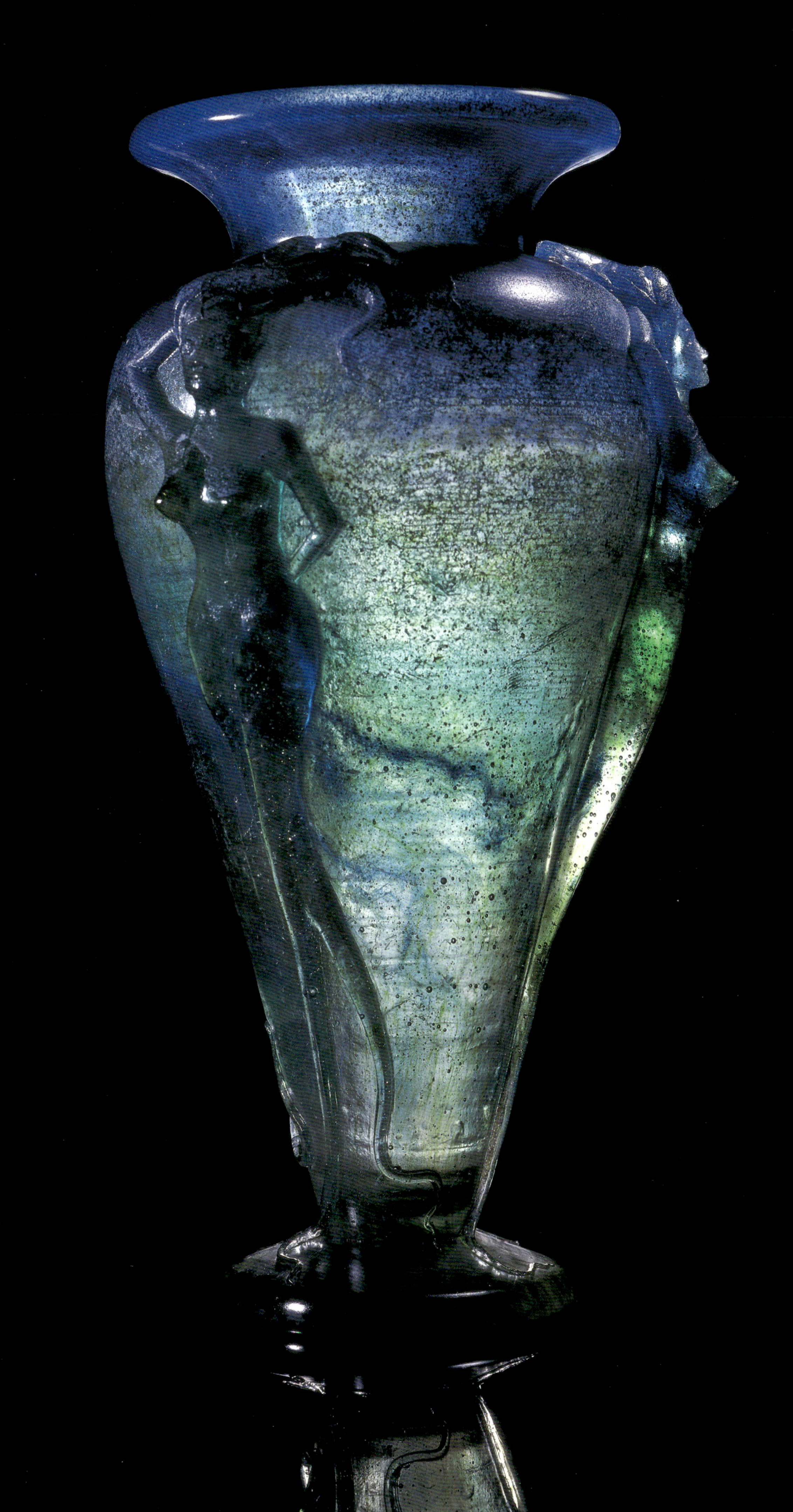

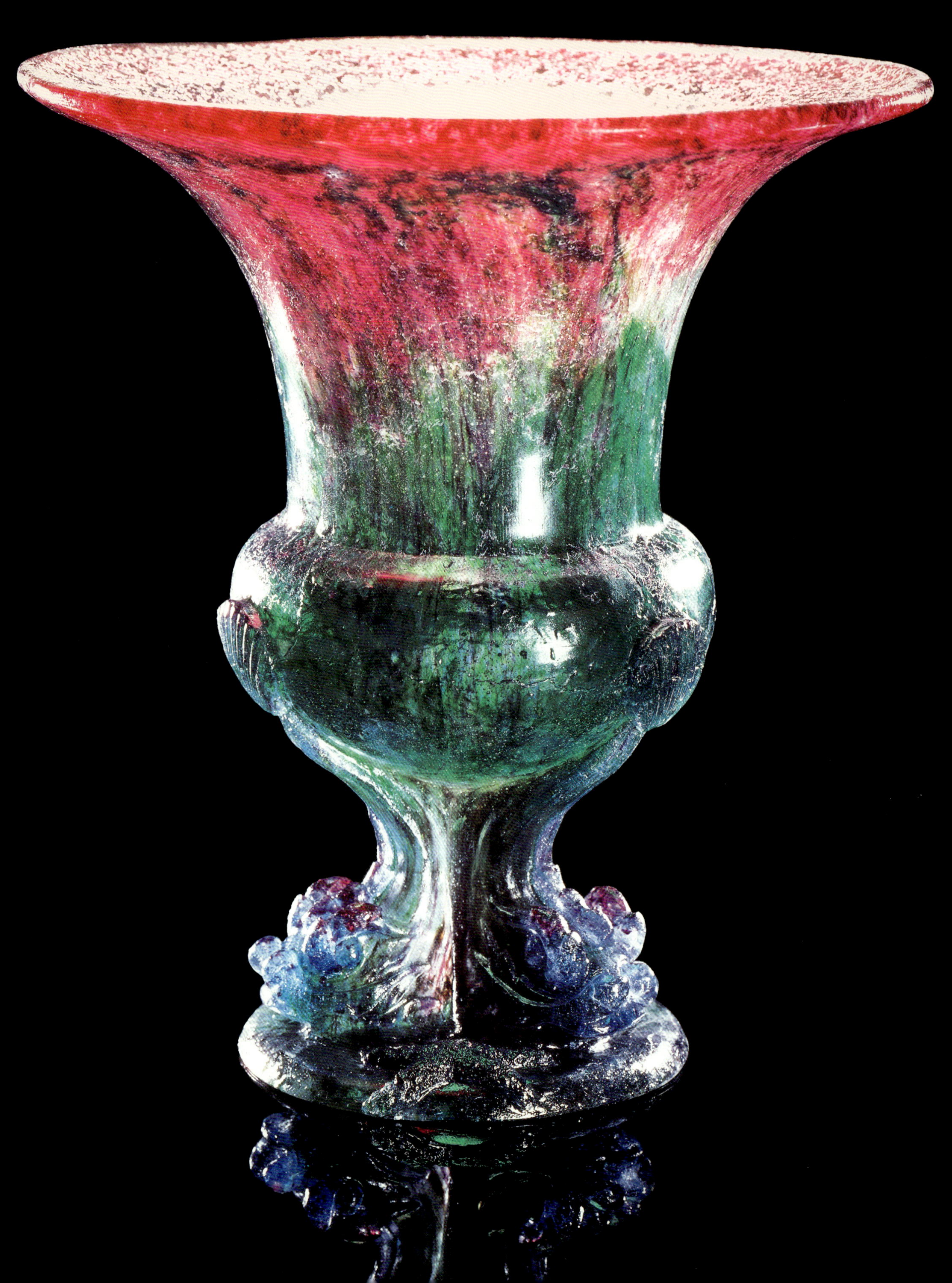

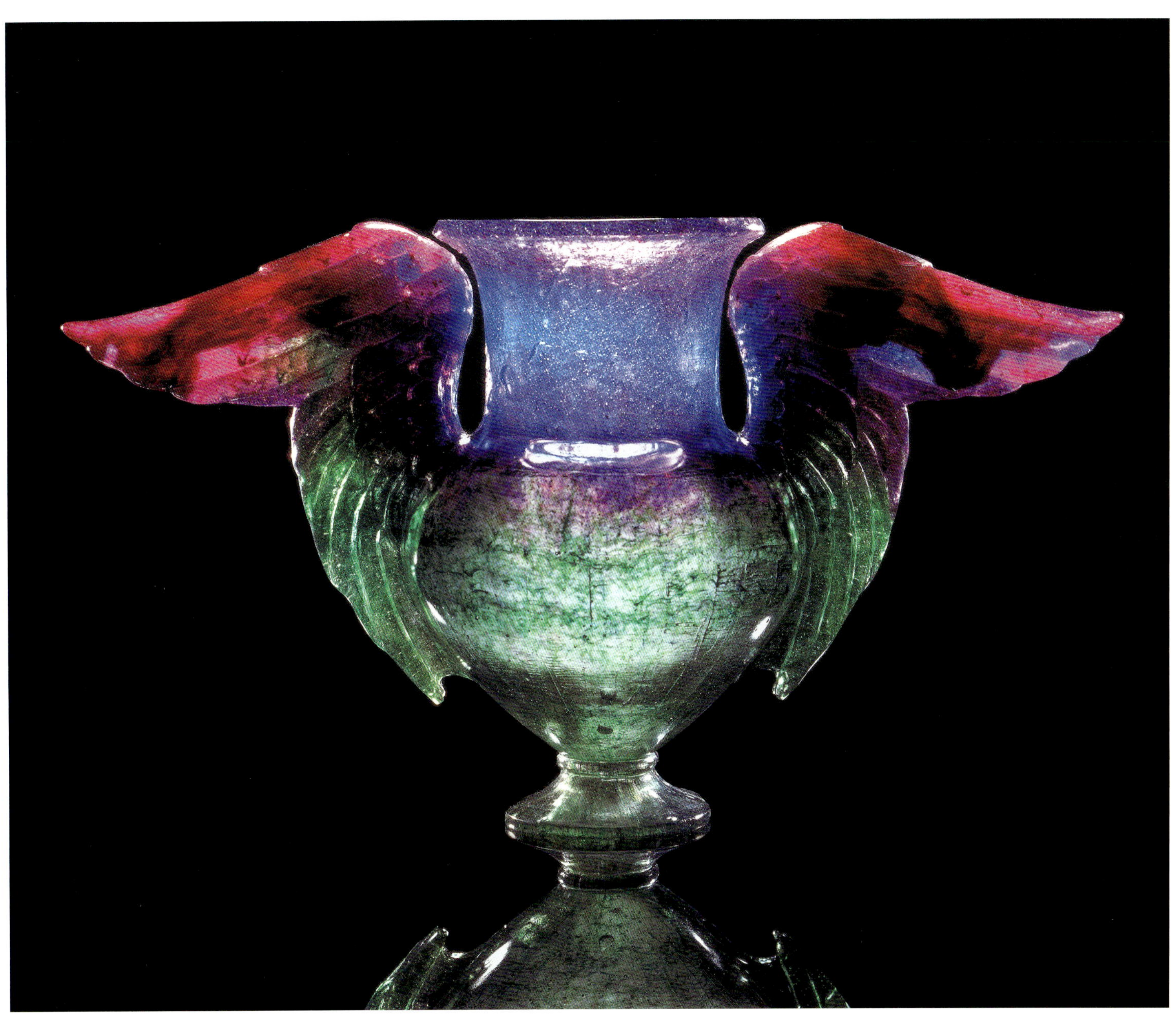

Trois Dauphins, 1990

Amphore de Liberté, 1992

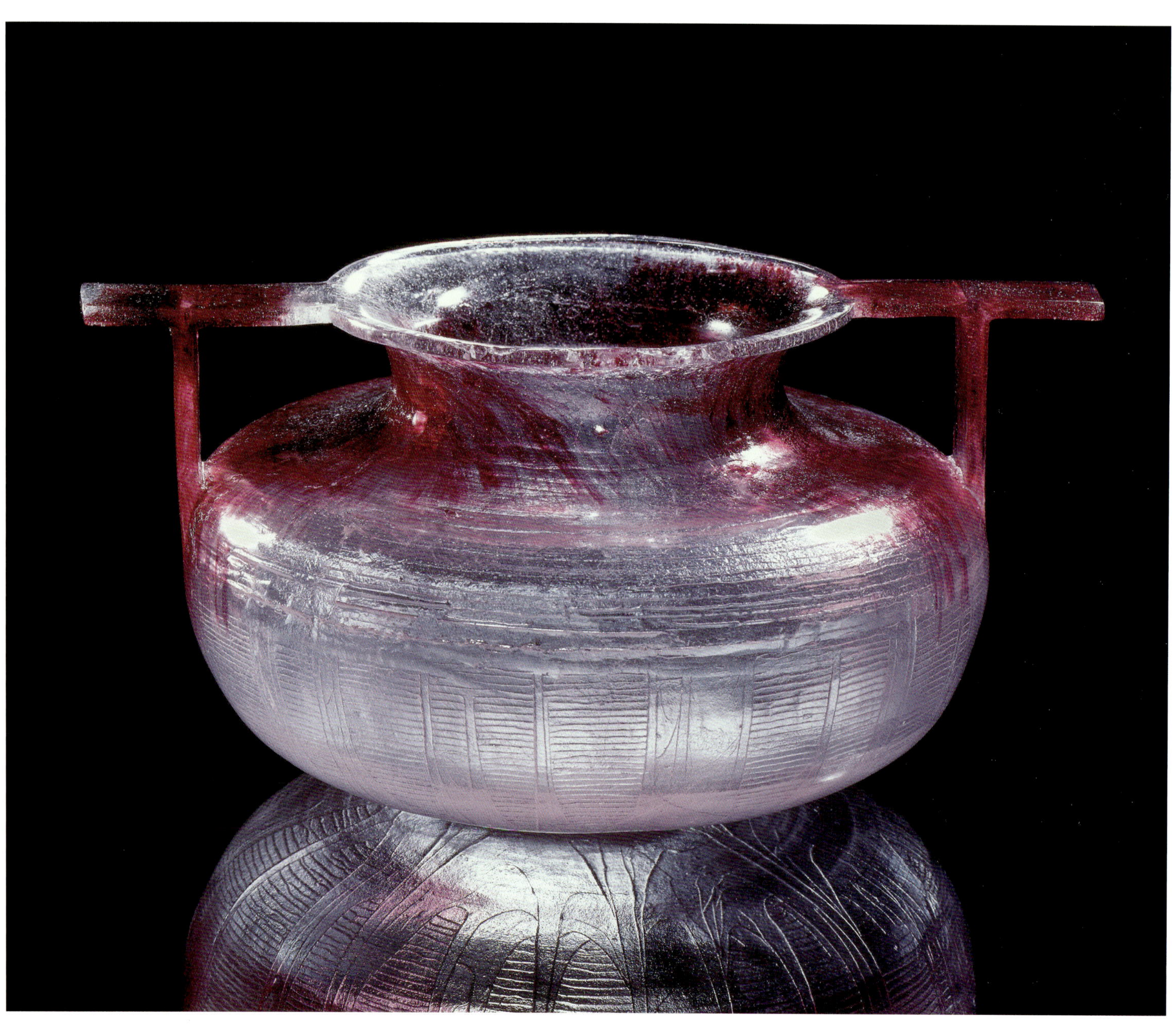

   Japonaise Rouge d'Or, 1990   Le Chardon, 1993

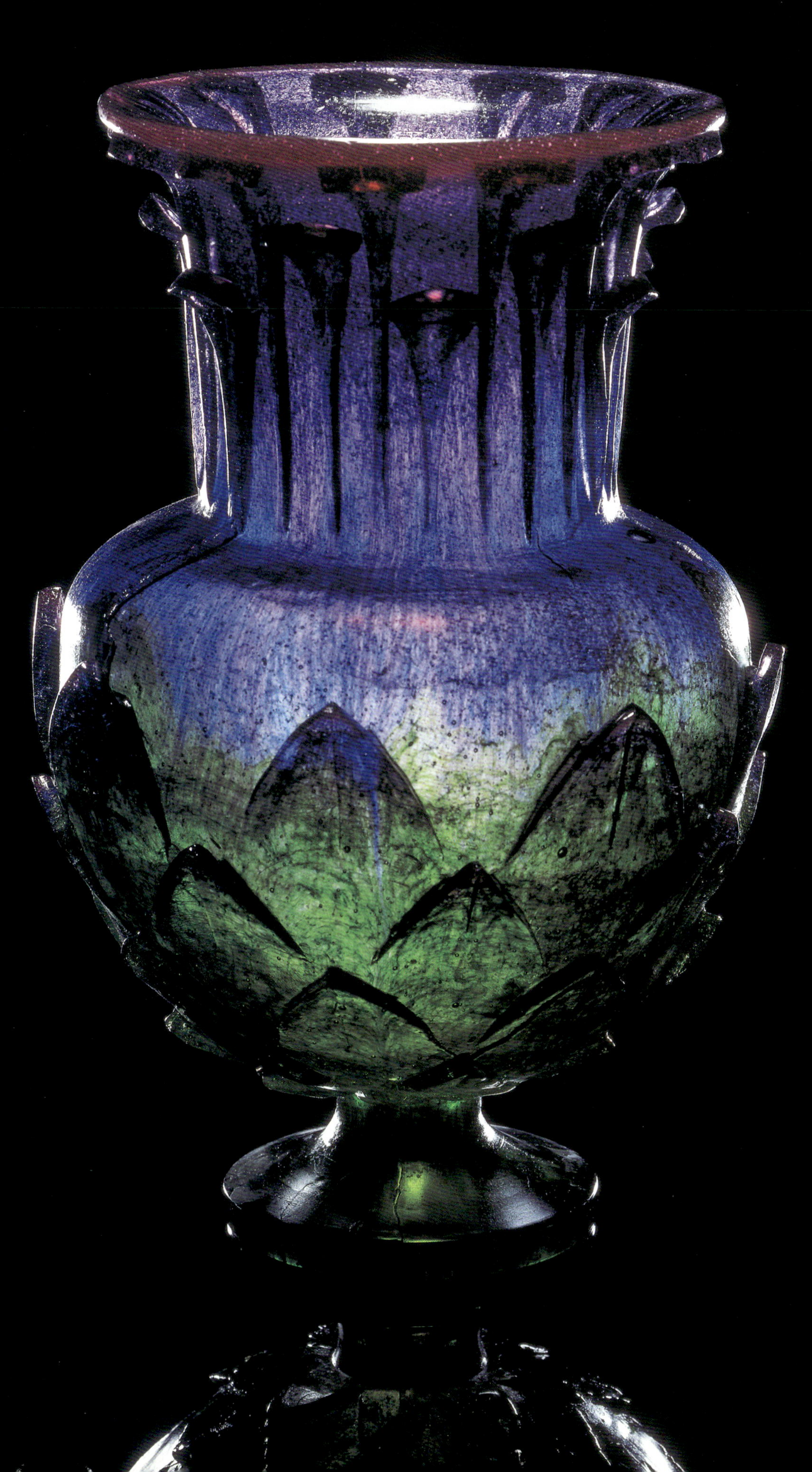

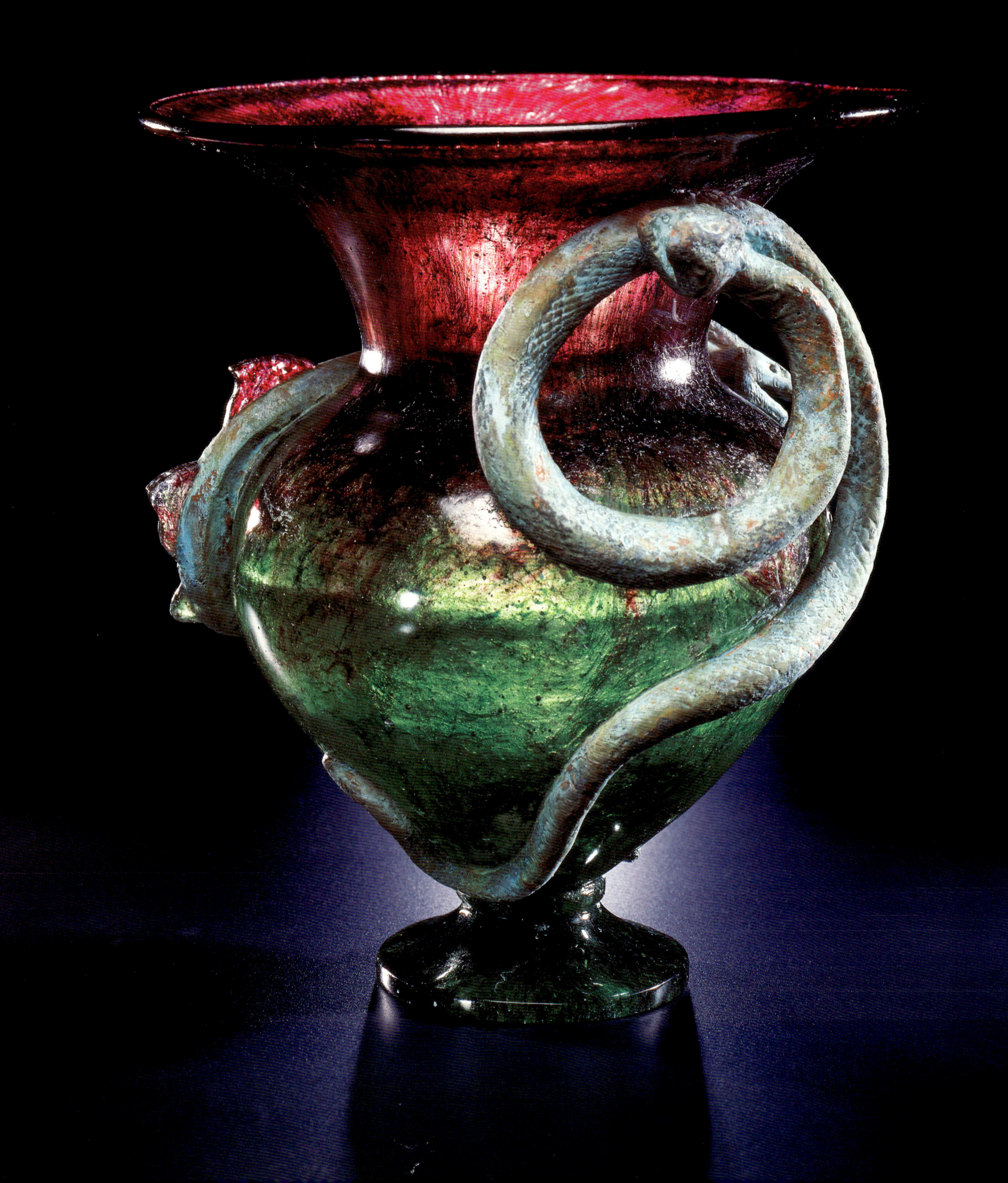

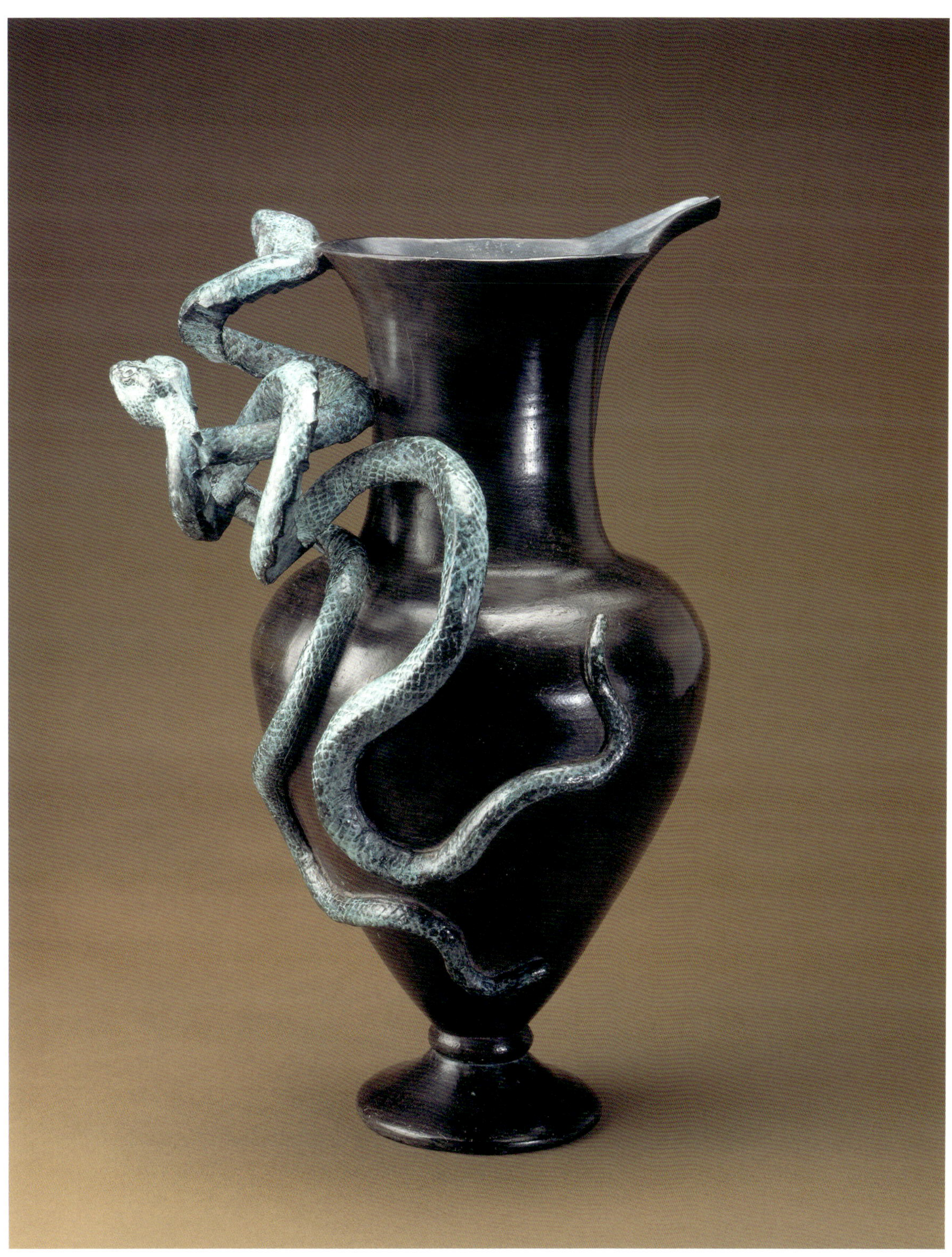

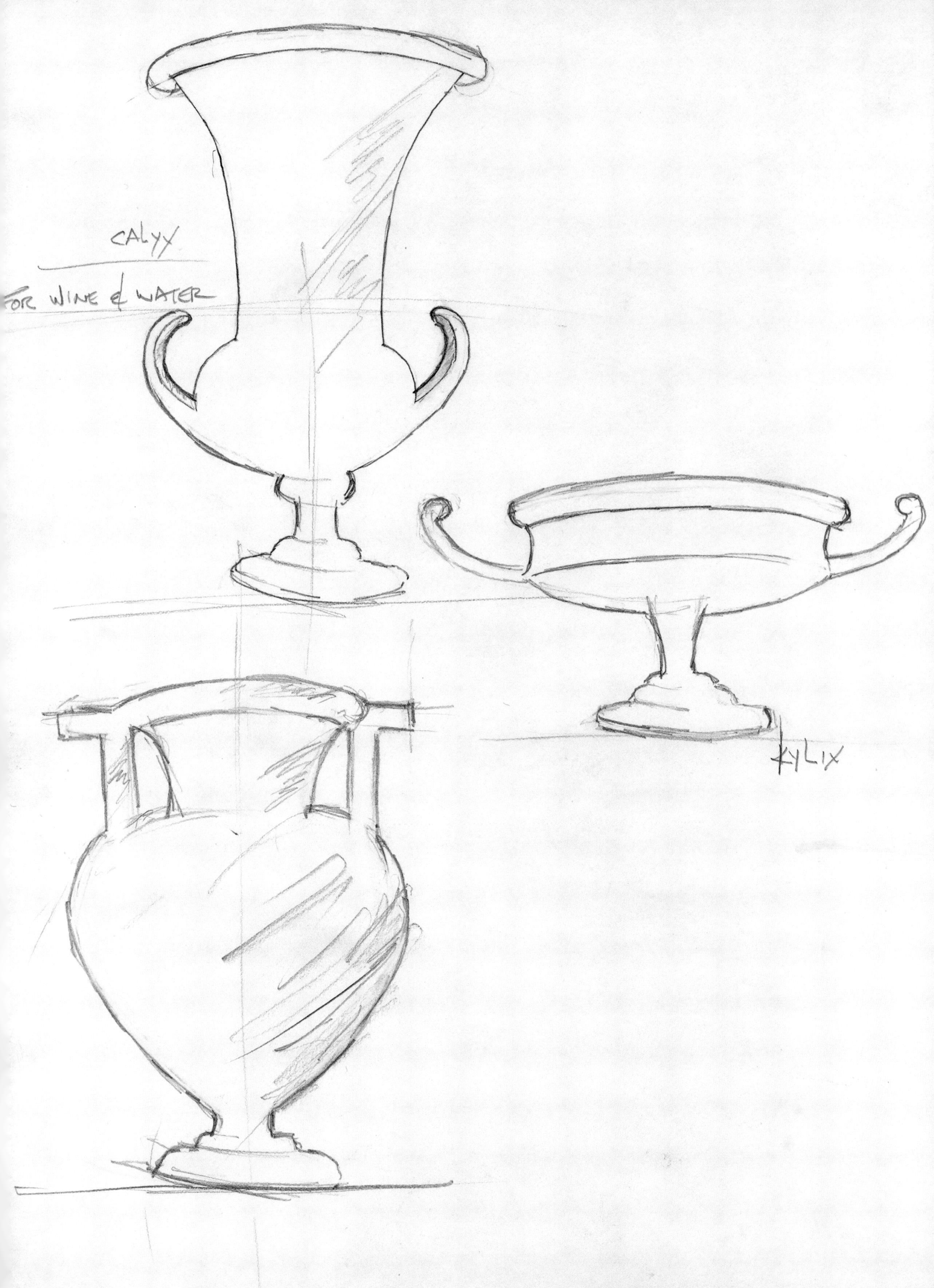

CALYX
FOR WINE & WATER
KYLIX

ODE TO A

GRECIAN URN

The beautiful is that which is desirable in itself.

—Aristotle

The next several years for Randal were a period of finding his creative niche. Right after his graduation from Parsons—in fact the very day he completed his final examinations—he left New York City. Overwhelmed by the pressures of the dense, fast-paced urban environment, he longed for a place where he could work without distraction. After a six-month artist-in-residence program at the Espace Verre school and glass studio in Montreal, he headed west to Seattle to visit his close friend (and fellow glass artist) Ginny Ruffner. Despite the unwelcoming weather—he arrived during one of the city's worst winters—his "visit" lasted seven years.

Randal immediately set up a studio in Seattle to continue working on his kiln-cast sculptures. He became involved in the artistic life of his adopted city, first through teaching fine arts and then by serving as a trustee on the board of the Pratt Fine Arts Center. He also curated several biannual masterworks auctions and organized shows in local galleries for Pratt's artists and instructors. But he did not allow these activities to detract from the development of his own work: "As I concentrated on exploring and mastering new casting techniques, I would encounter a steady stream of technical problems. As my pieces became larger and more complex, the amount of work involved, and ultimately the failure rate, increased exponentially. I would lose one piece for one reason and then lose the next for another totally different reason. In 1995 I made twenty-three pieces, out of which only seven were successful. I've very nearly quit more than once. And to this day, just when I think I've sorted out all my technical and design problems, another will come along. Fortunately, not all problems have ended in disaster. Most, but not all, have—for some of my best discoveries and

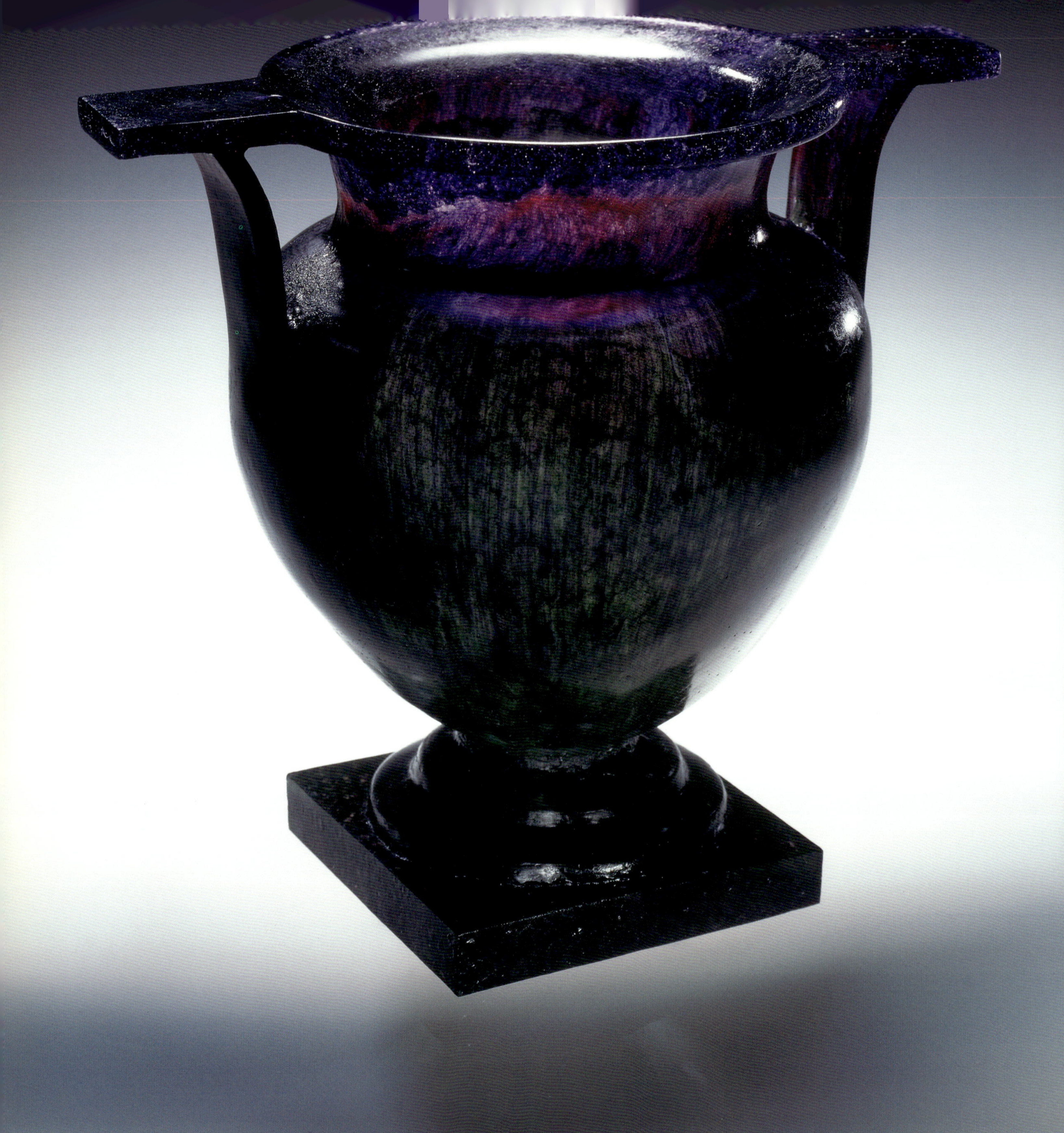

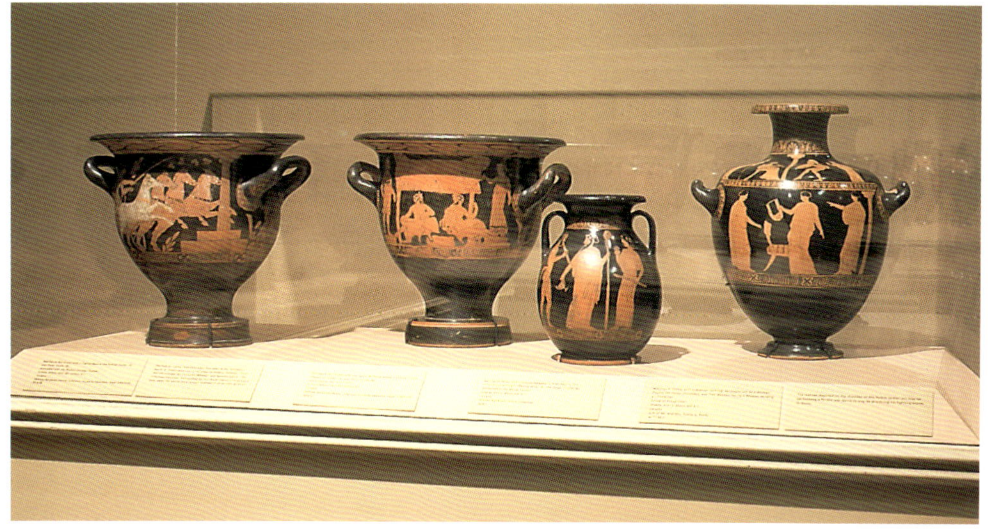

Installation view, Attic red-figure pottery at the Los Angeles County Museum of Art

most closely guarded secrets have come to me through trial and error." Once he was confident that his skills could sustain an involved body of new work, he was ready for the spark of a fresh idea.

Before leaving New York City, Randal had spent many hours in the ancient art galleries of the Metropolitan Museum of Art. Entranced by the beauty of the Attic Greek vases on view (black-figure and red-figure pottery from the fifth to third centuries BC), he made studies of the shapes of these ancient vessels, carefully recording their distinctive profiles. He became aware of the cultural significance of Greek pottery and learned about its multiplicity of uses—domestic, funerary, ceremonial, and export. He identified each design with its specific function: the wide-shouldered *amphora* and *hydria*, intended for the storage of water and other liquids; the open-mouthed and cylindrical *krater*, produced for the mixing of water and wine; the tall-handled *oinochoe*, created as a pitcher for pouring wine; the shallow, two-handled *kylix*, shaped to serve as a drinking cup; and the slender, long-necked *lekythos*, formed to hold oils and other unguents.

Randal brought this source material with him to Seattle and began to analyze it: "I studied these vessels. I looked beyond their painted surfaces. Something about their shapes really spoke to me. I recognized their beauty. I *saw them, understood them*, as works of art." His contemplation of the fabled aura of the Grecian Urn led him to meditate on the meaning of *kalos*, the Greek word signifying "beautiful" and "handsome," and to launch an investigation into the guiding principles of Greek classicism and its ideals of beauty.

Randal discovered that the principle that bestows beauty on material things was first defined by the Greek philosopher Plato in the fourth century BC, and was subsequently developed by Plotinus in the third century AD. Fundamentally Plato viewed the beauty of

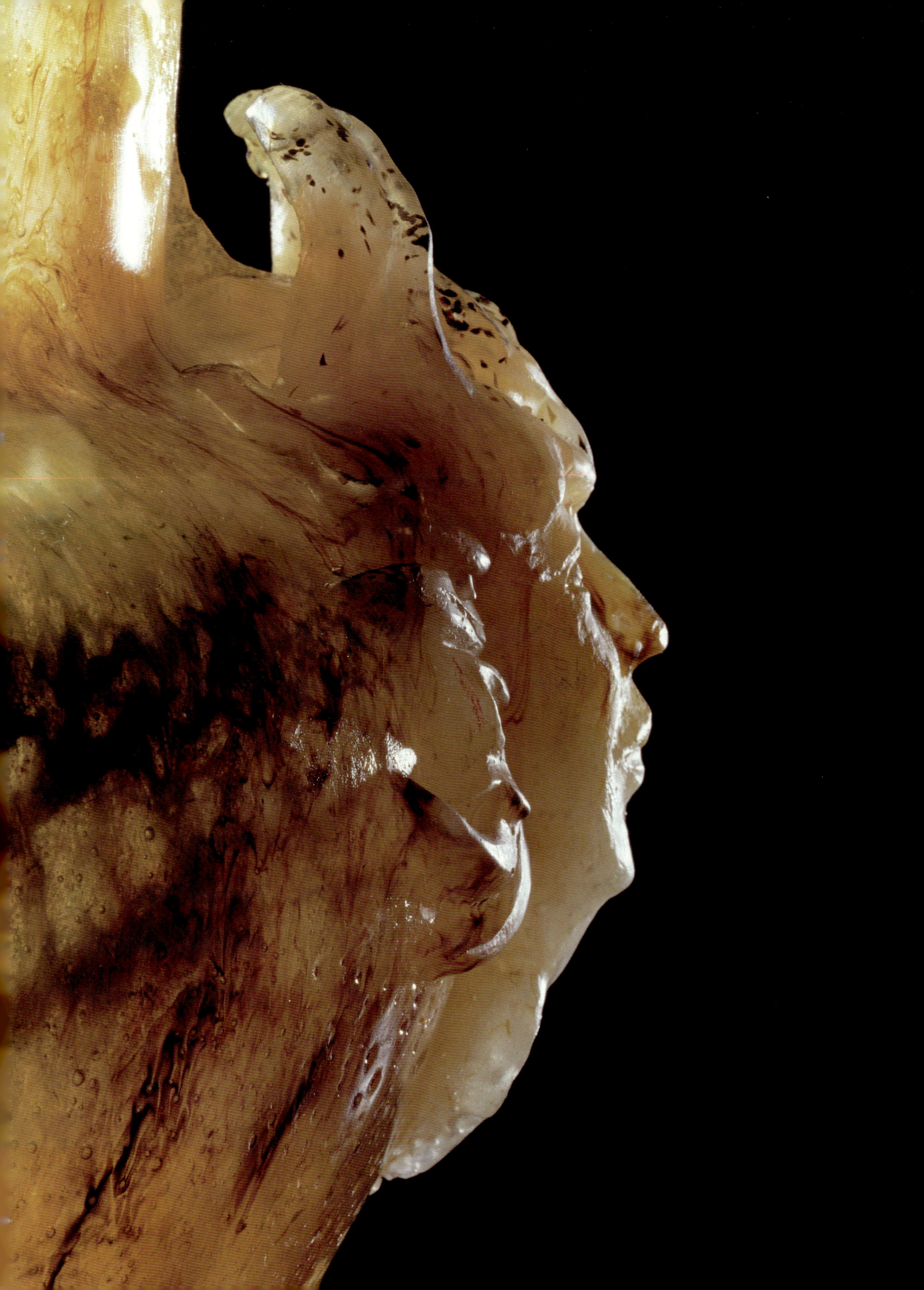

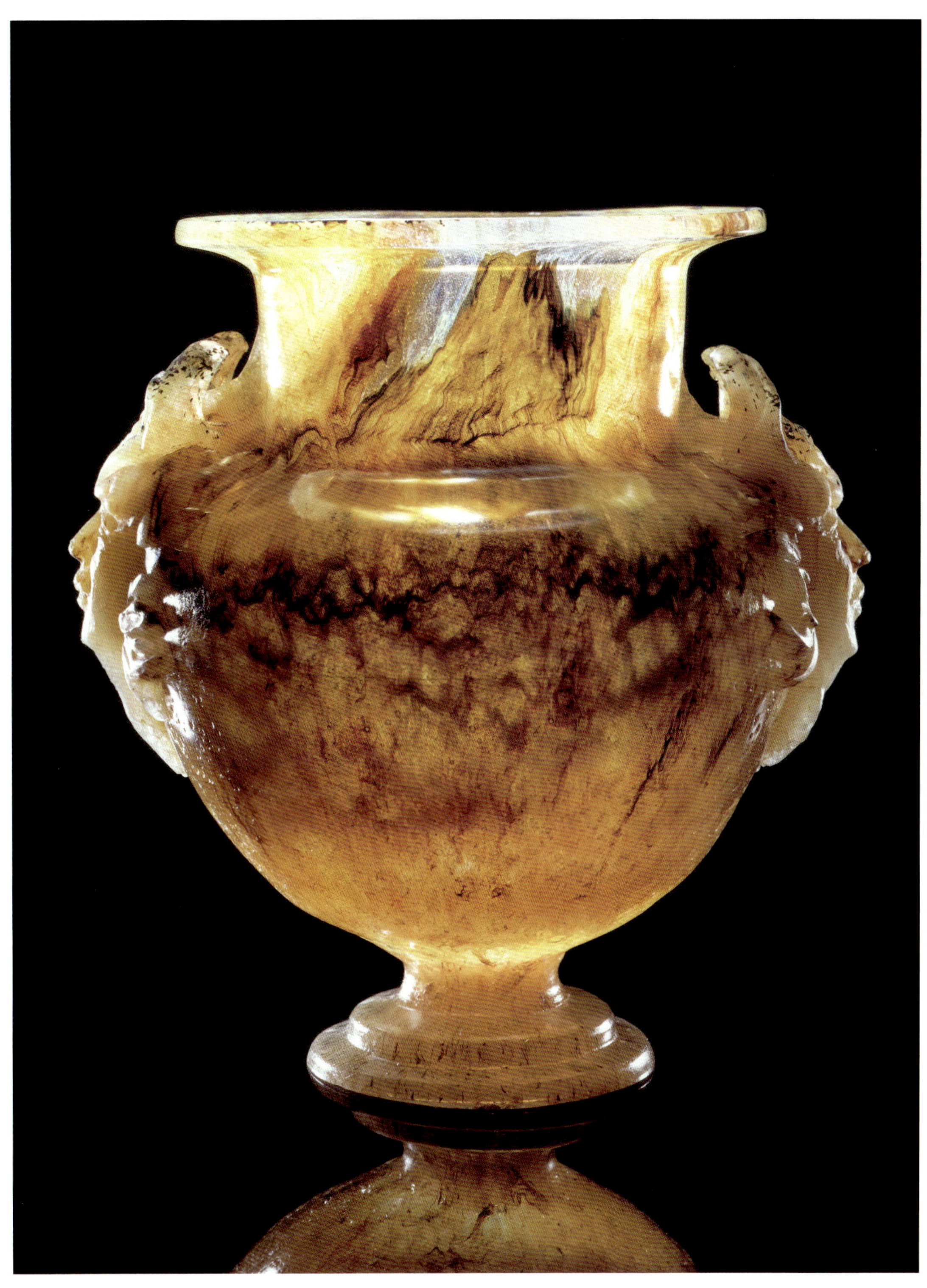

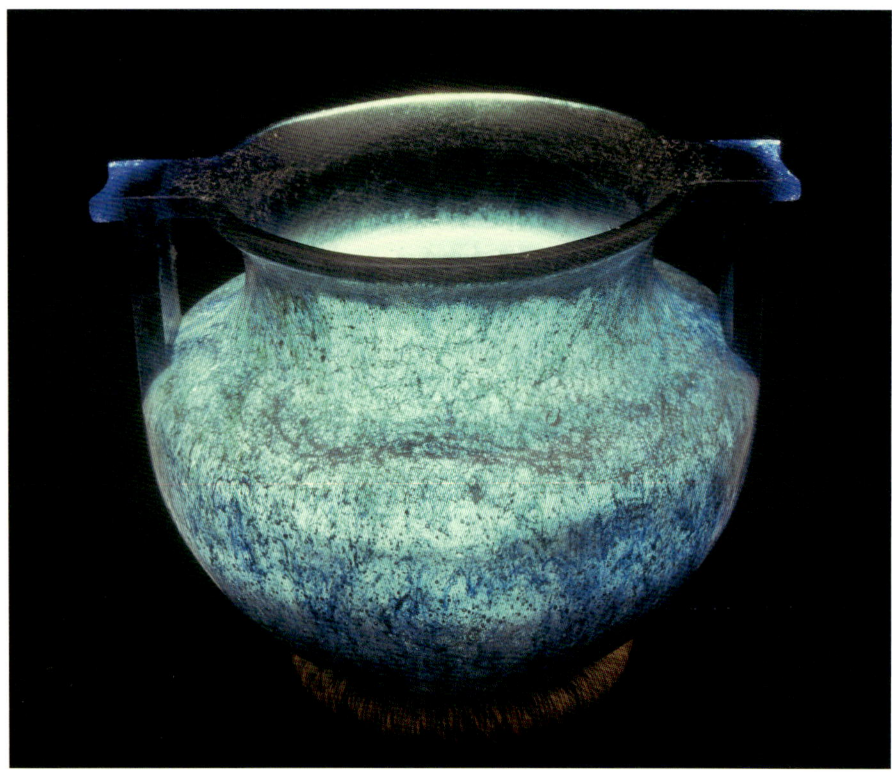

Amphore au Bleu, 1989

objects and nature as inherent. He believed that beauty is part of an object, that beauty possesses the object and cannot be separated from it.[8] In an attempt to codify the qualities of a beautiful thing, he identified the concepts of simplicity, symmetry, order, discipline, restraint, balance, and serenity. Above all, a harmony of these elements must be achieved in order for beauty to be excellent, perfect, and satisfying.

Plotinus extended these ideas in *The Enneads*: "The symmetry of parts towards each other and towards a whole . . . constitutes the beauty recognized by the eye . . . [Beauty] has grouped and coordinated what from a diversity of parts was to become a unity: it has rallied confusion into cooperation: it has made the sum one harmonious coherence: for the Idea is a unity and what it moulds must come to unity as far as multiplicity may."[9] Plato and Plotinus agreed that beauty provokes pleasure, that a beautiful object attracts the eyes, calls to and lures its viewer toward it, and "fills them with joy at the sight."[10]

Aspiring to enter this communion with Ideal Form, Randal embarked on his Attican Series. His objective was to reinterpret classical forms in a contemporary manner. He hoped to create objects that would evoke the same pleasure in others that he experienced while enraptured by the beauty of Attic Greek vases. In this body of work Randal quoted the purity of line, potent symmetry, and exquisite articulation of silhouette that came so vividly to life in Attic pottery. He executed his classically shaped vases in cast crystal infused with a luminous chromatic splendor and overlaid with historical and architectural elements.

Individual works within this series exhibit a progression, as they adapt and amplify the ancient principles governing ideal form and proportion. Consider *Jardinière Classique*

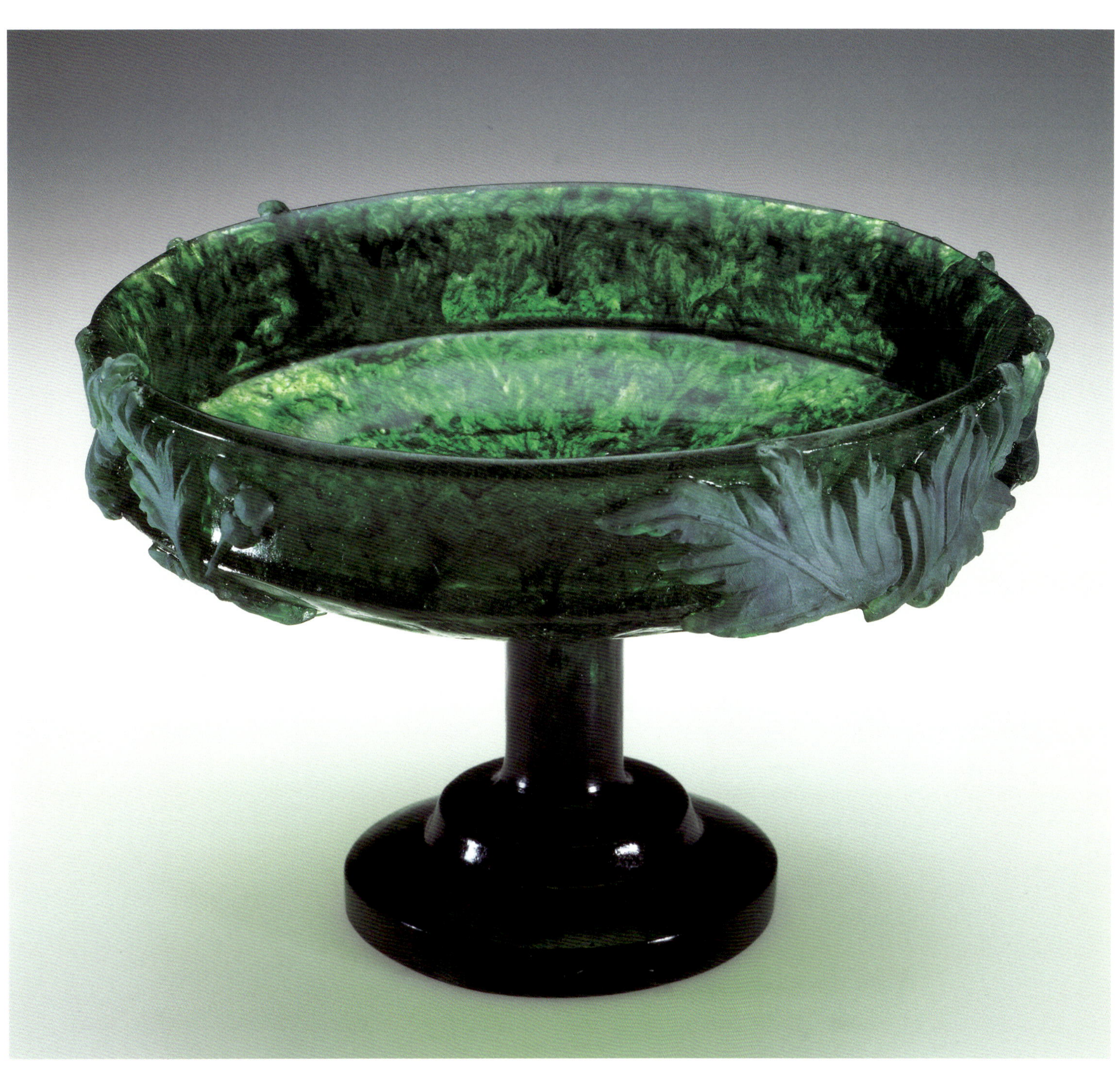

Coupe des Feuilles, 1990

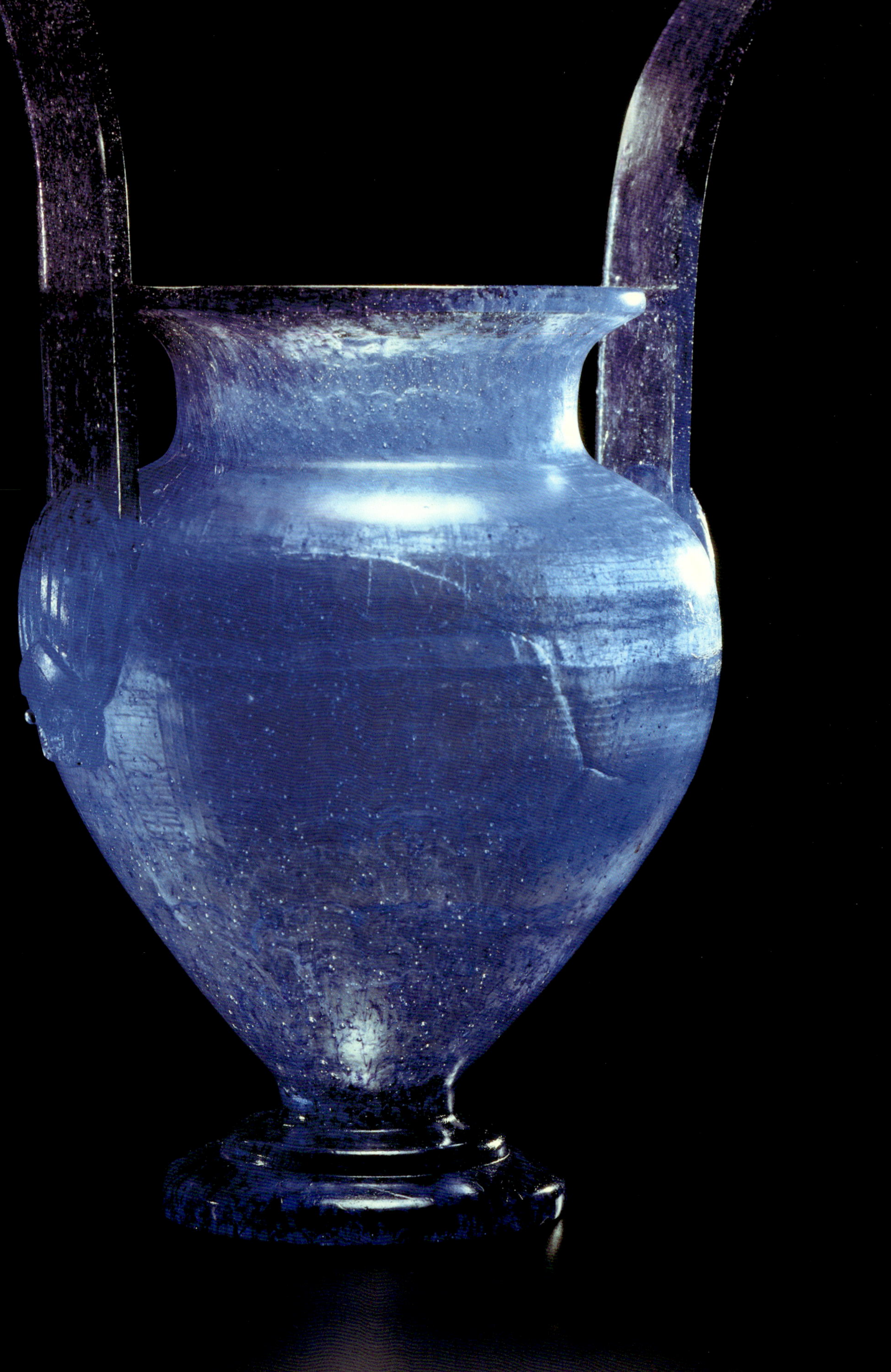

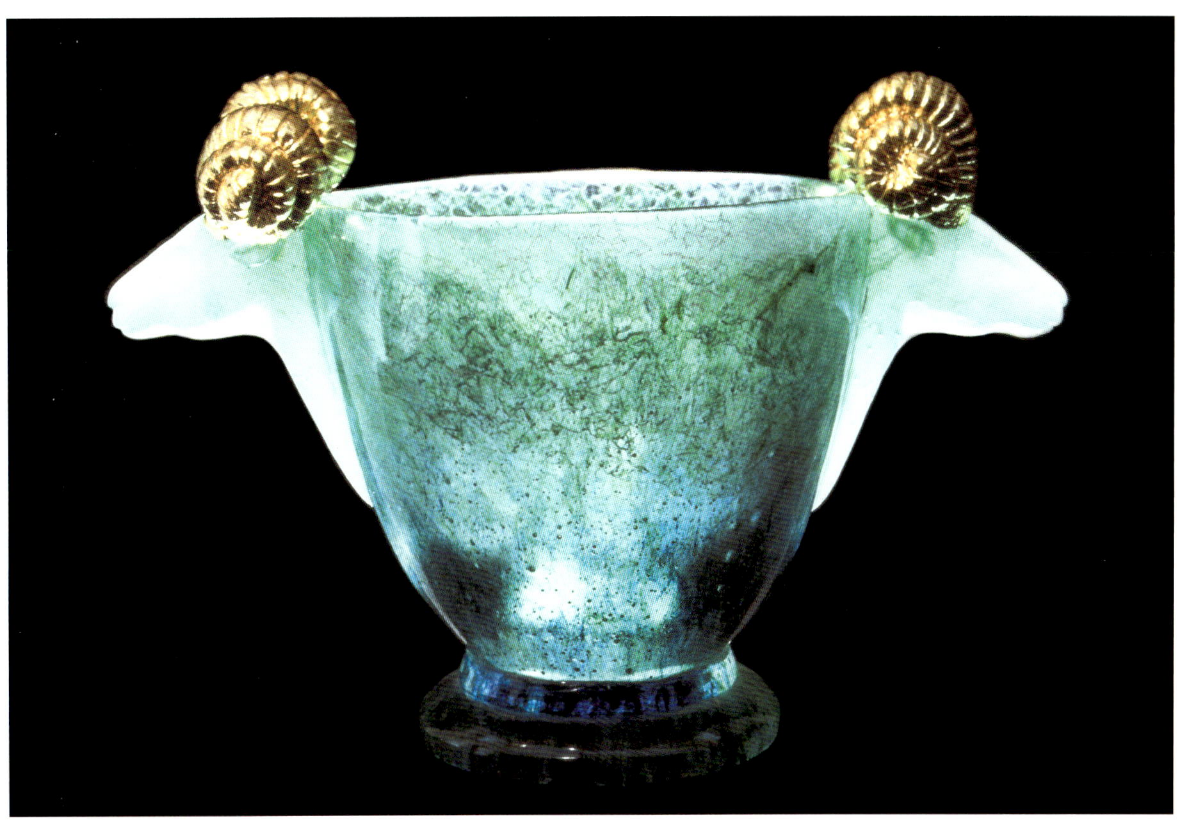

(p. 34) and *Amphore Classique d'Albâtre* (p. 48): both forms are based on the Athenian neck-amphora shape, where the neck is set off from the capacious body of the vessel by a deliberate change in contour. The neck-amphora is the quintessence of classical form, exhibiting refined proportions, calculated volumes, and a crisp silhouette. Randal didn't slavishly copy this model; instead, he used it as a starting point to which he applied his individual aesthetic. Eschewing the straightforward, sturdy, thick-walled characteristics of Attic wares, he fashioned elongated, delicate, elegant handles that rise gracefully from the main belly of the vase. In addition, he cleverly exploited the optical properties of his material, using the translucency of glass as a window to reveal the interior structure and volume of the vase, creating another level of harmonic balance.

Randal also appropriated Greek motifs, such as scrolling acanthus leaves, architectural columns, coiled rams' horns, writhing serpents, and stylized wings in flight. However, he used this ornamentation as sculptural enrichment—to articulate handles, finials, and base supports—rather than as painted imagery or decorative pattern. In deploying these motifs to enhance the basic shape of the vessel, Randal demonstrated a sculptor's control of form, adding a novel interpretation and an enriched vocabulary to the repertory of classicism.

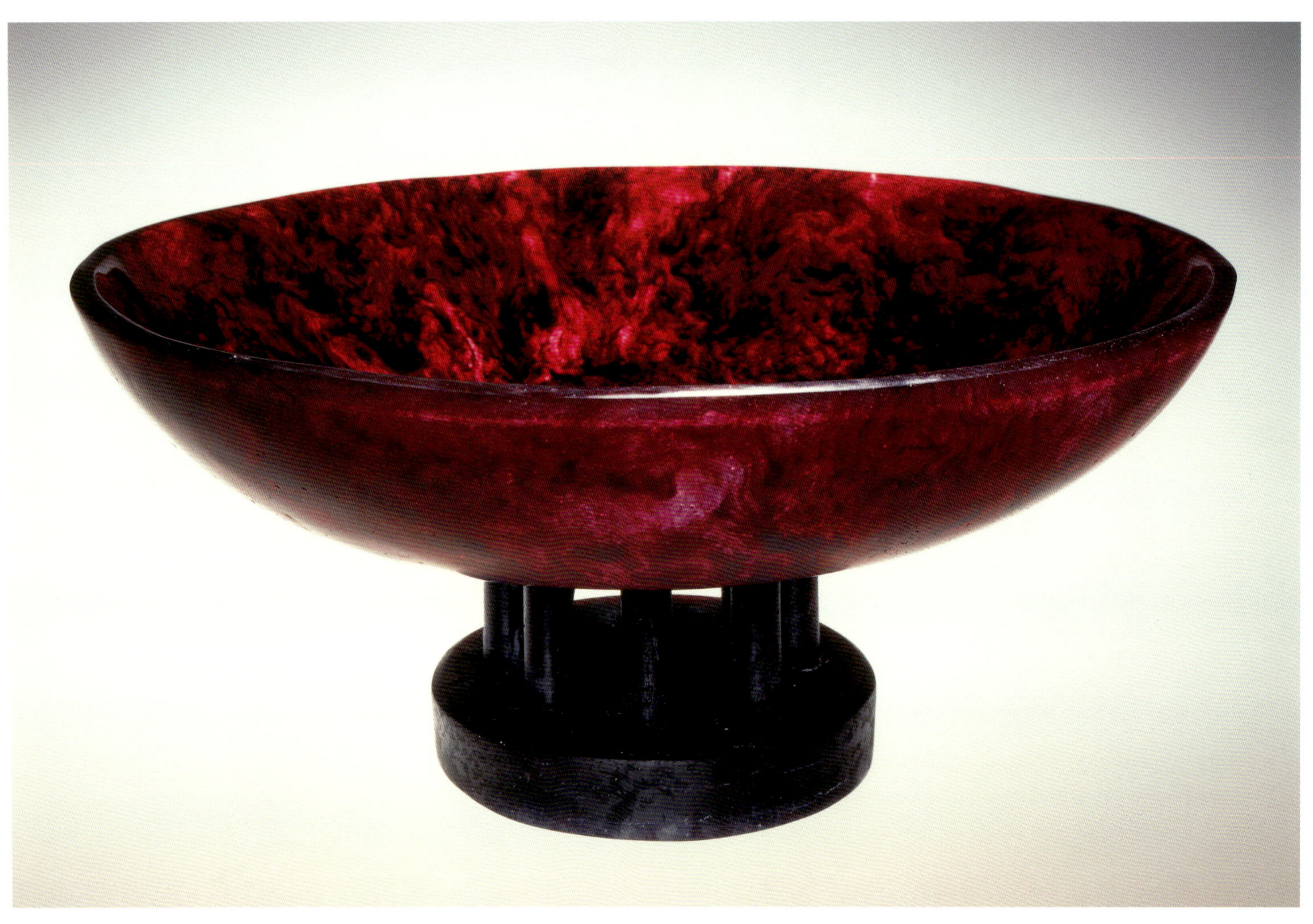

Maestro en Rouge, 1991   Les Moutons Brisés, 1991

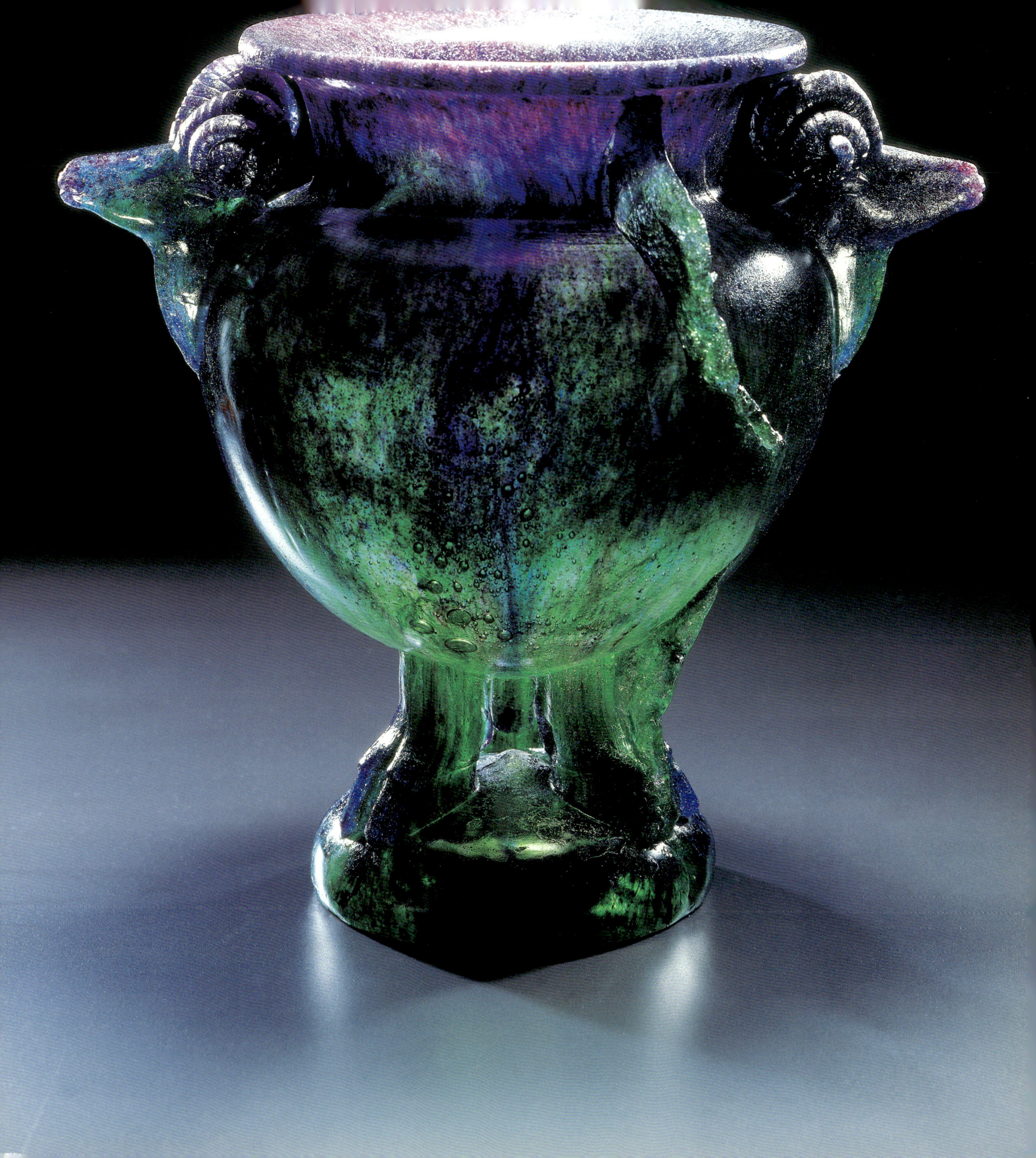

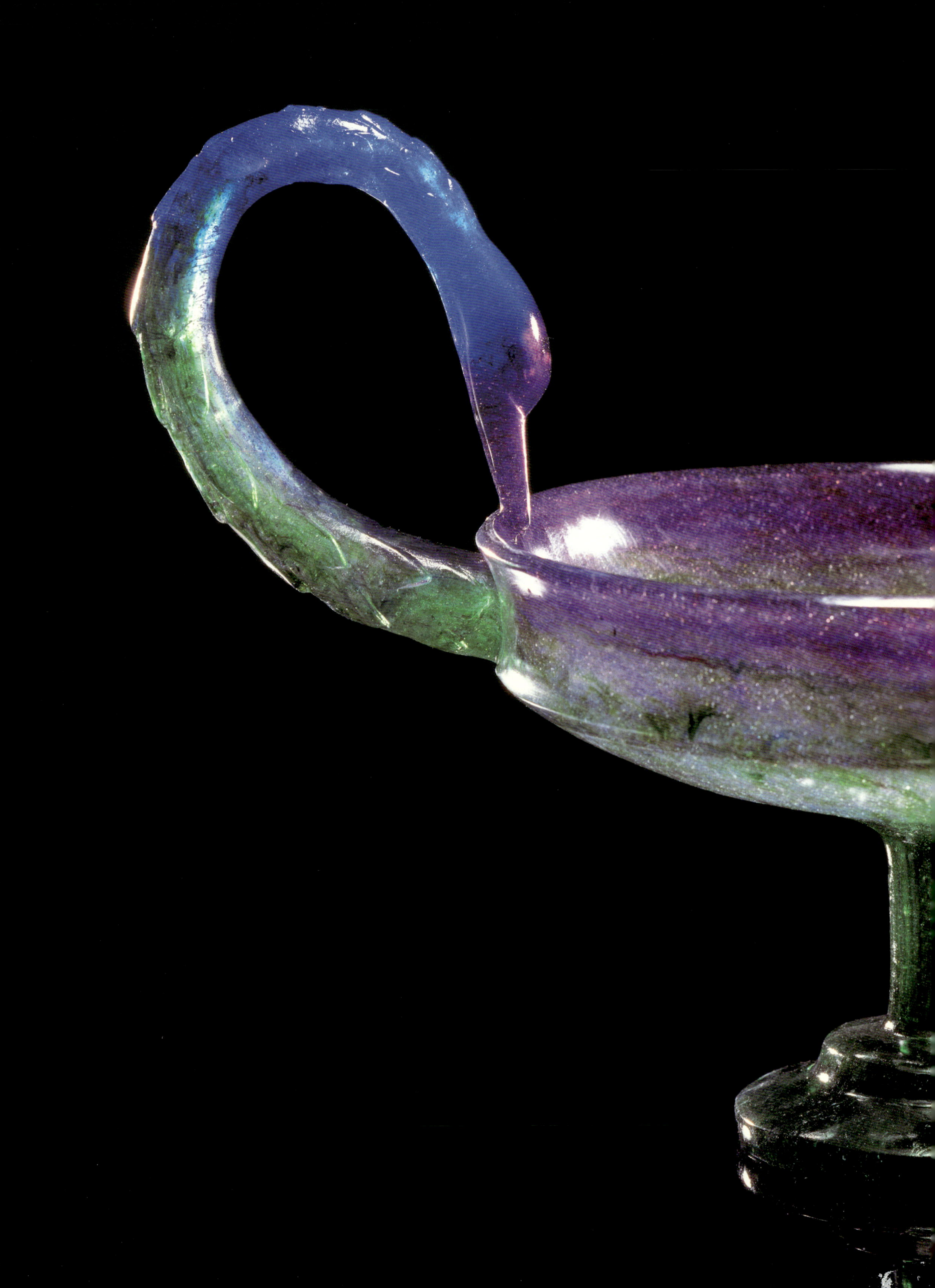

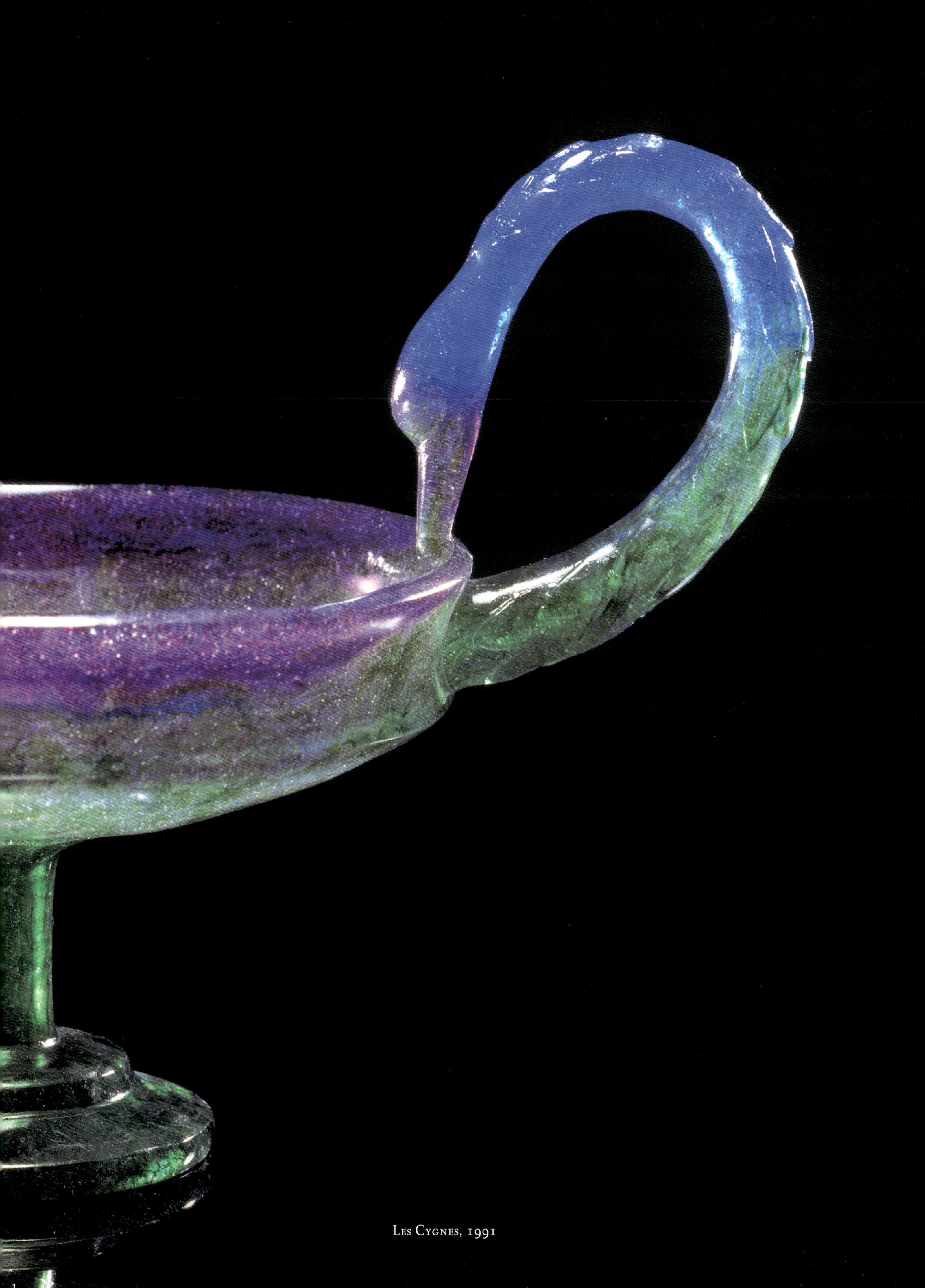

Les Cygnes, 1991

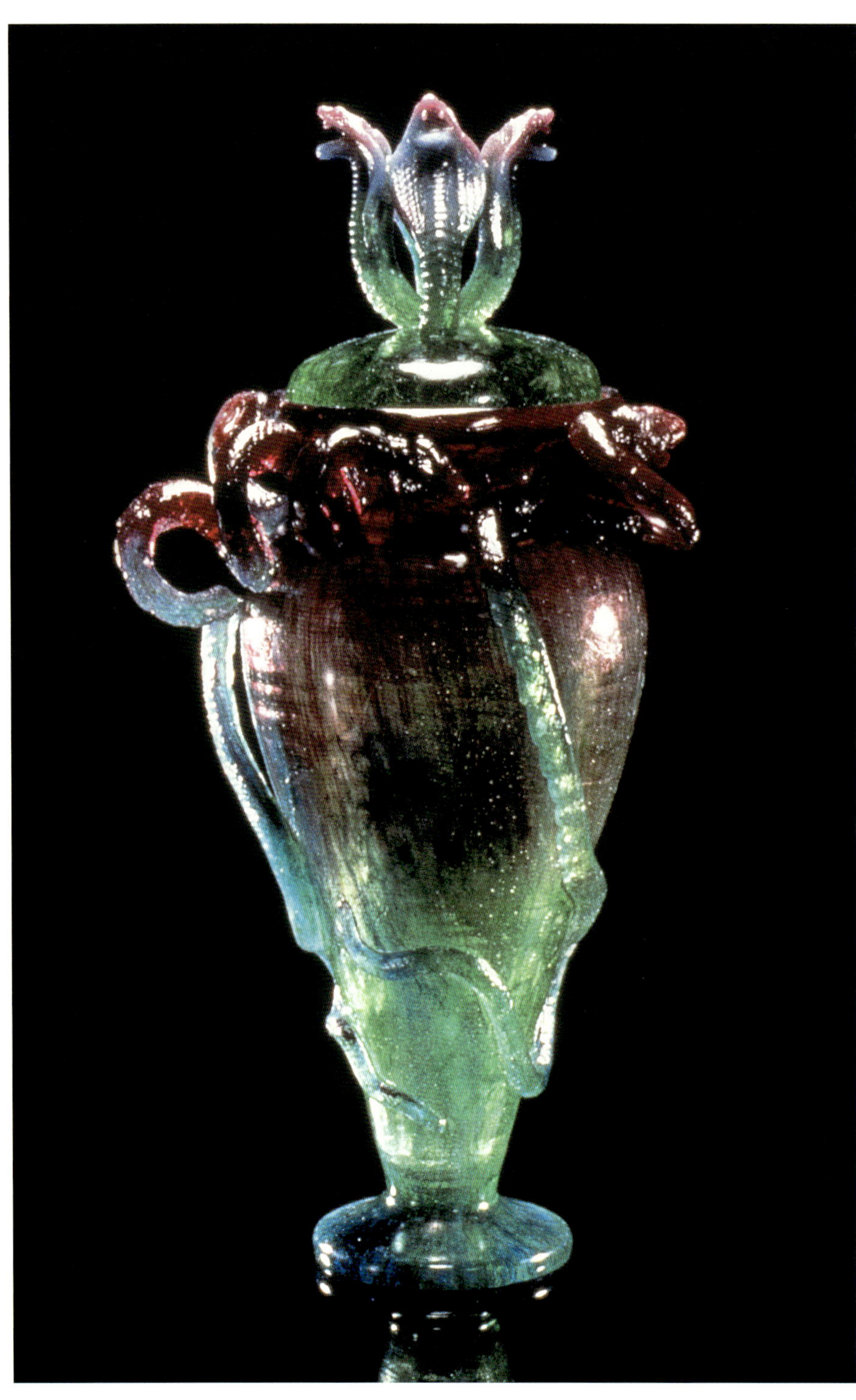

Un Chapeau Épouvantable, 1991   Pearl of Wisdom, 1992

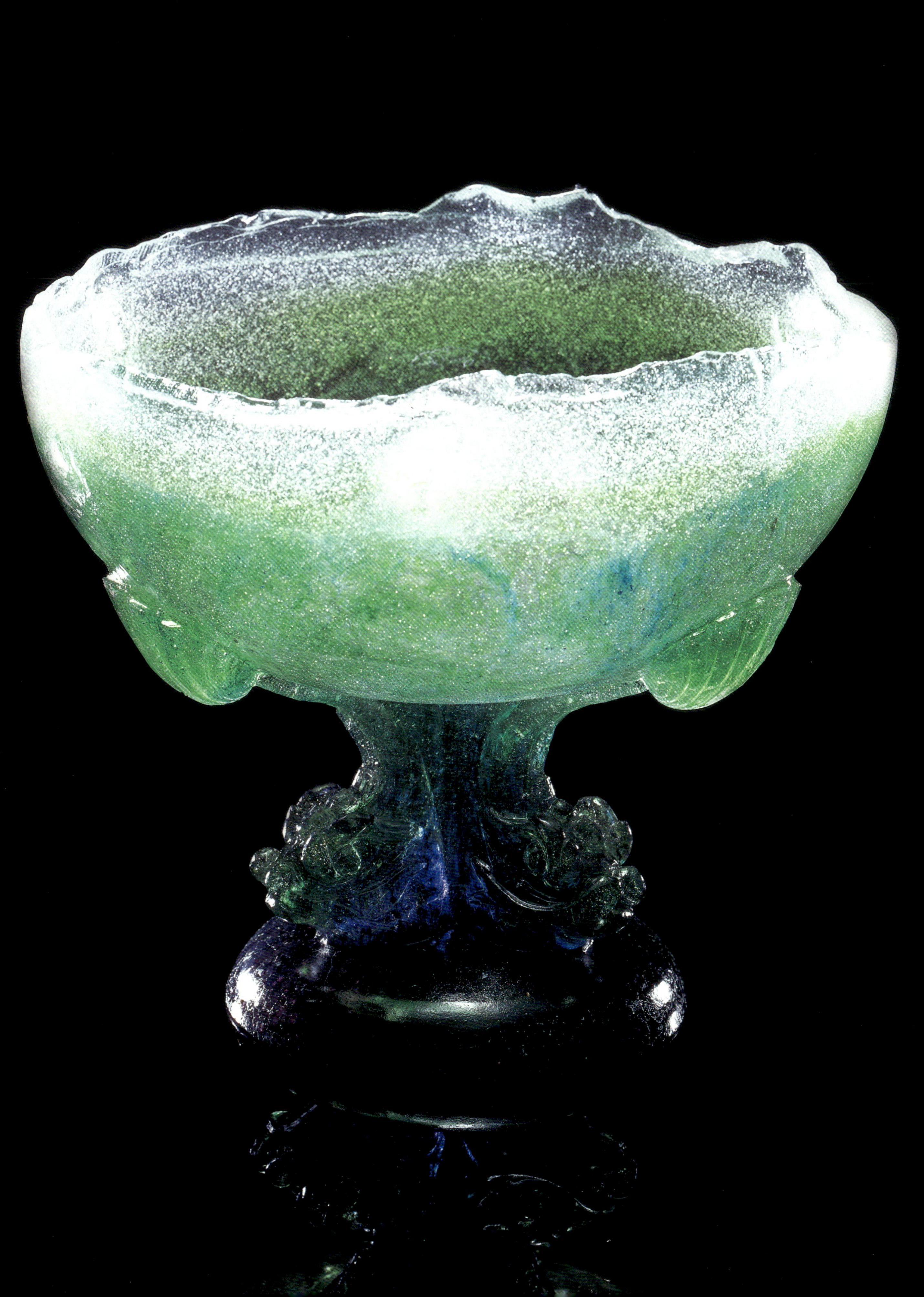

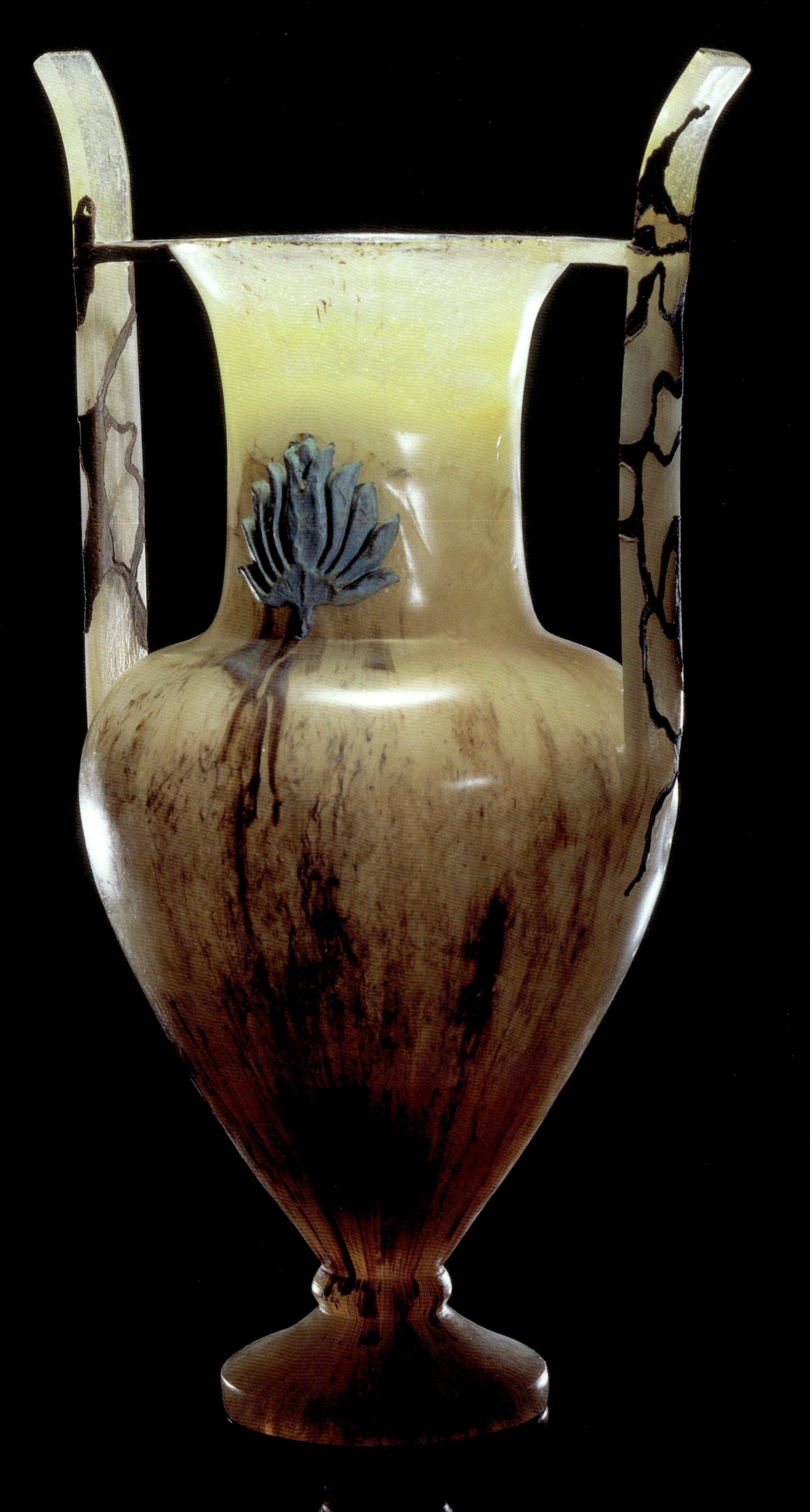

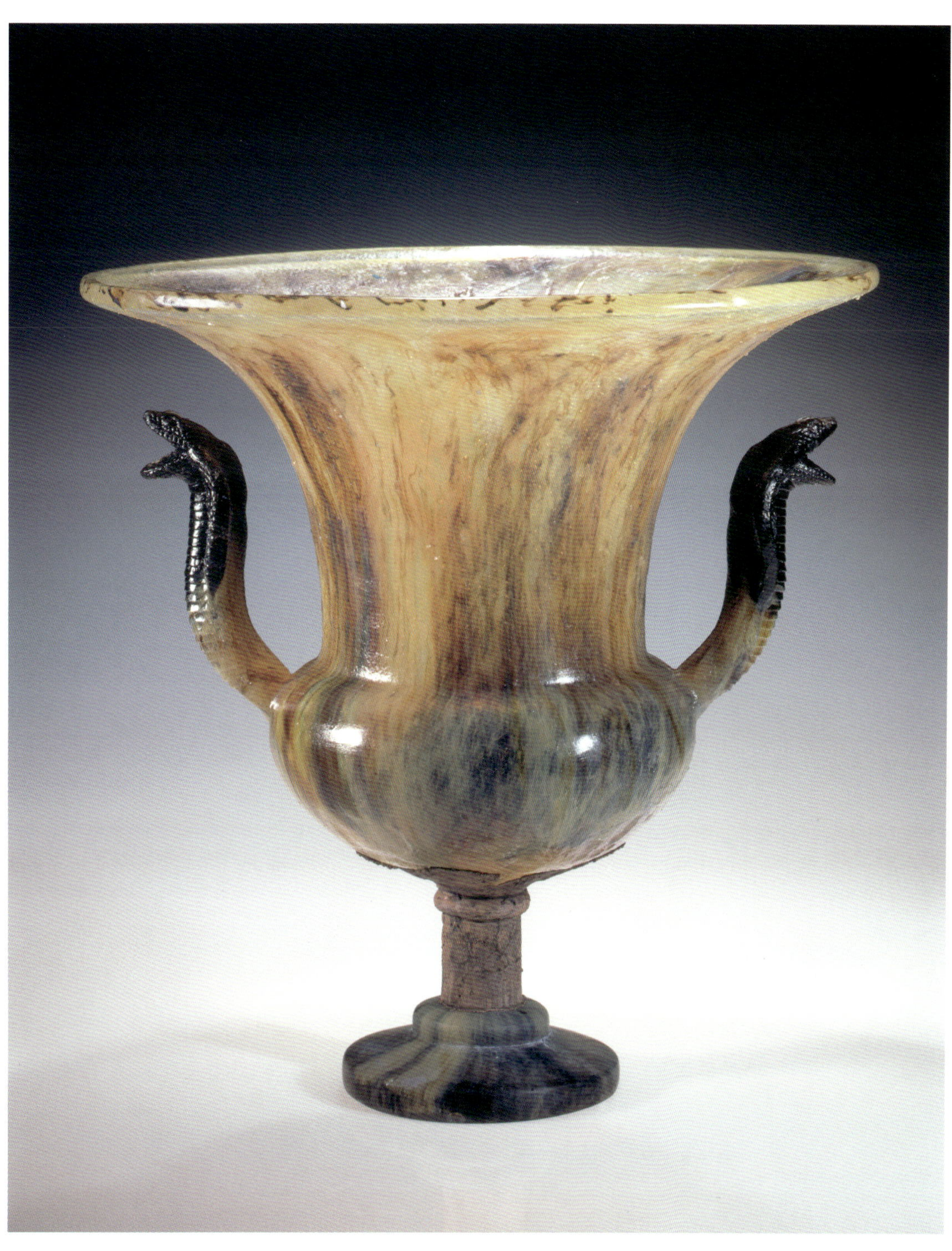

AMPHORE CLASSIQUE D'ALBÂTRE, 1993   LES SERPENTS D'ALBÂTRE, 1991   49

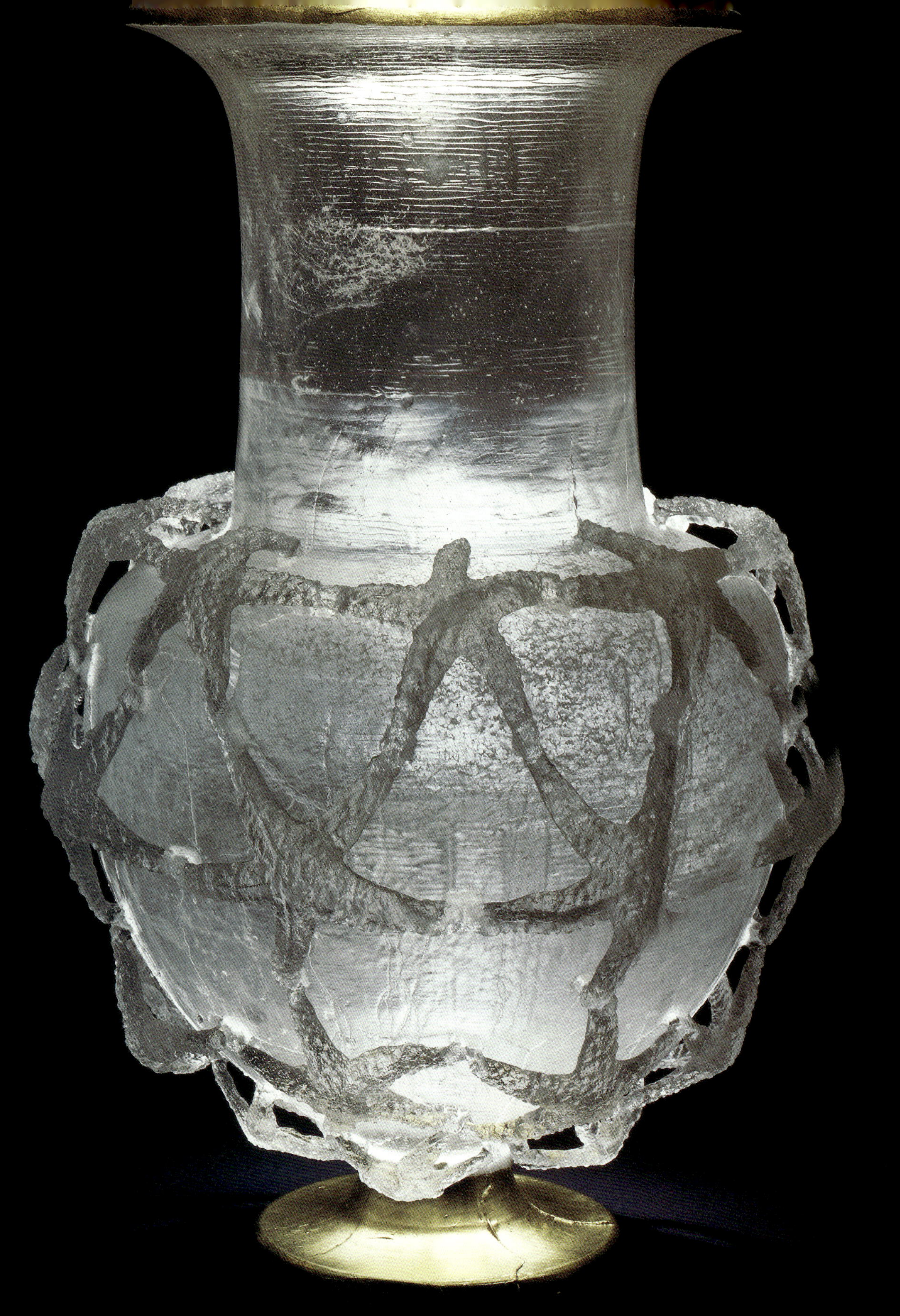

CAGE CUPS
THE THIRST
FOR PERFECTION

A masterpiece is a battle against death.

—Jean Cocteau

Randal's imagination was enlivened by the rich visual source material provided by his study of antiquity. His artistic trajectory next led him to Rome, and to further investigations of glassmaking in the ancient world. He discovered a fascinating type of vessel, the Roman *vasa diatreta*, and was immediately inspired to re-create it. Literally translated from the Latin, *vasa diatreta* means "open-work vessels." However, based on their appearance they are more commonly referred to as "cage cups."

The most complex vessels produced during the golden age of Roman glassmaking (fourth to fifth century AD), cage cups were made by a laborious and risky process that required the consummate skill of the glasscutter. A single thick-walled blank, either a handblown or mold-blown shallow bowl, was carved with intricate undercut decoration that stood free from the body of the piece. This decoration was usually in the form of a net or cage attached to the vessel by strategically hidden supporting struts. The vessel thus appeared to be enclosed in an openwork cage.[11] Cage cups required absolute precision in cutting, as any break in the mesh meant that the entire piece had to be discarded. So delicate was the labor and so uncertain the outcome that a clause was written into Roman law to protect the glasscutter, stating that the "craftsman was to be permitted to accept the work only on condition that he took no risk whatsoever."[12] Cage cups were the finest and most luxurious glasswares of their time, and only the privileged class could afford them.

Randal went to the Corning Museum of Glass in 1990 to see the famous cage cups in its collection. On exhibit was the renowned *Roman Cage Cup* from 300 AD, a shallow bowl with metal fittings around the rim, probably used as a hanging lamp, which was made in the traditional manner. Randal admired the virtuoso

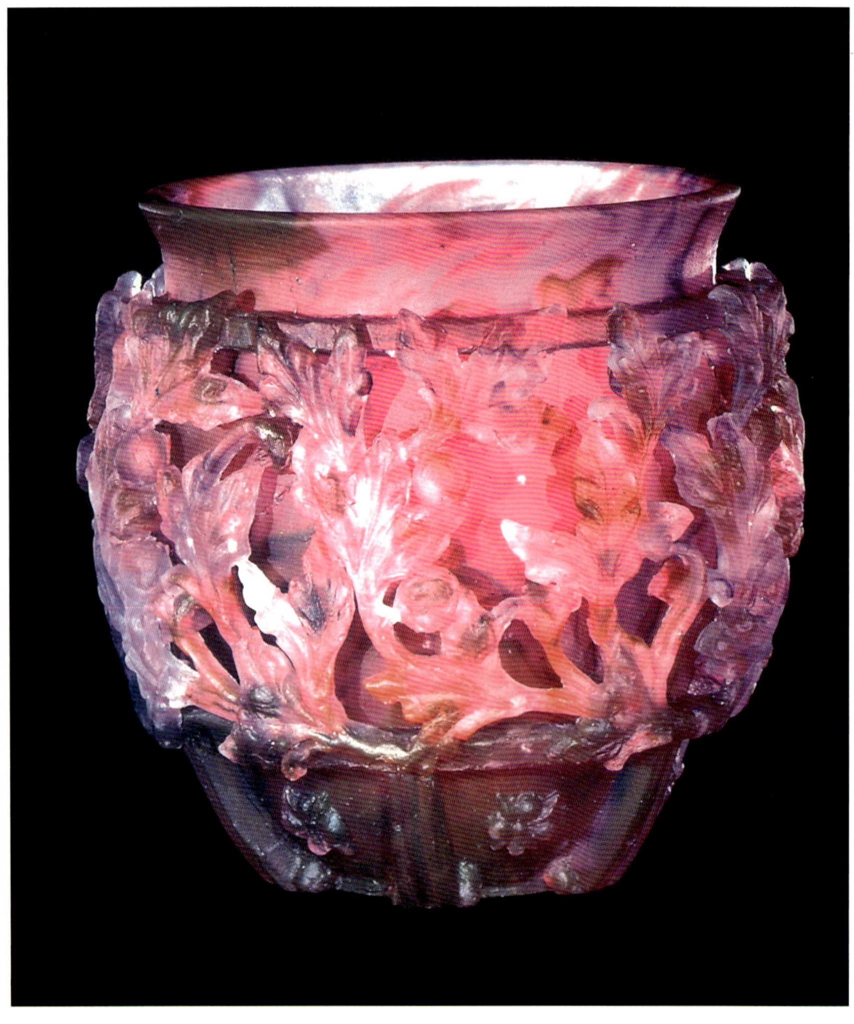

Frederick Carder, *Diatretum Vase*, 1953

carving of this ancient cup, but found himself even more in awe of several pieces from the 1950s that were not cut, but cast by the *cire perdue* (lost wax) process. These modern cage cups, inspired by the Roman *vasa diatreta*, were designed by Frederick Carder for Steuben Glass.

Carder, a brilliant innovator of glass techniques, perfected his version of the cage cup by adapting the lost-wax casting process—progressing through a series of complex steps that involved mold-making and the *pâte de verre* method—to produce vessels with overlaid ornamentation in high relief. This outer layer was fused to the body by small hidden glass struts, thus imitating the cut openwork of antique cage cups.

Emboldened by the success he had achieved in casting his Attican vases, Randal decided he was ready to undertake the challenge of casting cage cups. The key was to consider the negative space—the "open" part of the openwork—to be as important to the design as the positive space. Randal recalled an exercise he had been given while a student at England's Hampstead College that helped him understand this principle: "The headmistress of my college was a small, wiry woman, built rather like a sparrow, and she was a bundle of enthusiasm and energy. A tremendous lover of the arts, she taught most of the art classes in the school. We spent many afternoons on Hampstead Heath practicing life drawing and

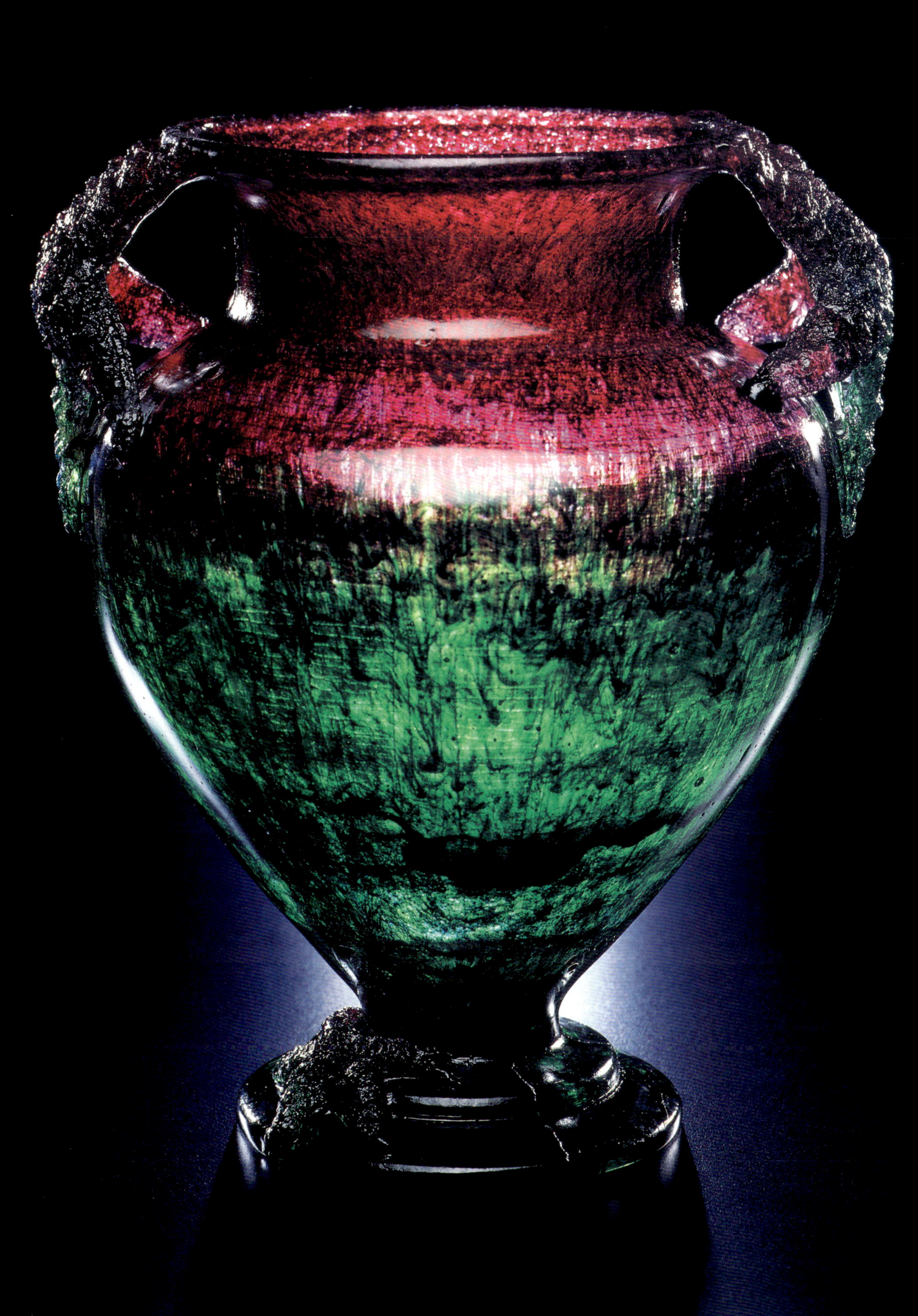

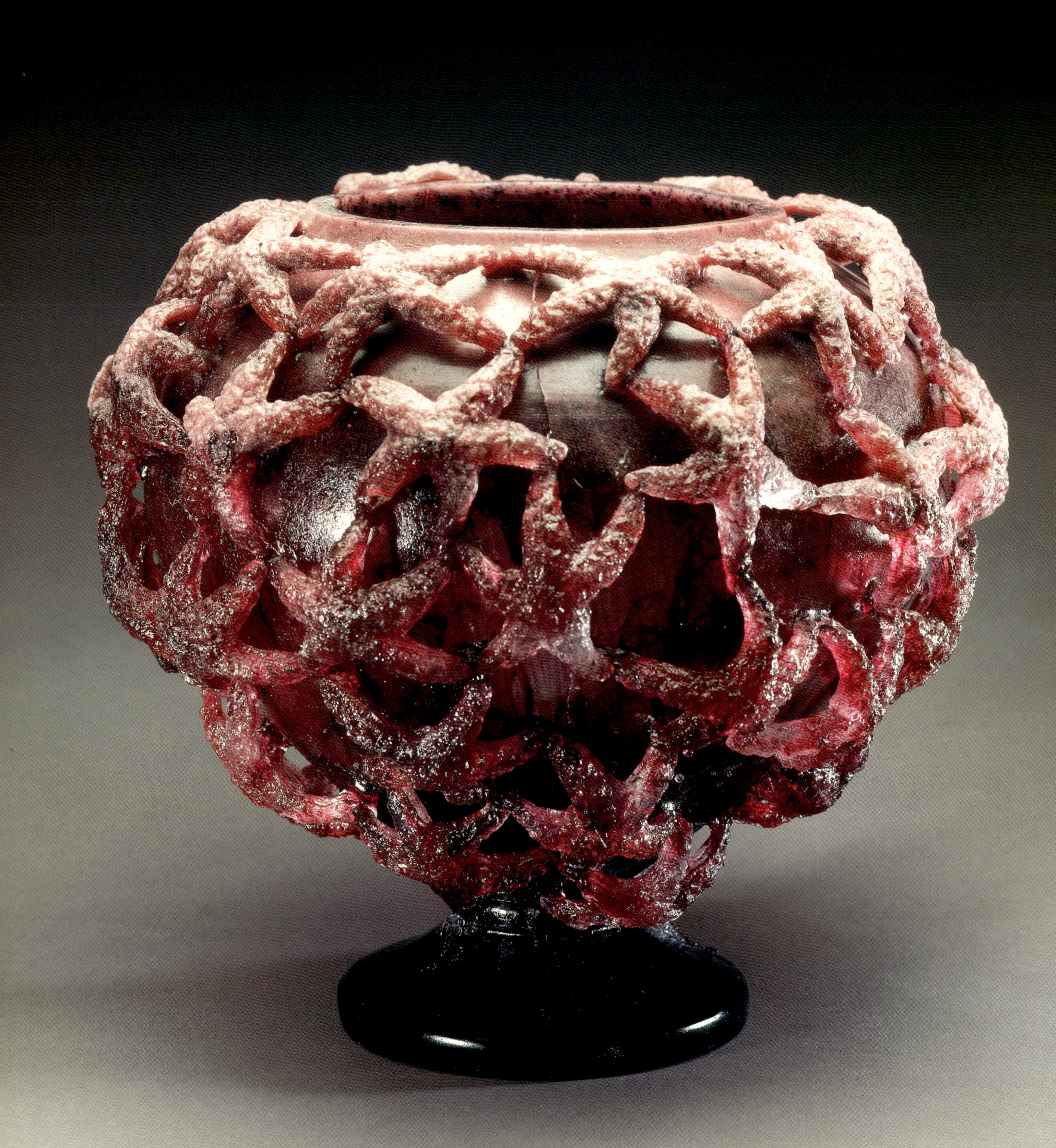

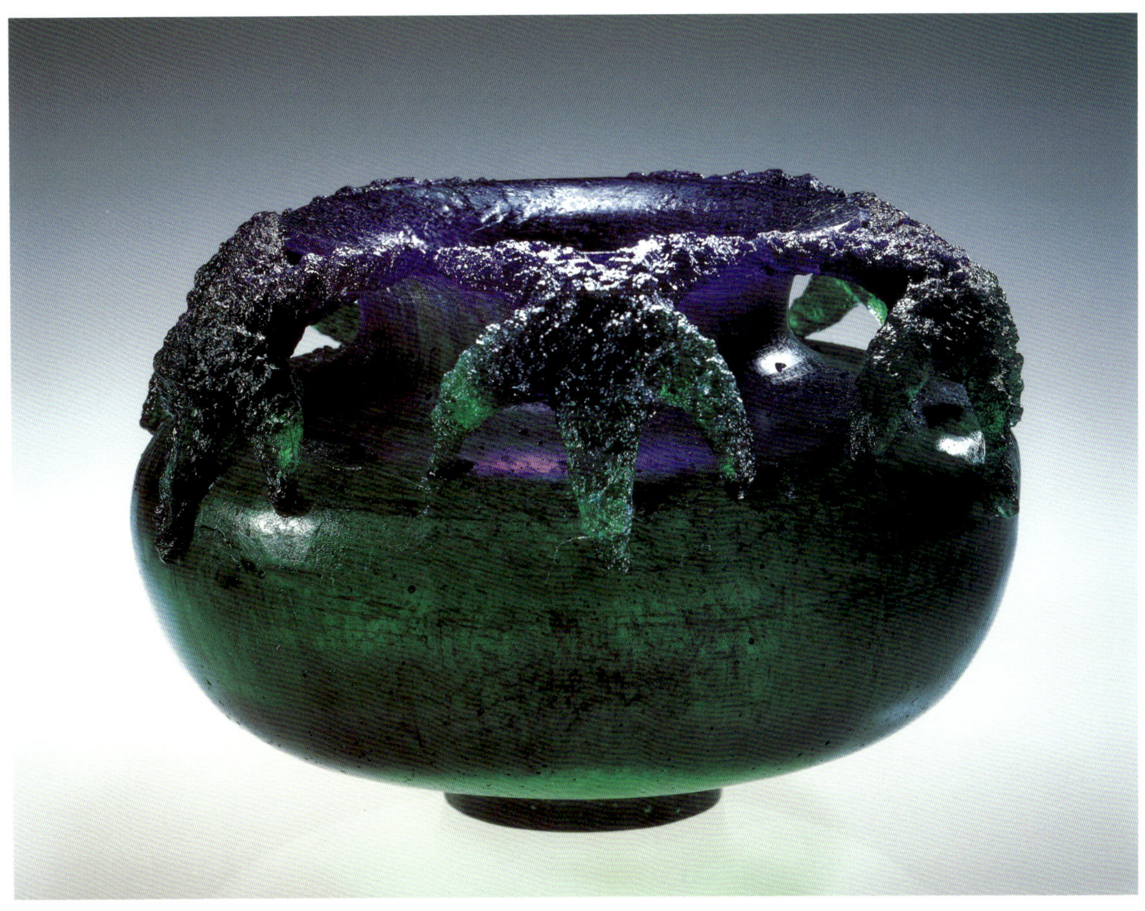

nature studies. One day I remember coming back from lunch to find all the chairs stacked in a huge pile in the center of the room. We were told to get out our pads and pencils and draw—not the stack of chairs, but the negative spaces between and around the chairs. It was a really compelling exercise, as it made me realize that negative space can actually define and delimit an object."

Following Carder's lead, Randal designed and cast a series of vases with an attached outer layer of ornamentation, using a starfish motif as the central sculptural element. His first castings, *Danse des Étoiles*, *Les Étoiles*, and *Danse des Étoiles II* (all from the early 1990s), were promising, although modest, attempts to fully realize the cage effect. In these pieces the starfish were primarily used as sculptural handles or rim designs. More accomplished and finer cagework followed in *Diatrète de la Mer* and *Diatrète de Nuit* (p. 56). Here the spiny creatures were linked at their tips and encircled the vessel completely in an undulating net of stars. In *A Vintage Cage Cup* (pp. 68, 69) Randal reached the zenith of his accomplishment in the form. This vessel is fully encased in a spiraling trellis laden with grapevines and bunches of grapes ripe for harvesting.

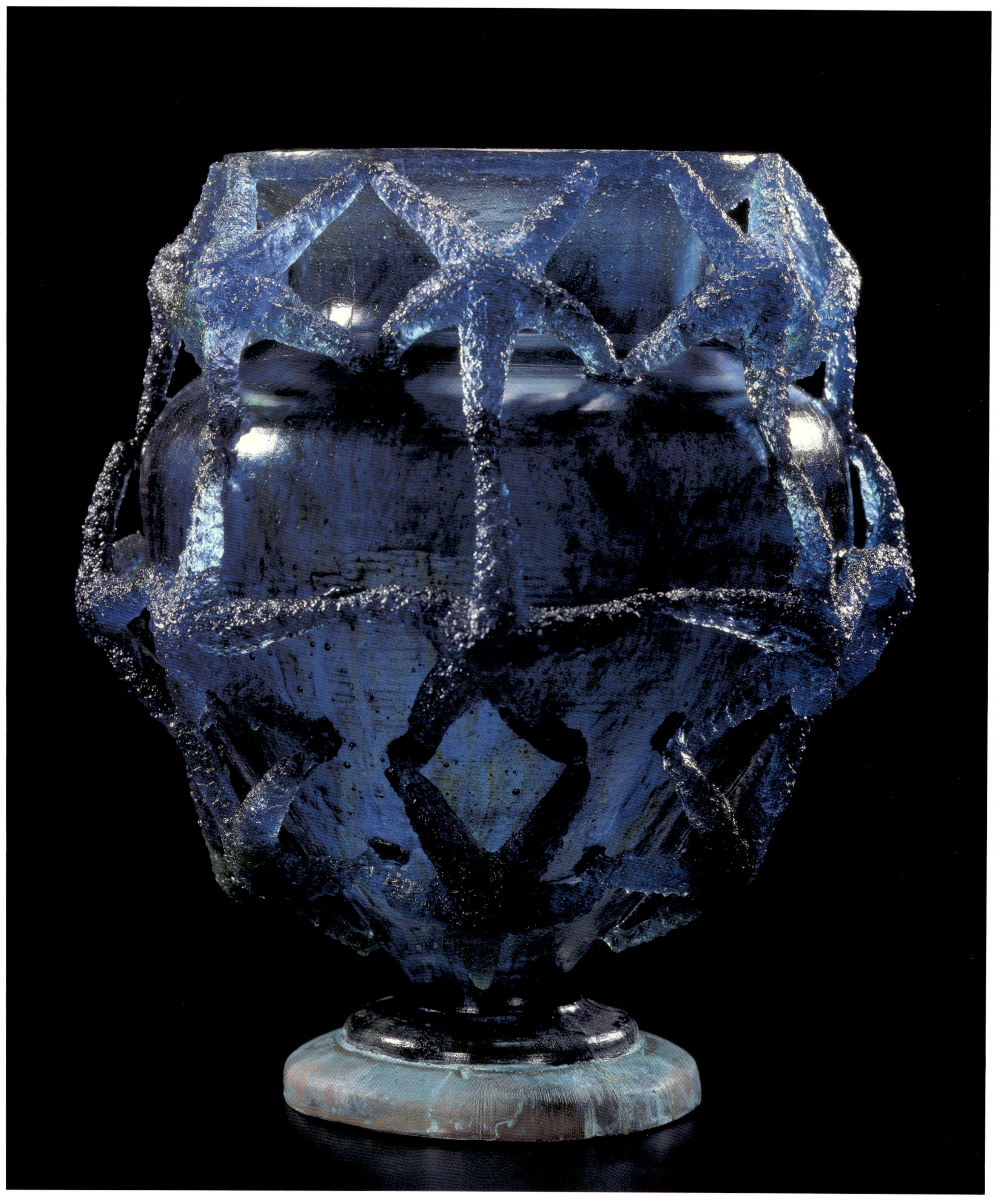

Diatrète de Nuit, 1995

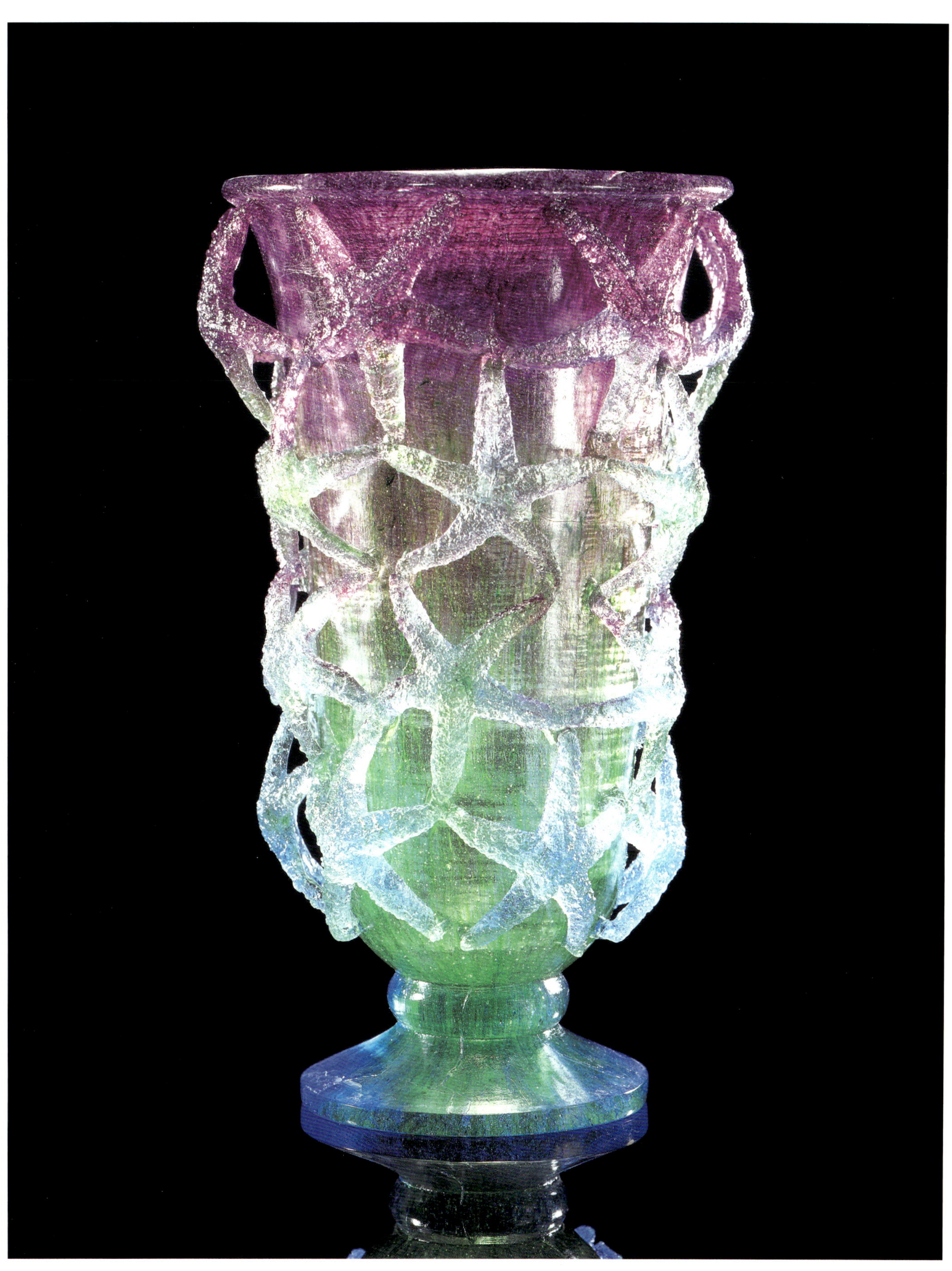

Grand Diatrète de la Mer, 1991

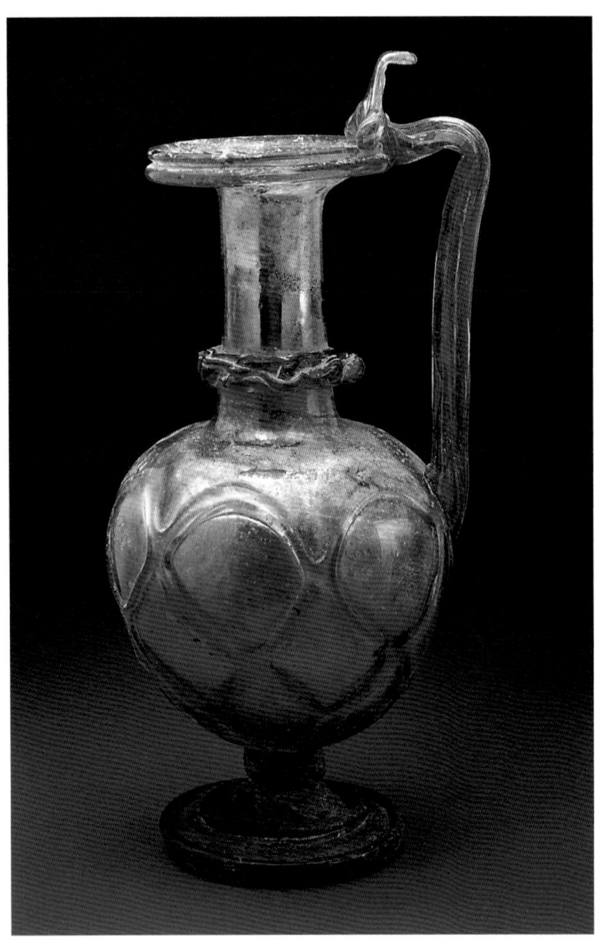

Jug, n.d., Syria or Palestine

But Randal did not remain content with his achievement. In what he now admits was a "fit of sheer madness" he developed a casting technique to produce "double cage cups," vessels surrounded by two layers of latticework crossing each other in opposing directions. For such a concept he could find no antecedents, and Randal believes he is the only artist to achieve this technical feat in glass. *Grand Double Helix Diatreta* (p. 60) and *Autumn Double Helix Diatreta* (p. 63) are classic Attic-shaped vases cast in vivid hues. They shimmer behind graceful arching struts woven into splendidly intricate nets.

The total effect is one of visual theater. Dramatic and commanding in their presence, double cage cups engage both the eye and the intellect. Randal soon learned, however, that these glass "superstars" were not only highly temperamental, they were also exceedingly fragile. The utmost attention to detail in fabricating the multipart mold, and a deft hand at divesting the mold after the firing, were required to produce a successful casting. Out of the fifteen double cage cups he attempted, only six survived the process. He realized that he would have to abandon this alluring pursuit and move on to a more gratifying, and more forgiving, casting process. Once again he cast his net deeply into creative waters to capture the next inspiration.

     DIATRÈTE GLACÉ, 1993

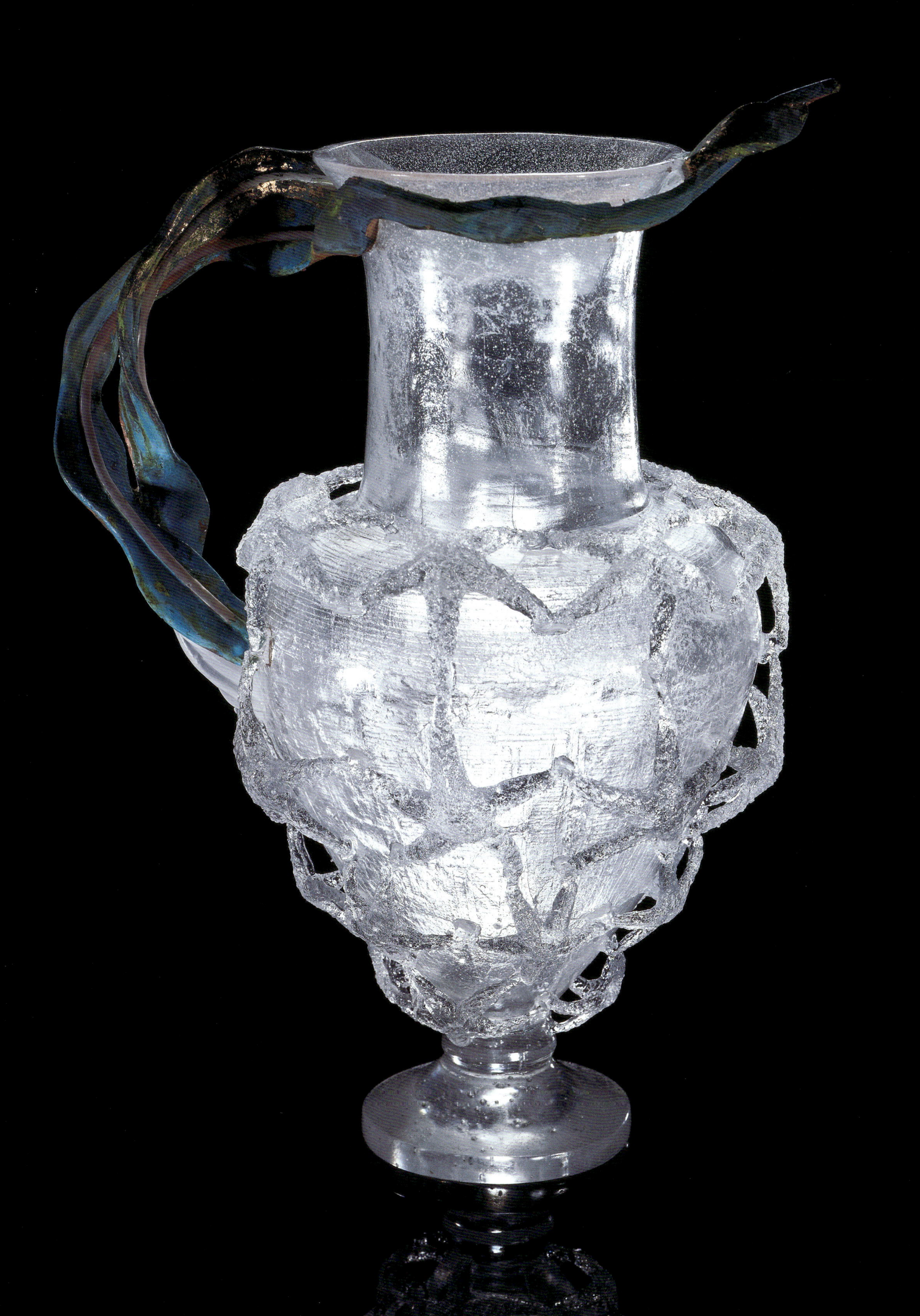

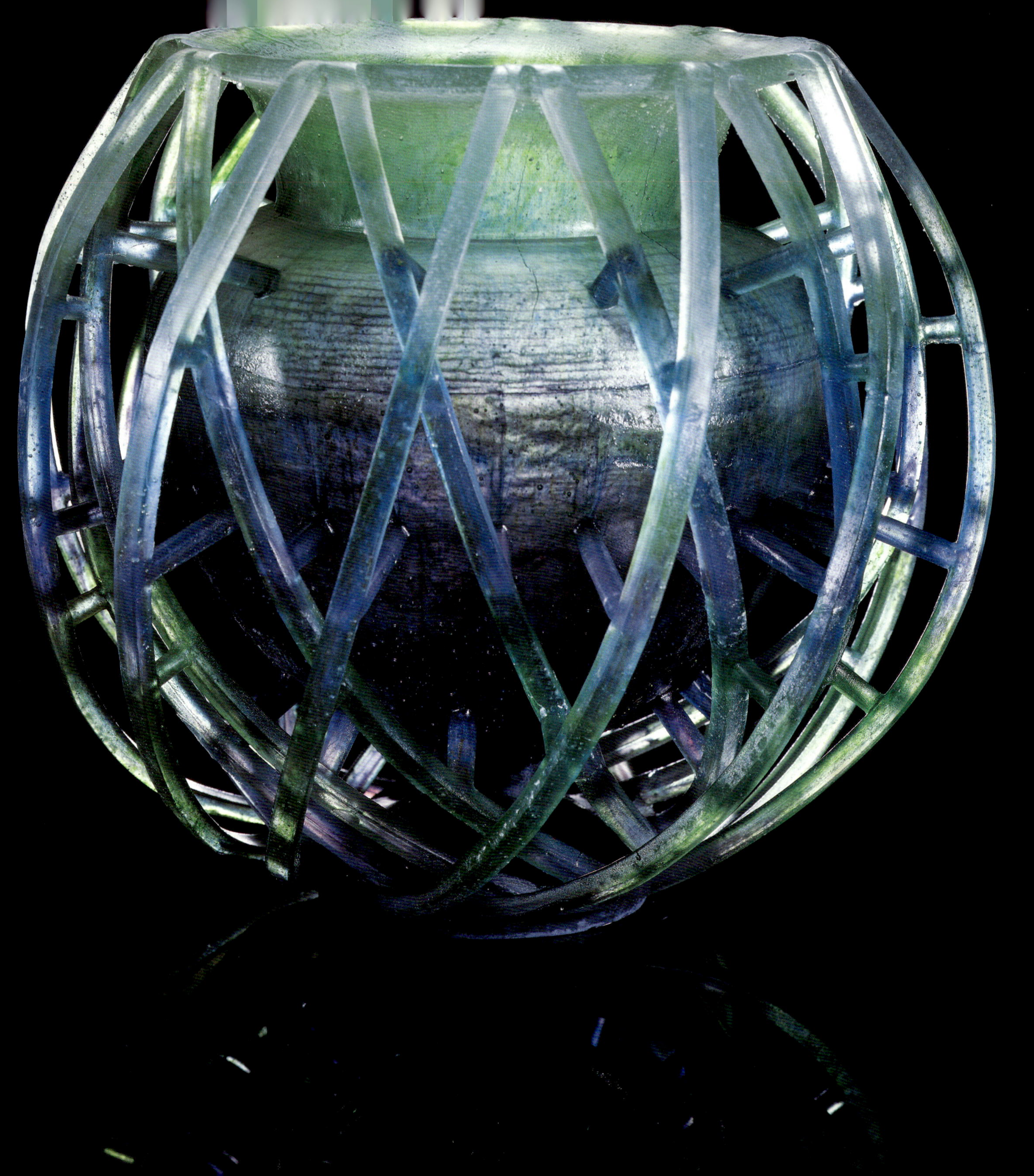

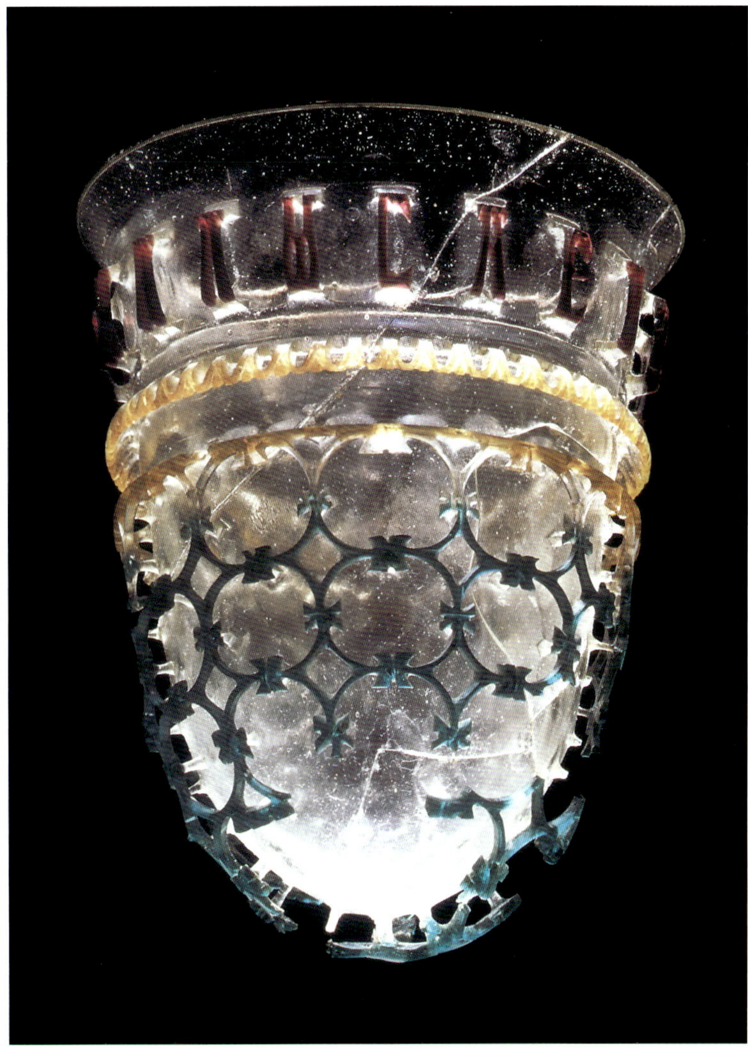

Diatreton glass, 1st half 4th century
The glass is inscribed ΠΙΕ ΖΗΣΑΙΣ ΚΑΛΩΣ ΑΕΙ
("Drink, live well forever.")

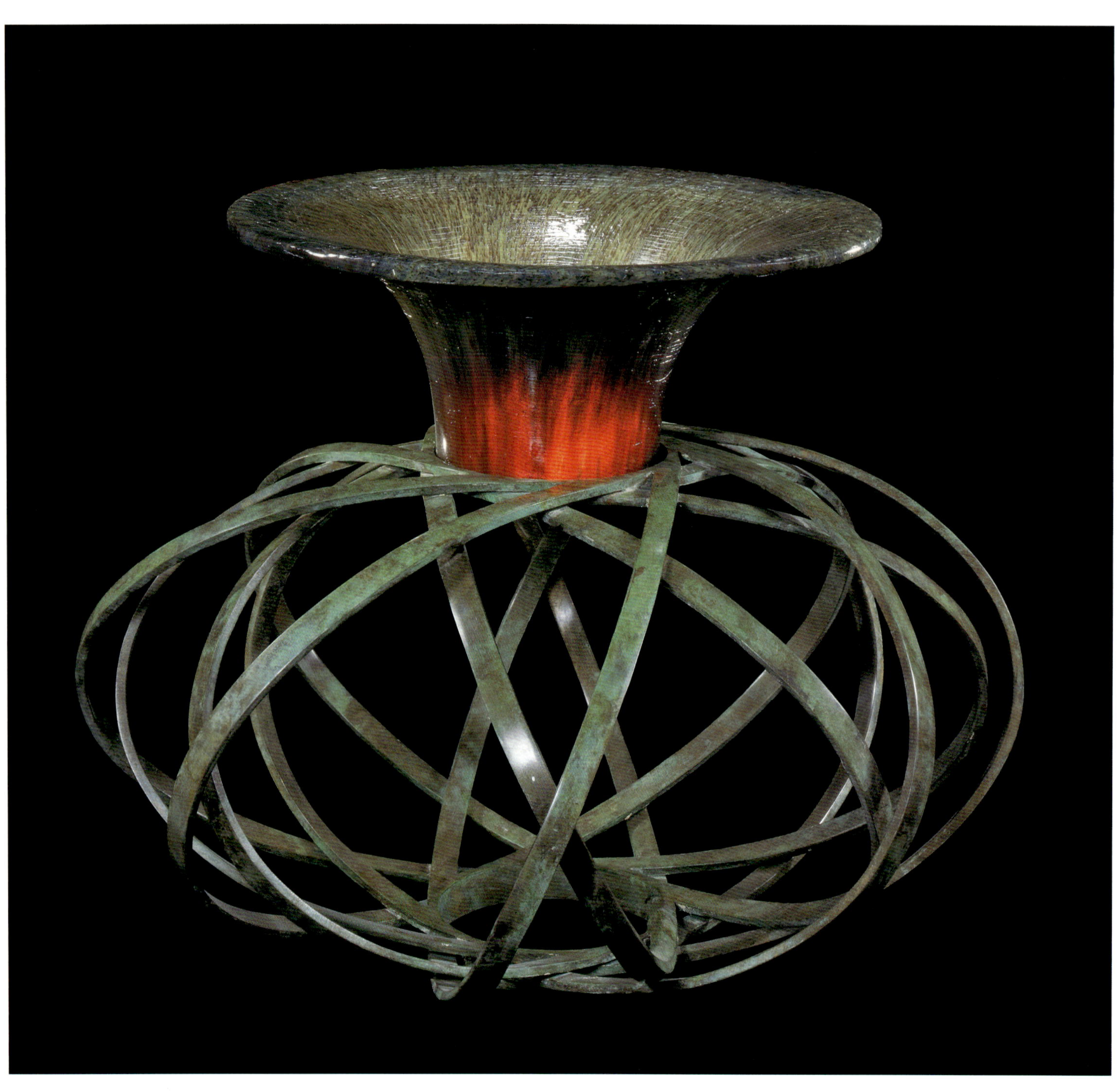

DOUBLE HELIX TABLE LAMP, 2001

AUTUMN DOUBLE HELIX DIATRETA, 1997

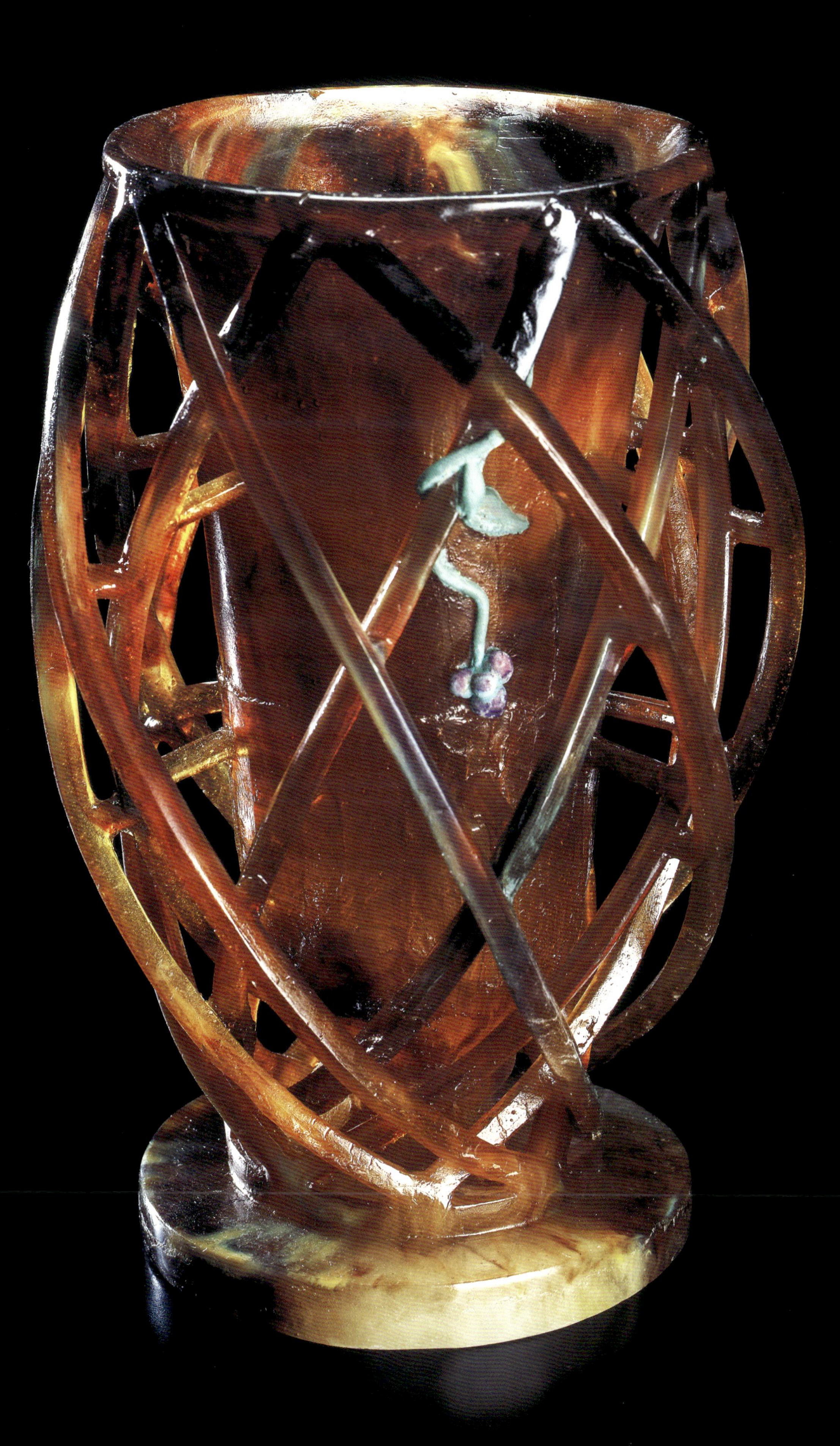

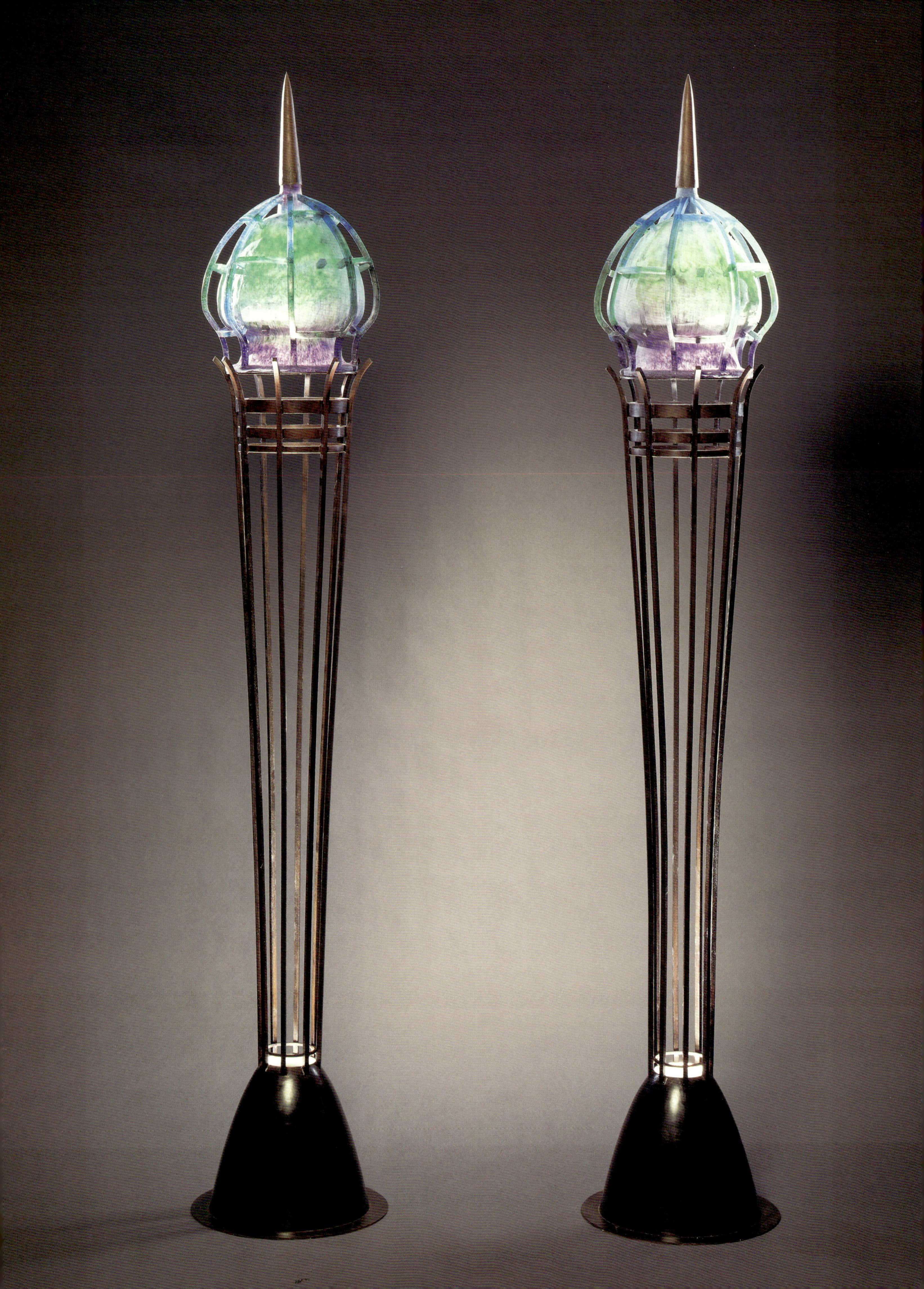

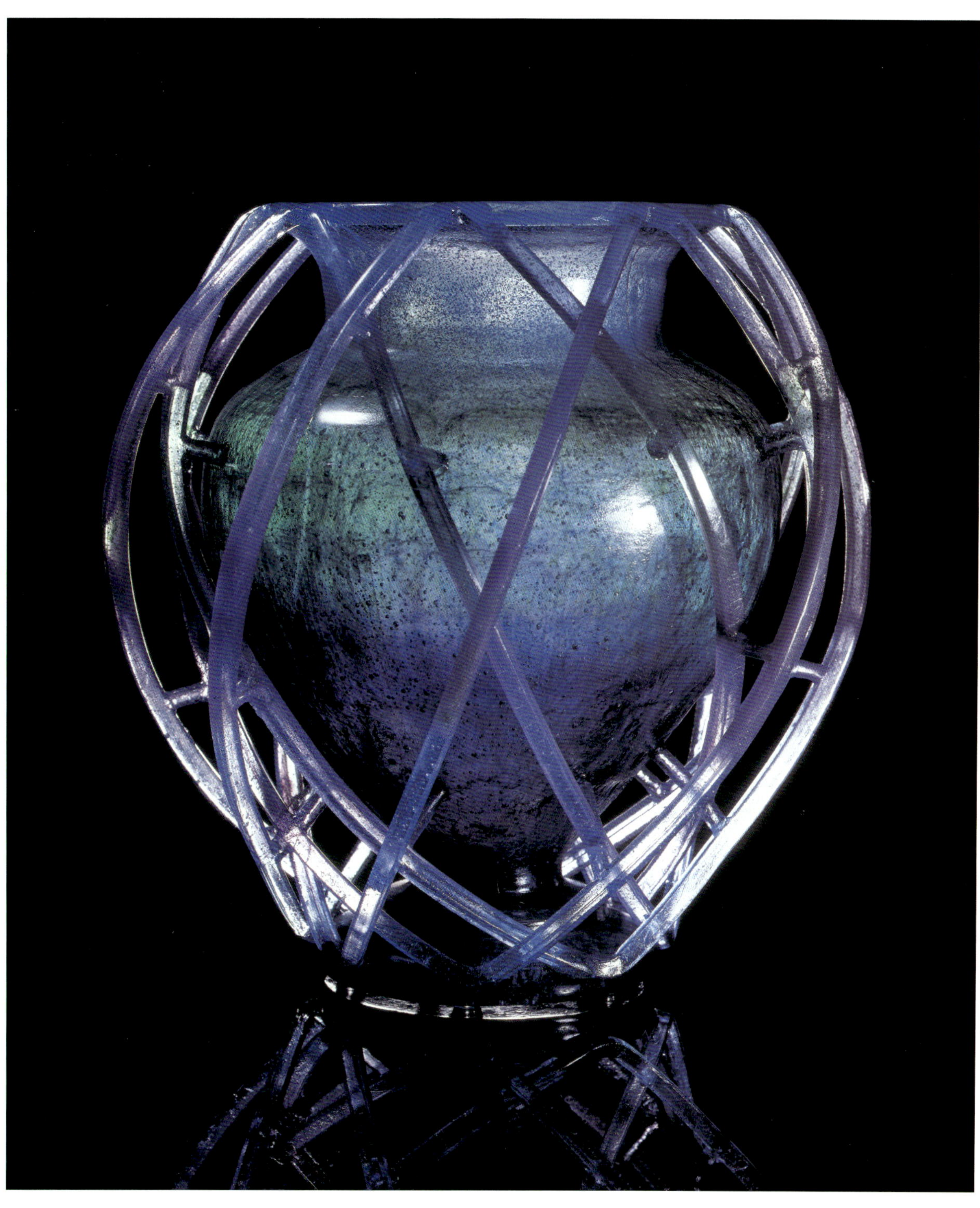

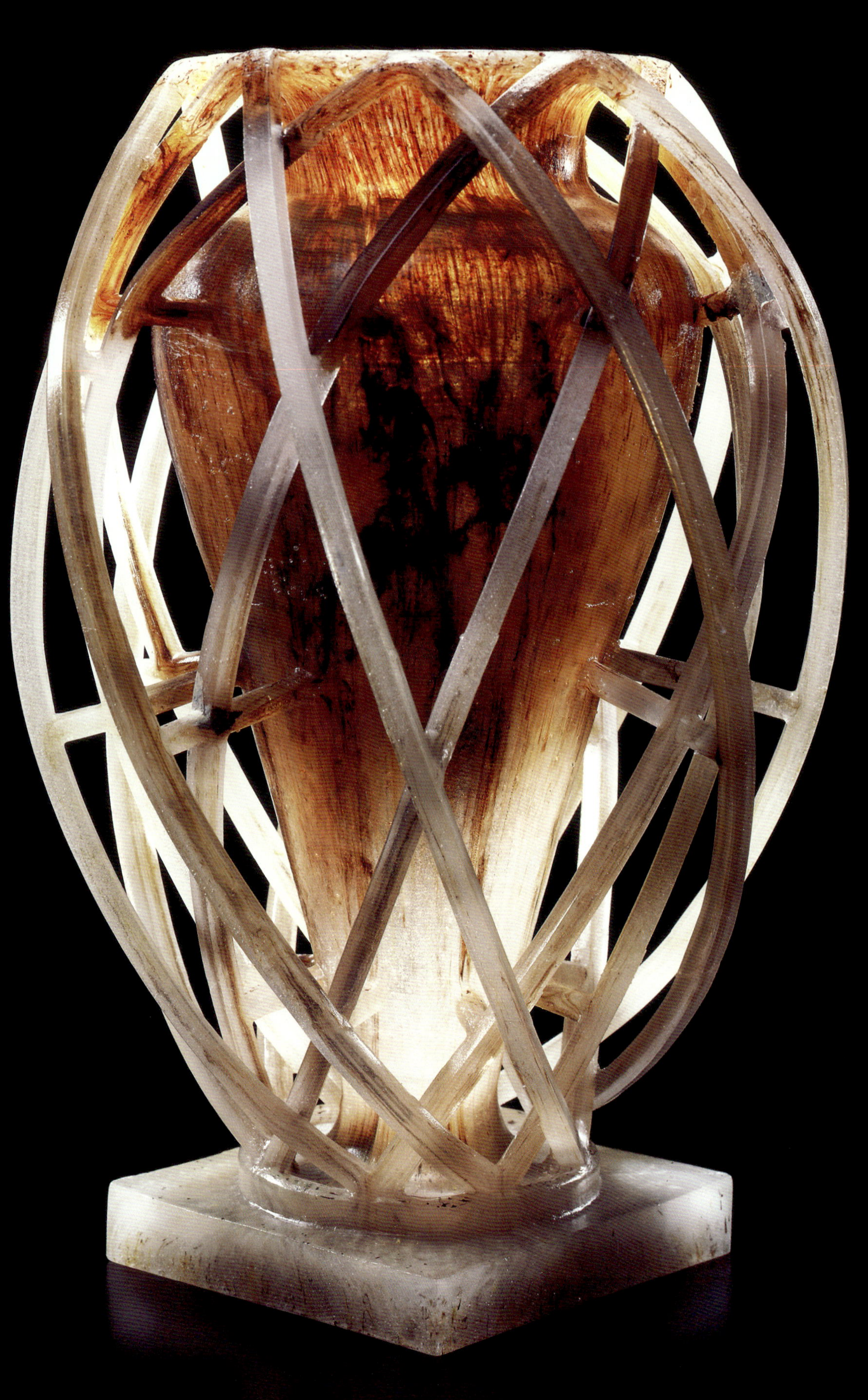

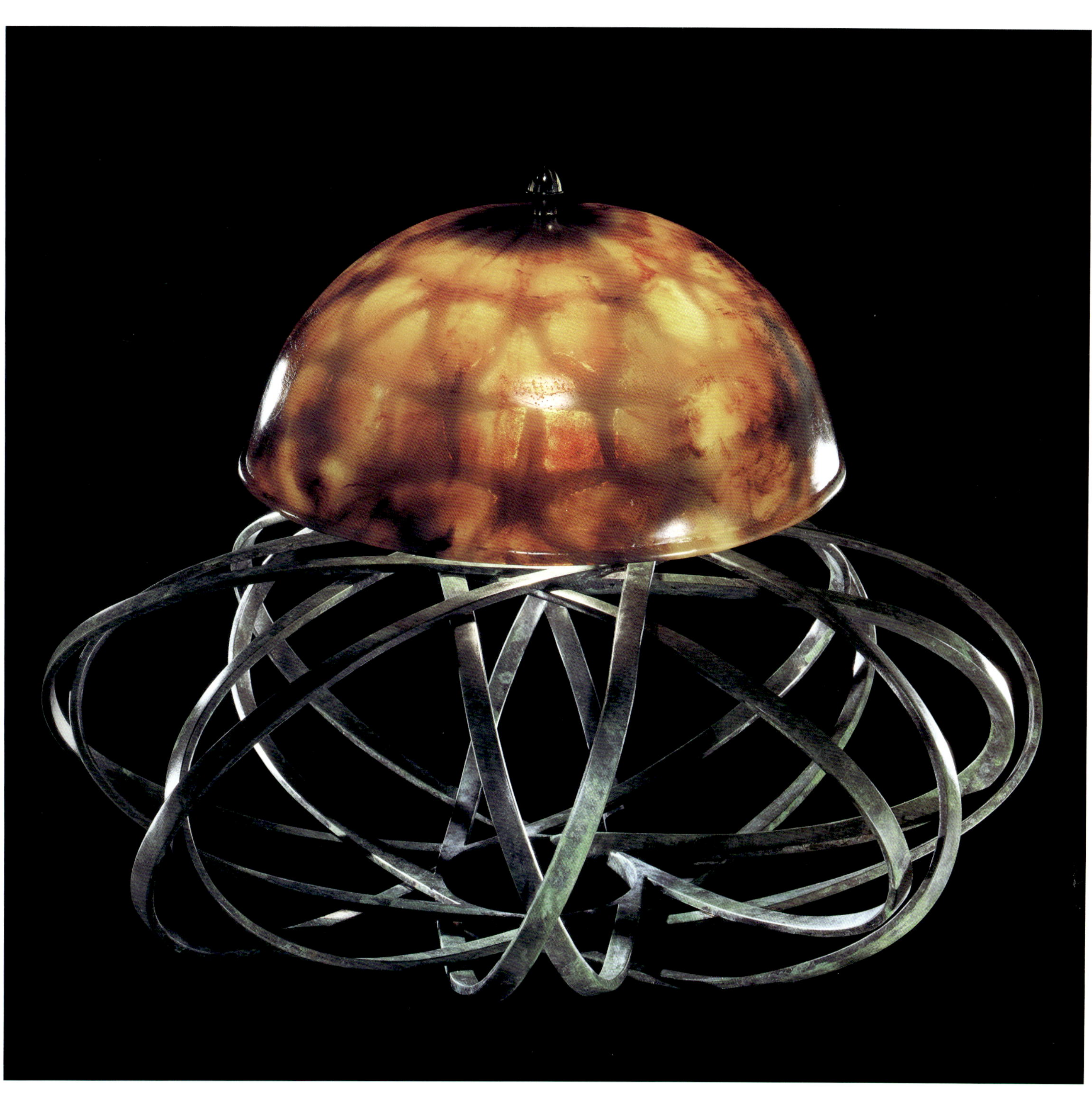

Alabaster Double Helix Diatreta, 1996   Starfish Table Lamp, 2000

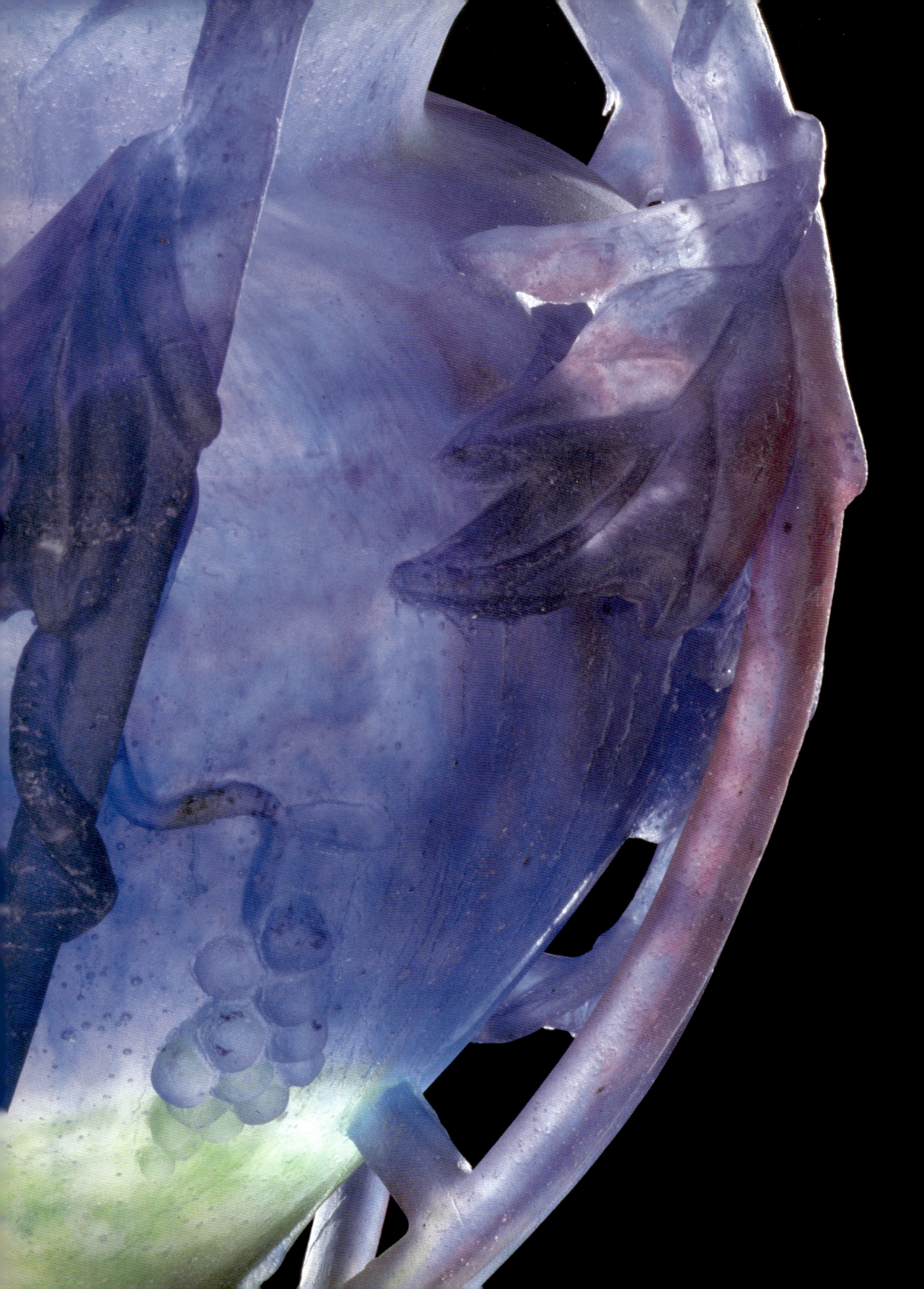

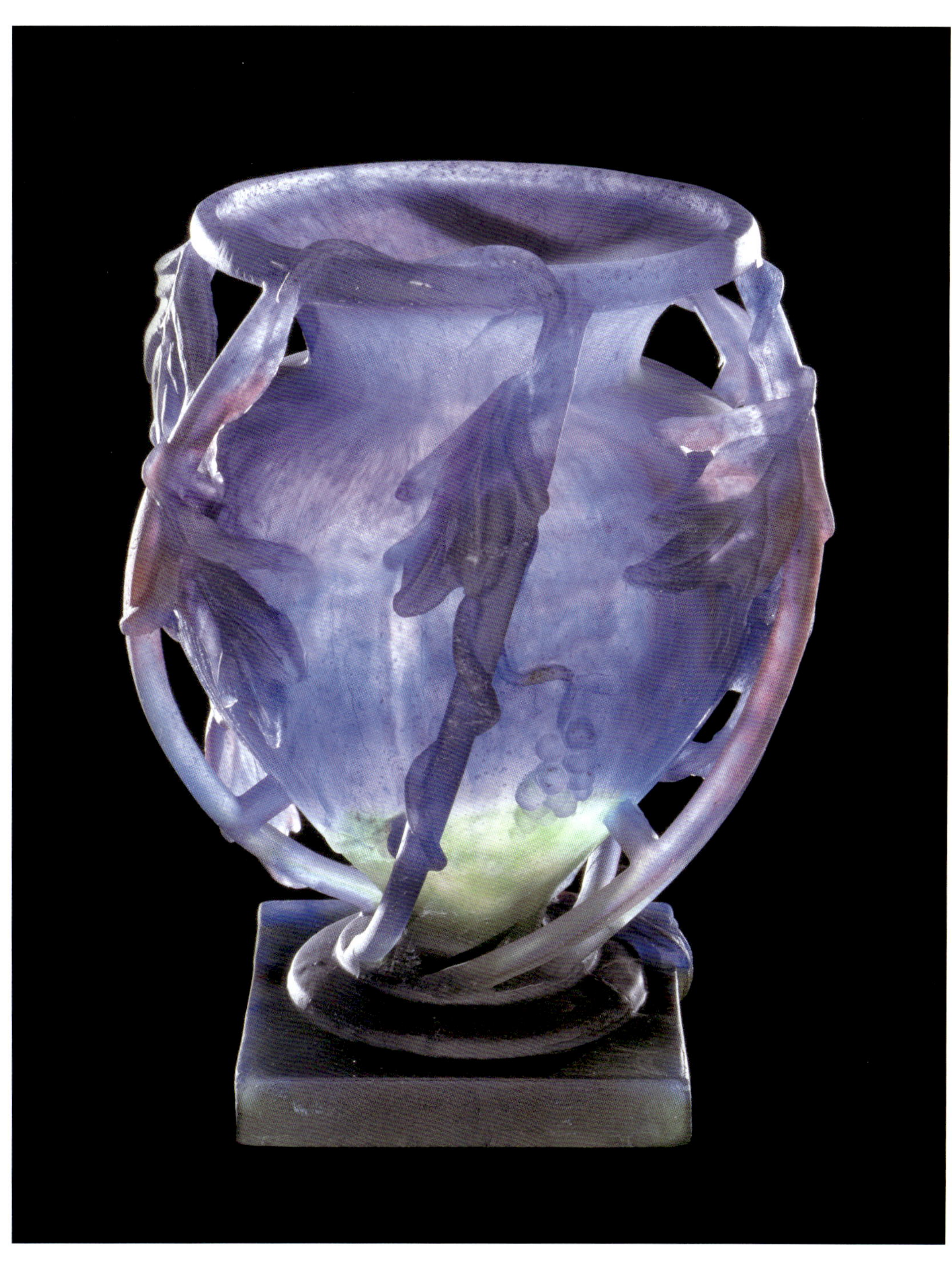

A Vintage Cage Cup, 2001

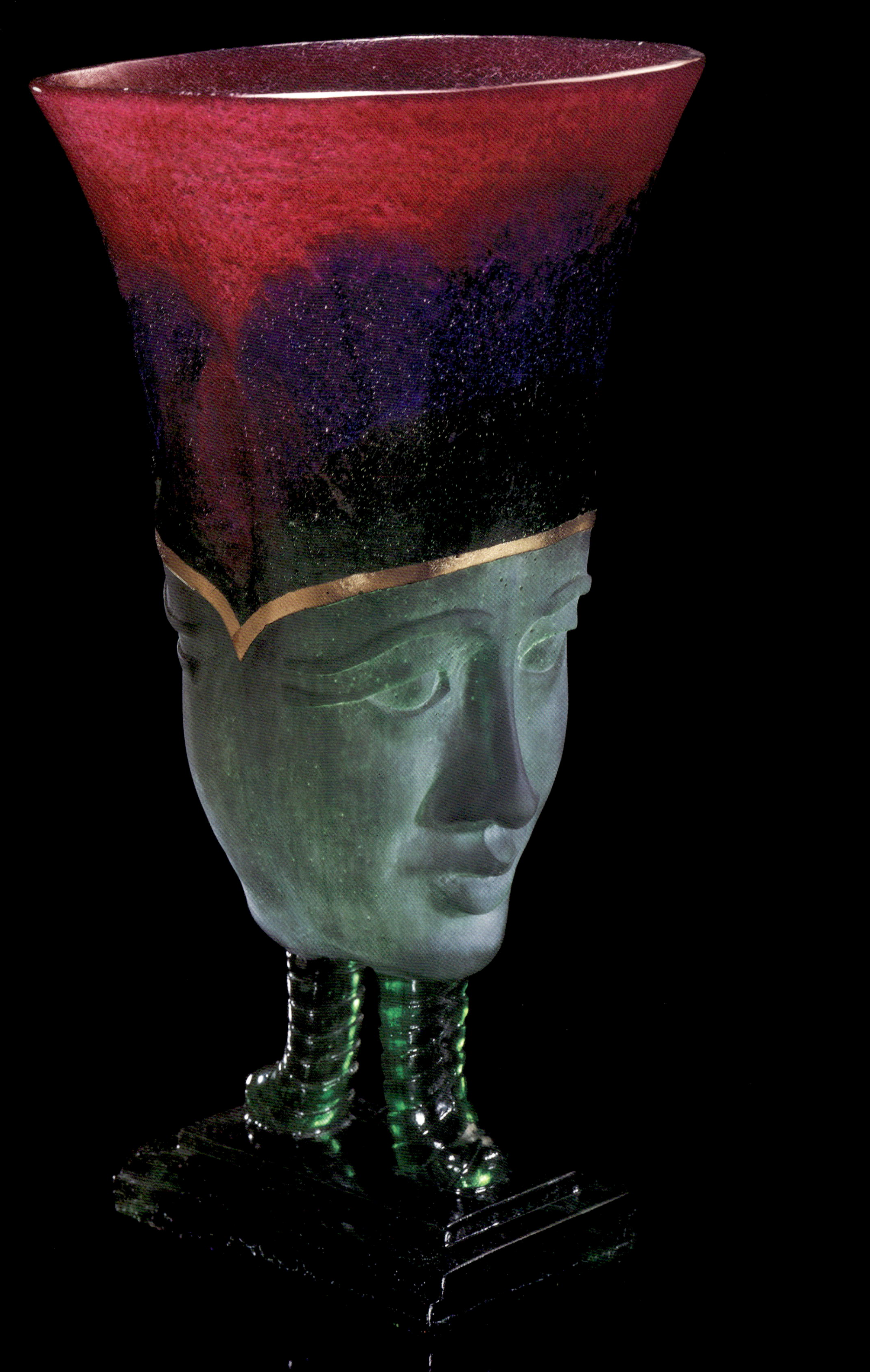

LARGER THAN LIFE
THE EFFIGY SERIES

Many are the wonders of the world, and none as wonderful as man.
—SOPHOCLES

IN HIS PREVIOUS SERIES OF VESSELS AND DESIGNS FOR LEADED and etched glass, Randal found both subject matter and meaning by cultivating the rich representations of the past. These historical references had exclusively been drawn from the decorative arts, from the language of ornament and utility. Although this work was sculptural in nature—one can indeed consider an Attic vase a sublime sculpture of curved stacking volumes—he had never before looked to the human figure for inspiration. In 1993, quite unexpectedly, a flood of images of ancient Egyptian and Greek gods, kings, queens, royal personages, and venerated priests marched into Randal's artistic vision, conjuring forth memories of an expedition he had taken with his mother in 1988.

Together they had traveled southeast through Venice and Florence, down to the heel of Italy, and on to Egypt and Greece. They visited Athens, Luxor, Cairo, the Valley of the Kings, and viewed all the major archaeological sites. "When I saw the colossal sculptures at the Egyptian tomb sites," Randal recalls, "I could feel the power emanate, as if the person represented by the sculpture were still embodied in the stone. It made my hair stand on end. I was transfixed. I knew these images would have a lasting effect on me, but I didn't know when, or how. I often tell people that my mind is like the hard drive of a computer. Things and images are captured in my head, like thousands of files that are randomly stored. These compelling images of Egypt and Greece incubated for years and then miraculously popped into my consciousness, presenting me with inspiration and material. That's when I created the sculpture *Gemini* and unwittingly began my next series, the Effigy vessels." Randal launched the Effigy Series with what was for him a new method—working from a clay model. "From the beginning of the piece in clay, modeling in three dimensions,

GEMINI, 1993

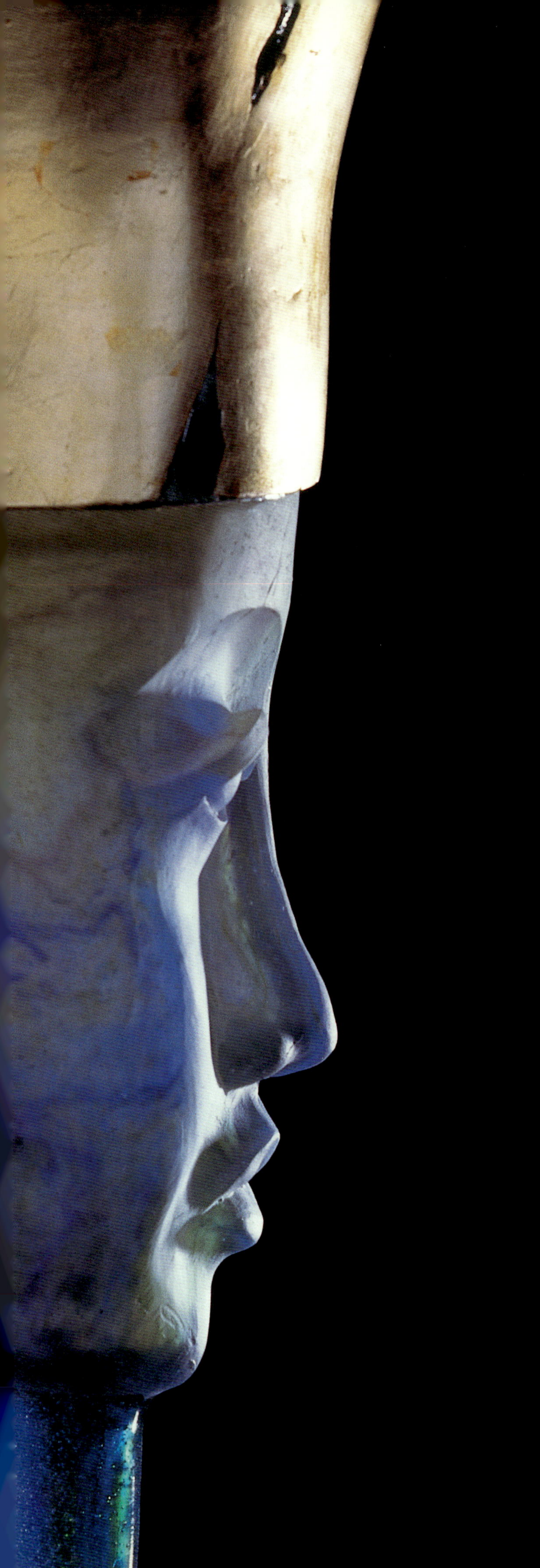

through all the ensuing steps, the process is *pure sculpture*. It gives me great pleasure to know that I am using almost the same process that great artists such as Rodin and Degas used for their bronze sculptures over a century ago."

In *Gemini* (p. 70) Randal created fantasy portraits of Castor and Pollux, the twins of classical mythology immortalized in the zodiac, sitting back to back. However, their strong features—the almond-shaped eyes, the broad band delineating the upper eyelids, the pronounced lips edged with a sharp ridge—are characteristic features of Egyptian sculpture from the New Kingdom (18th–20th Dynasty). Enthralled with Egyptology, Randal had studied the culture, religion, art, and architecture of this ancient civilization. In these sculptures he wanted to create effigies— invoking the spirits of the individuals represented to portray the achievements of these vital and influential people of the past.

One of Randal's next subjects was Ramses II, the potent pharaoh of the 19th Dynasty, rendered with deliberate historical accuracy. Ramses is depicted with the false beard of Osiris, the god of the afterlife. The wearing of this type of beard was reserved exclusively for the highest royalty. The false beard appears on many images of Egyptian pharaohs, although whether such a beard was actually worn or its portrayal was entirely symbolic is not known. The ruler also wears a tall funnel-like crown divided into two curling projections, one bending toward the front and the other toward the back. This headdress is known as the "double crown," and it signifies the unification of Upper and Lower Egypt. Ramses II ruled over an empire of unprecedented prosperity, and Randal has created his crown in shimmering white gold, underscoring the king's magnificence.

The idea for *Archaica* (p. 76) was rooted in Randal's desire to represent a personage from a specific time, recognizable from prevailing stylistic conventions. *Archaica* draws its inspiration from the Archaic period of Greek art (circa 700–480 BC), an important

RAMSES II, 1996

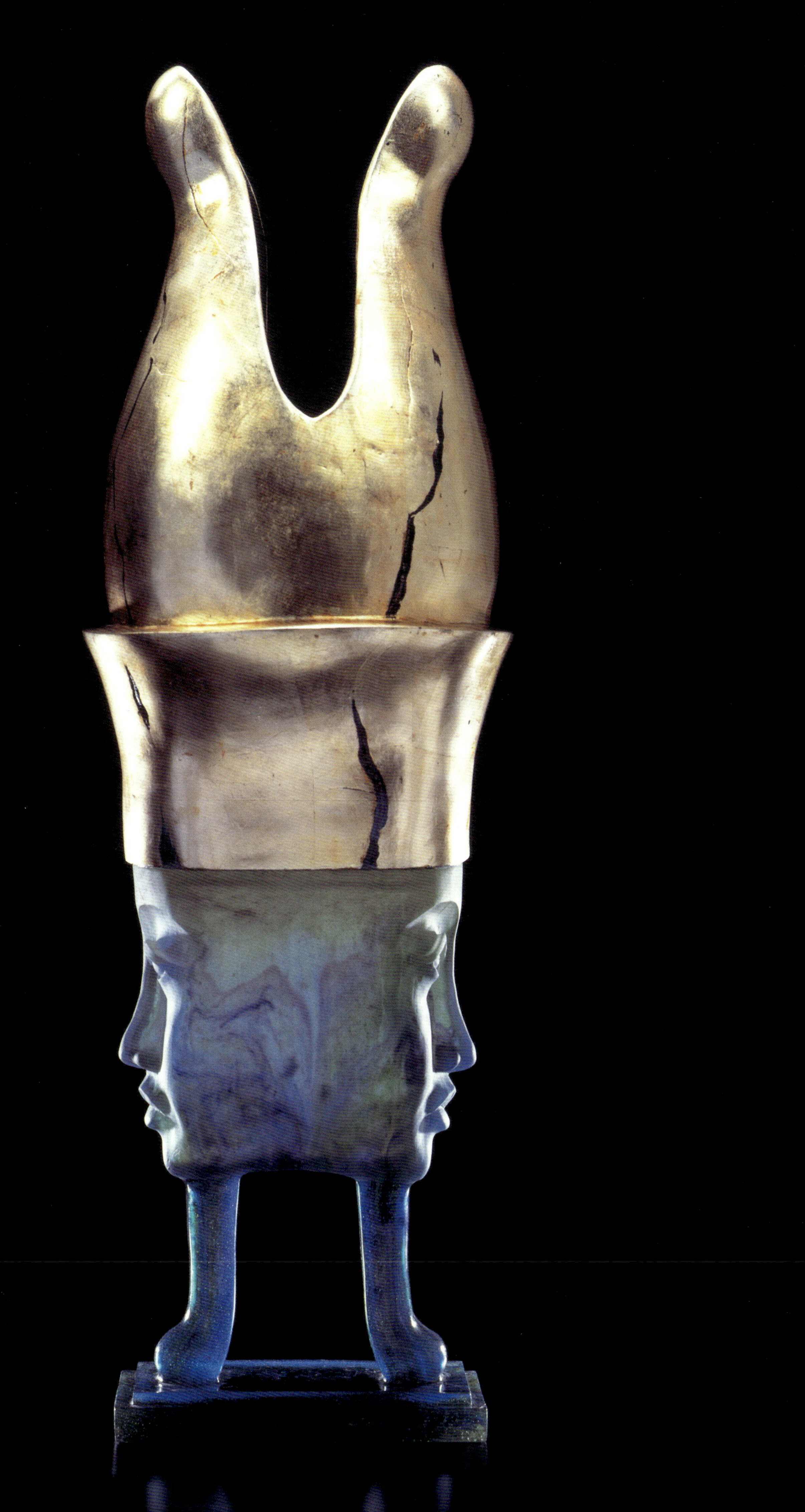

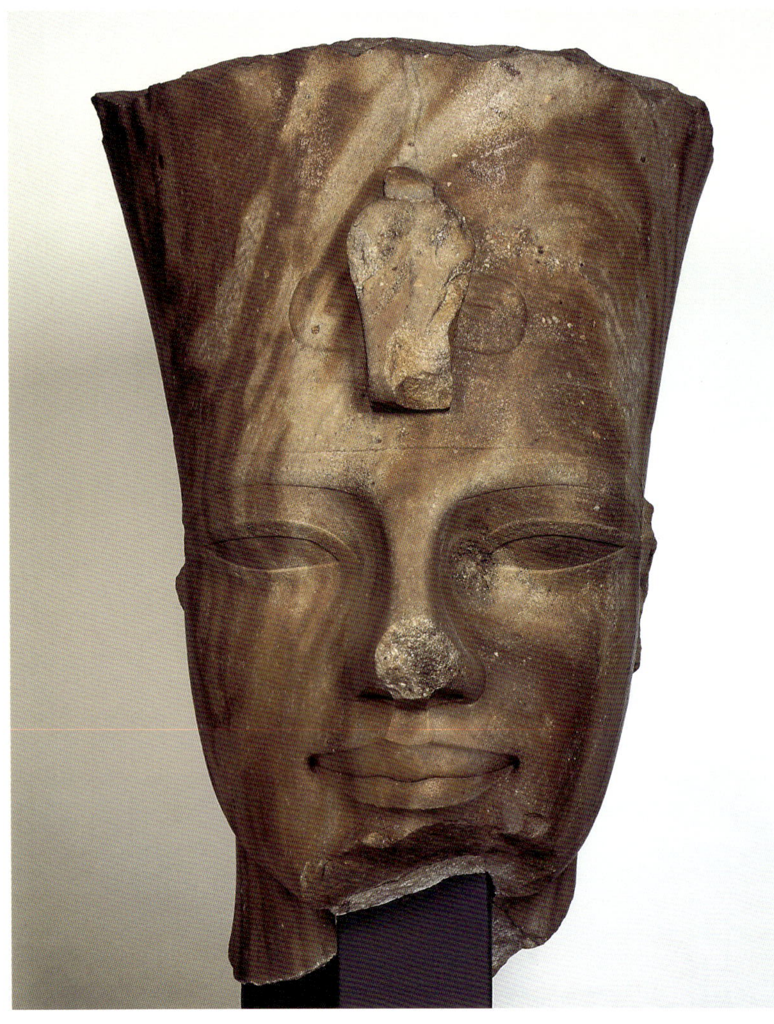

Colossal head of Amenophis III,
circa 1360 BC

Randal working on *Golden Ruin*

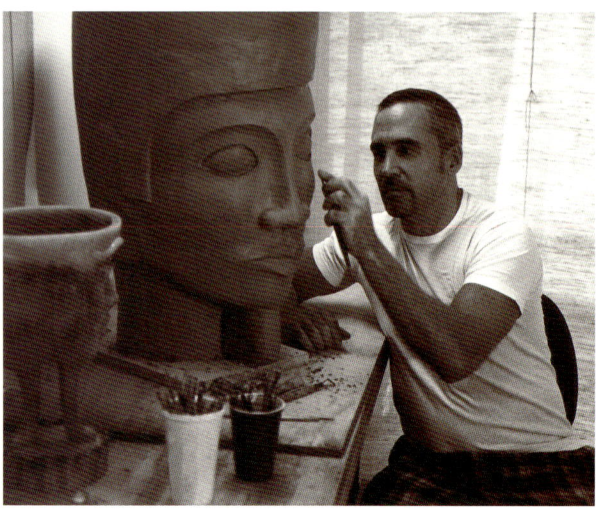

era of innovation and achievement during which artists made great strides in depicting the human form in sculpture. A new understanding of human anatomy led to a realistic softening of musculature, naturalistic facial expressions, and animated poses. According to classical scholar Mario A. del Chiaro, "Whereas the ancient Egyptian representation of the human form remained essentially unchanged throughout the millennia of Egyptian history, in Greece, within the relatively short span of less than four centuries—the representation of the human form evolved with startling rapidity from a rather stiff hieratic pose to one of convincing naturalism."[13] However, certain traits were conventionalized, such as almond-shaped eyes, incised pupils, a well-modulated mouth, "snail curls" in the hair and beard, and ringlets that would fall in gentle registers along the side of the head or nape of the neck.

Archaica, perched atop dual columns, conforms stylistically with Archaic Greek sculpture, and gazing at her one feels transported to a distant time and place. Randal explains: "In the Larger than Life—Effigy Series, I am portraying figures—both real and imagined—from different times in history, from diverse cultures and geographical locations. People who were placed on a pedestal, looked up to, and literally seen as larger than life, whether a king or a queen, a deity or a mythological figure. I hope the viewer will look at these figures and wonder: Who was this man? Who was this woman? Did they live a long and productive life, or were they assassinated before their prime? What kind of power did they wield? What is the meaning of the crown on their head? Were they loved and respected or despised and feared? In this way I am hoping to initiate an interactive experience; to encourage each person to delve into their imagination and write their own story."

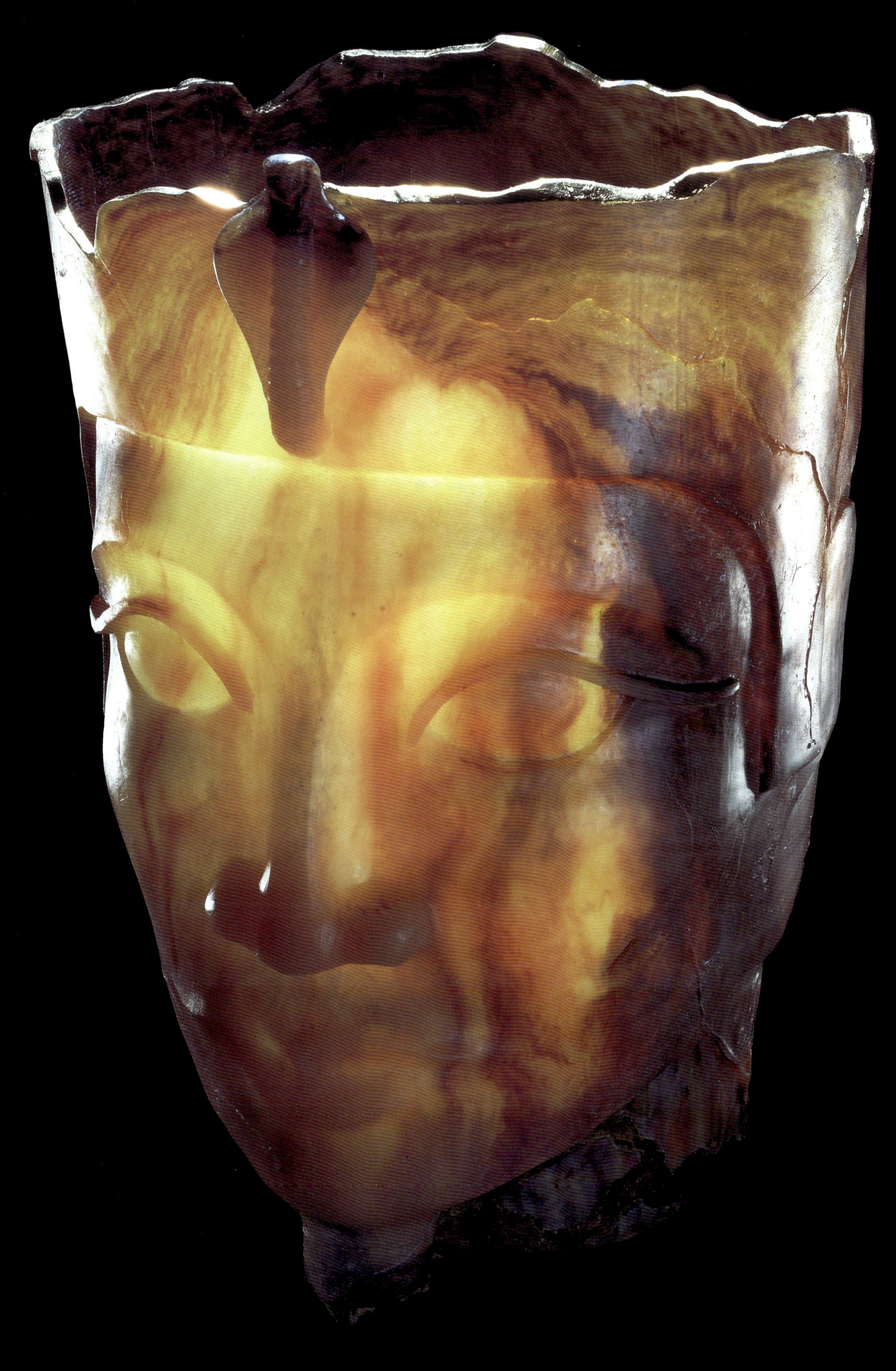

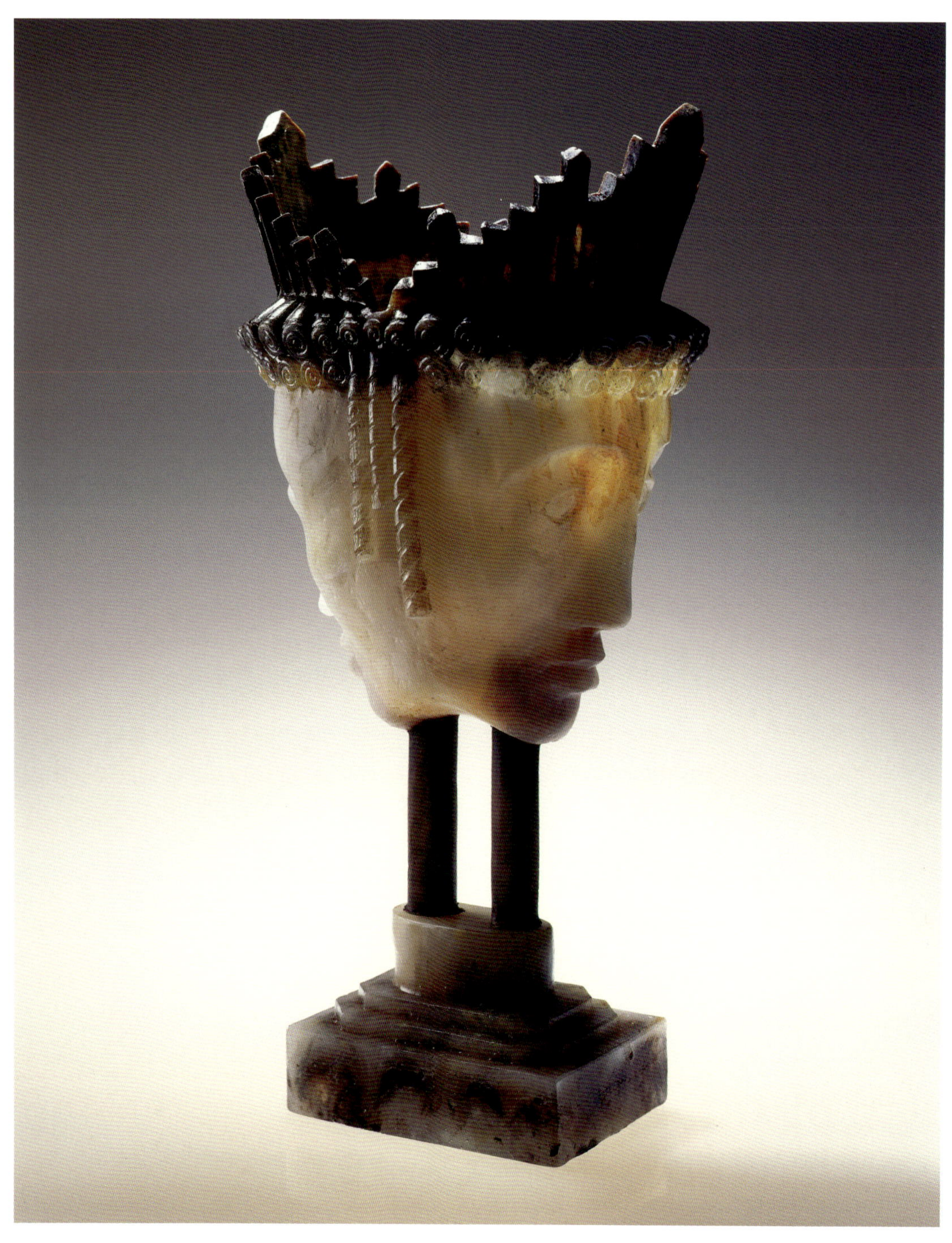

Archaiea, 1997

Nubia, 1995

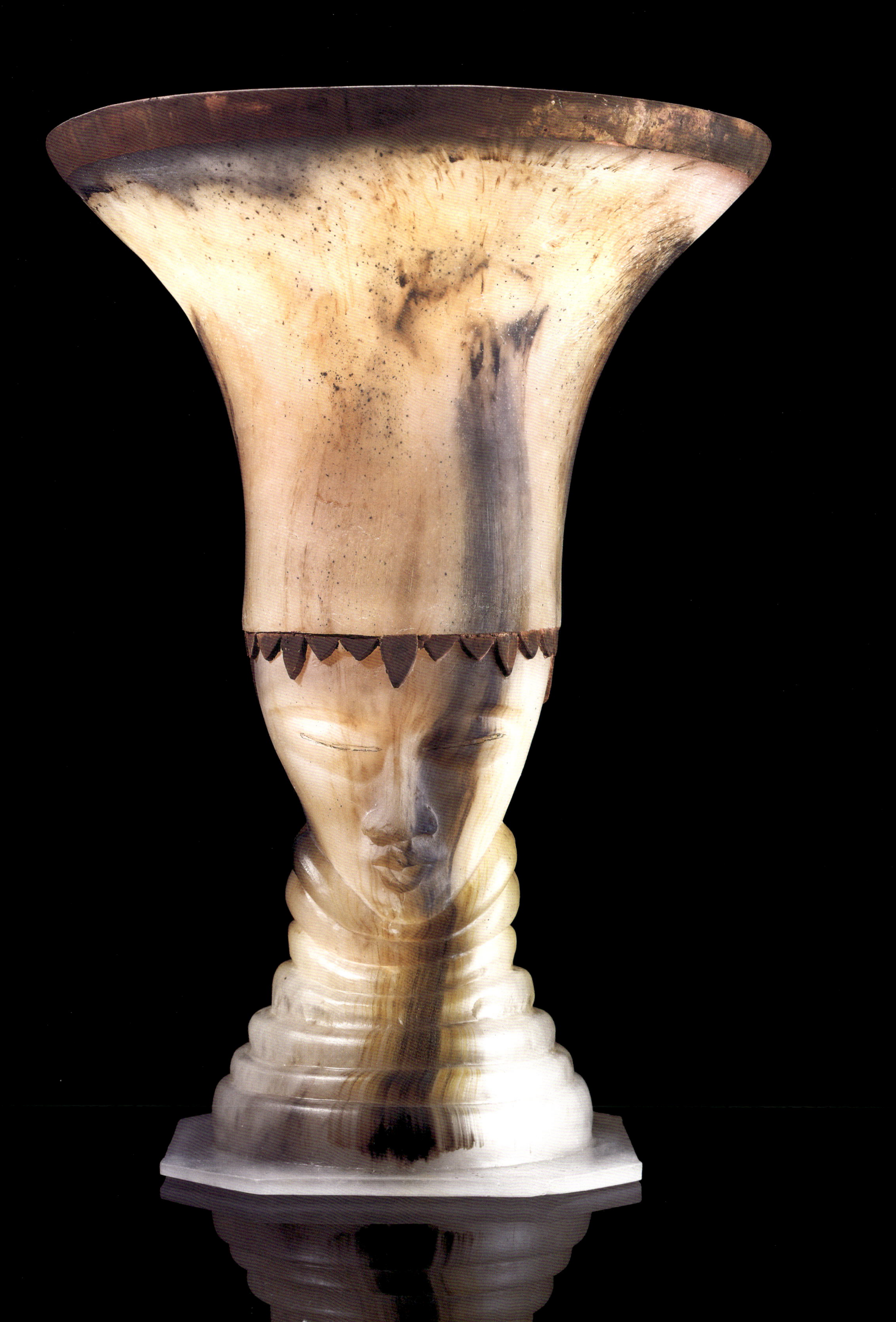

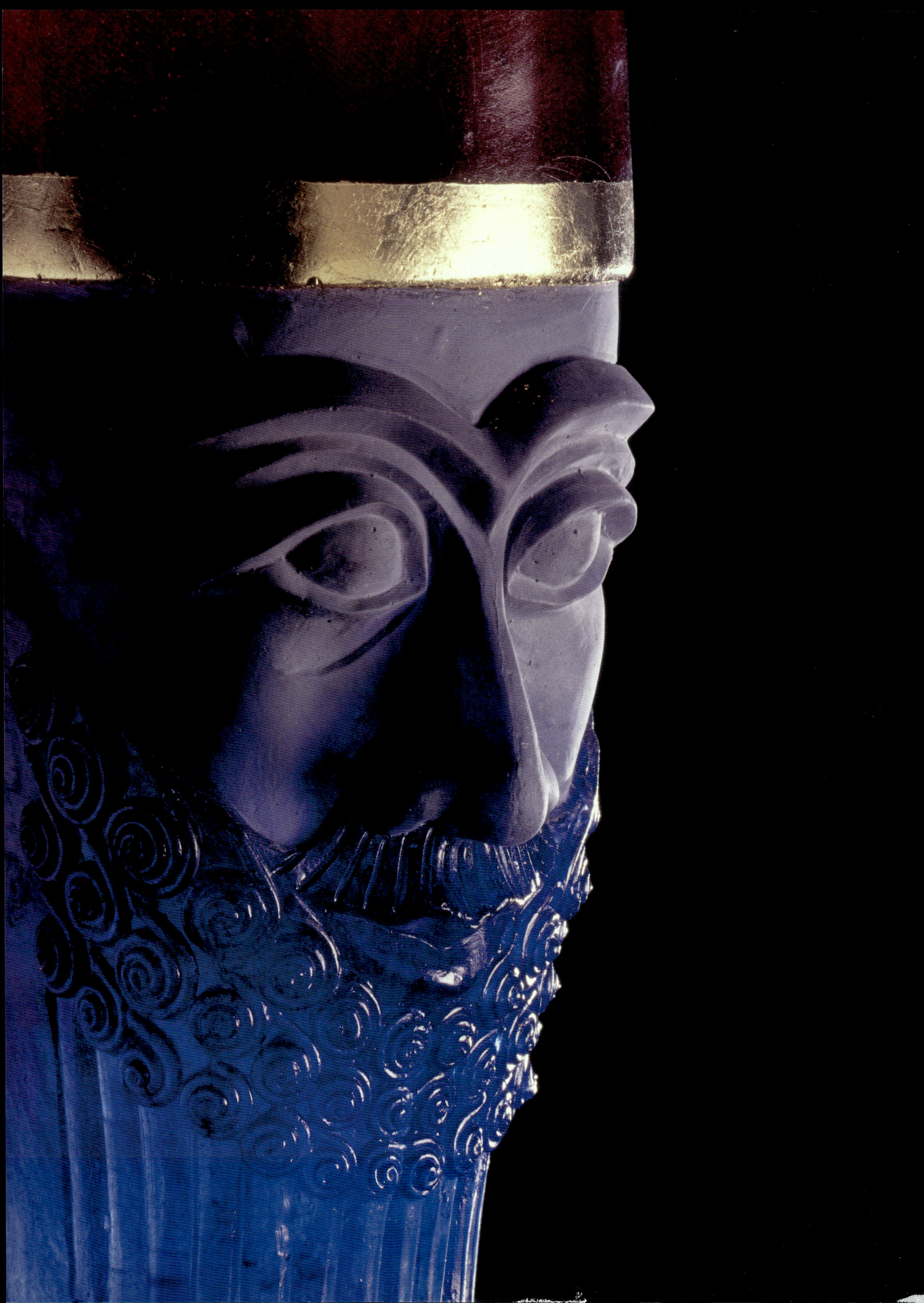

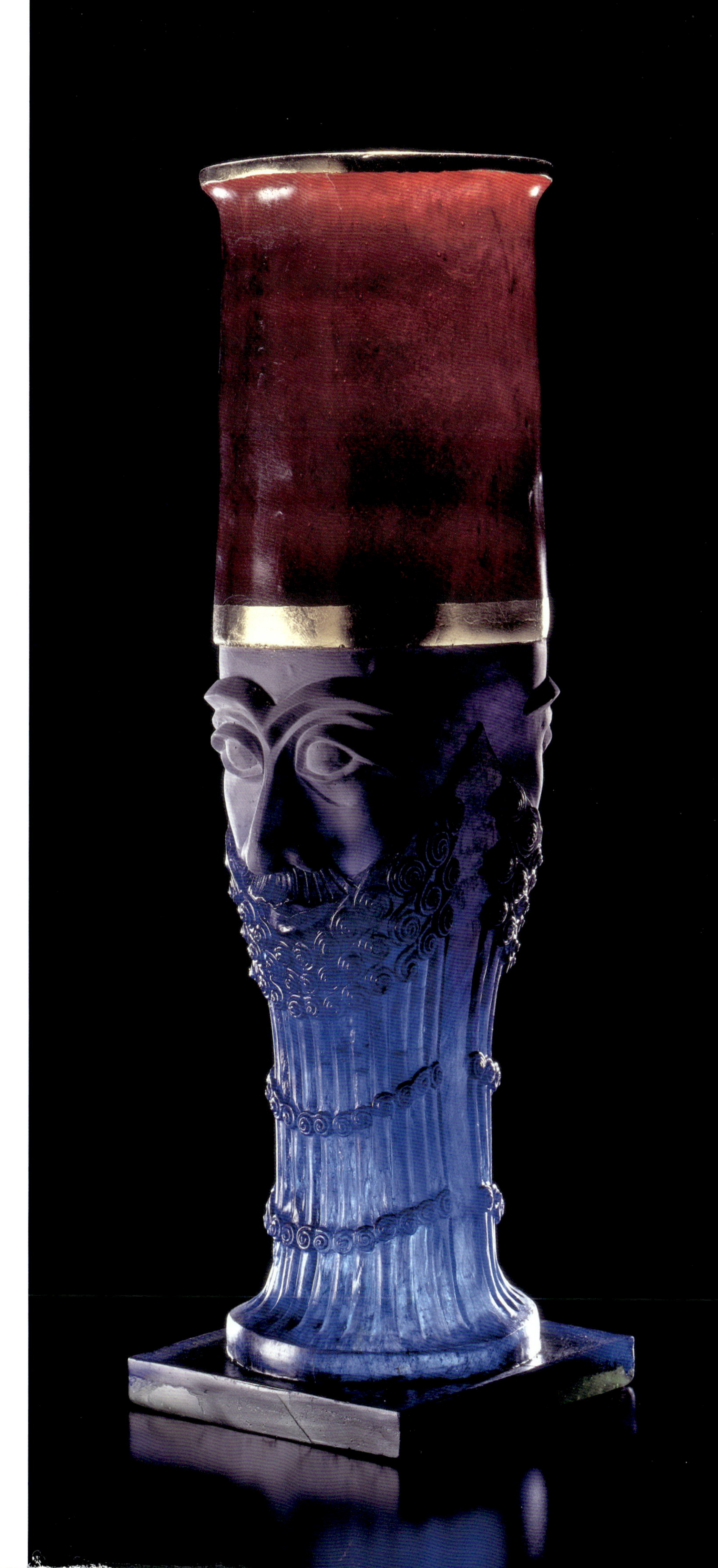

Holy Man, 1995

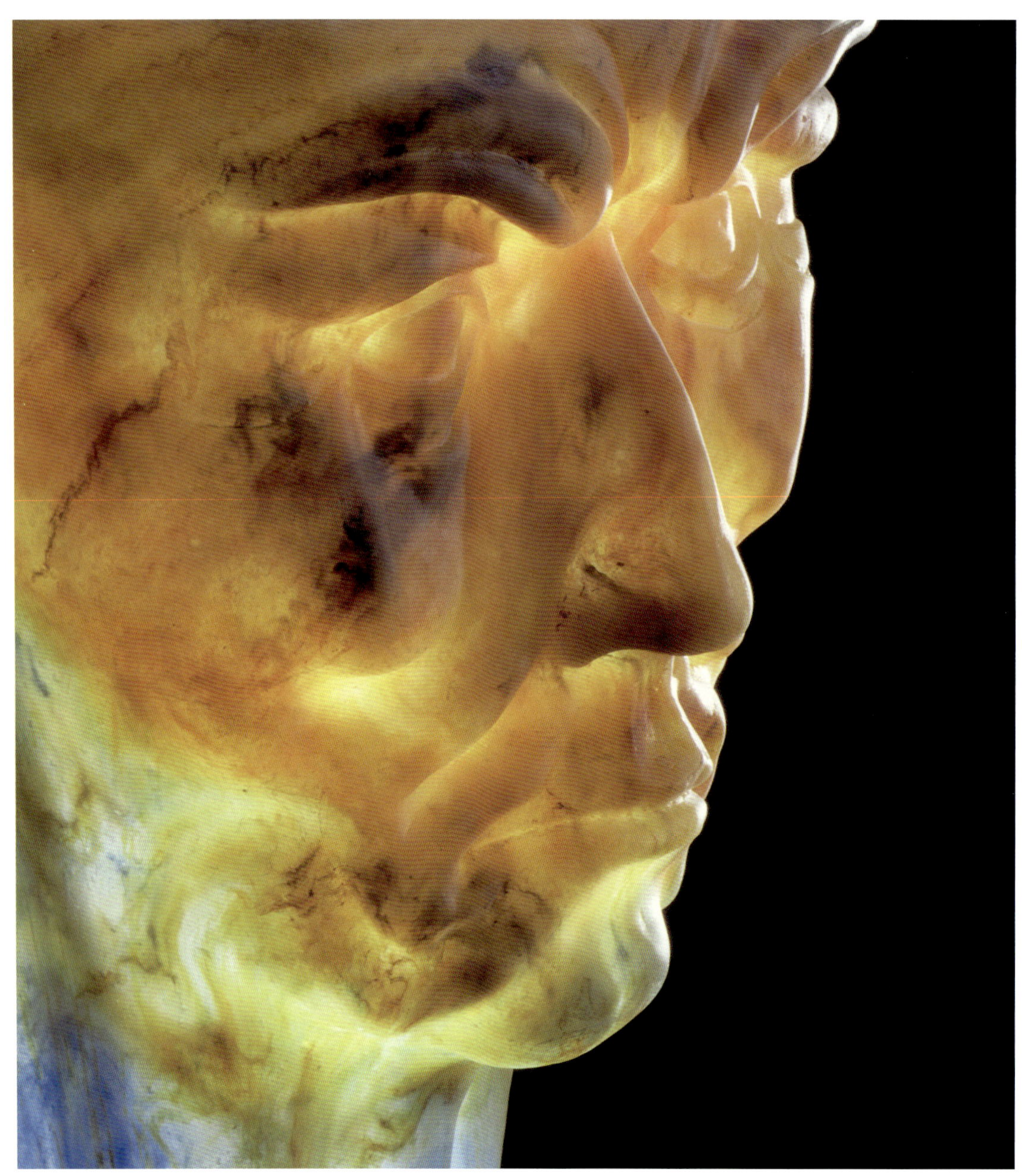

As Randal sifted and sorted through layers of reference, sometimes the result would be a synthesis of people, periods, and styles. In *Holy Man* (pp. 78, 79) the bust of an Abyssinian king, replete with the traditional attributes of curlicued beard, protruding brows, and boldly ridged eyes, is capped by a striking red fez, a hat worn in contemporary times by Turkish men. In *Acanthus King* the model was a terra-cotta bust of an Indian chief that adorned a turn-of-the-century bank building in Seattle; Randal crowned the figure with a wreath of stylized acanthus leaves, a motif associated with ancient Greek art. These playful assemblages tweak the viewer's perceptions, as they rearrange the references that serve as markers for a particular style, place, and time.

ACANTHUS KING, 2000

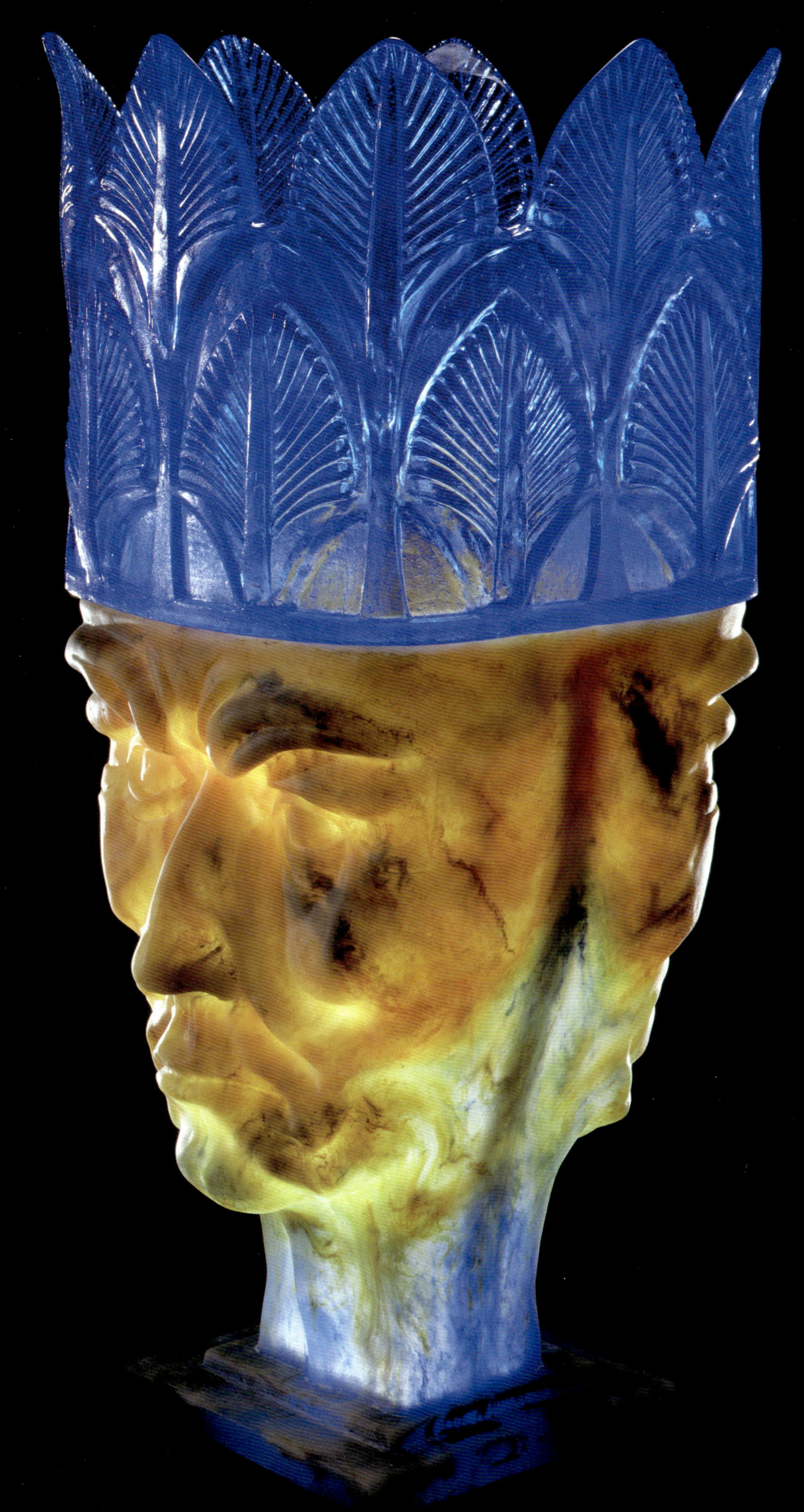

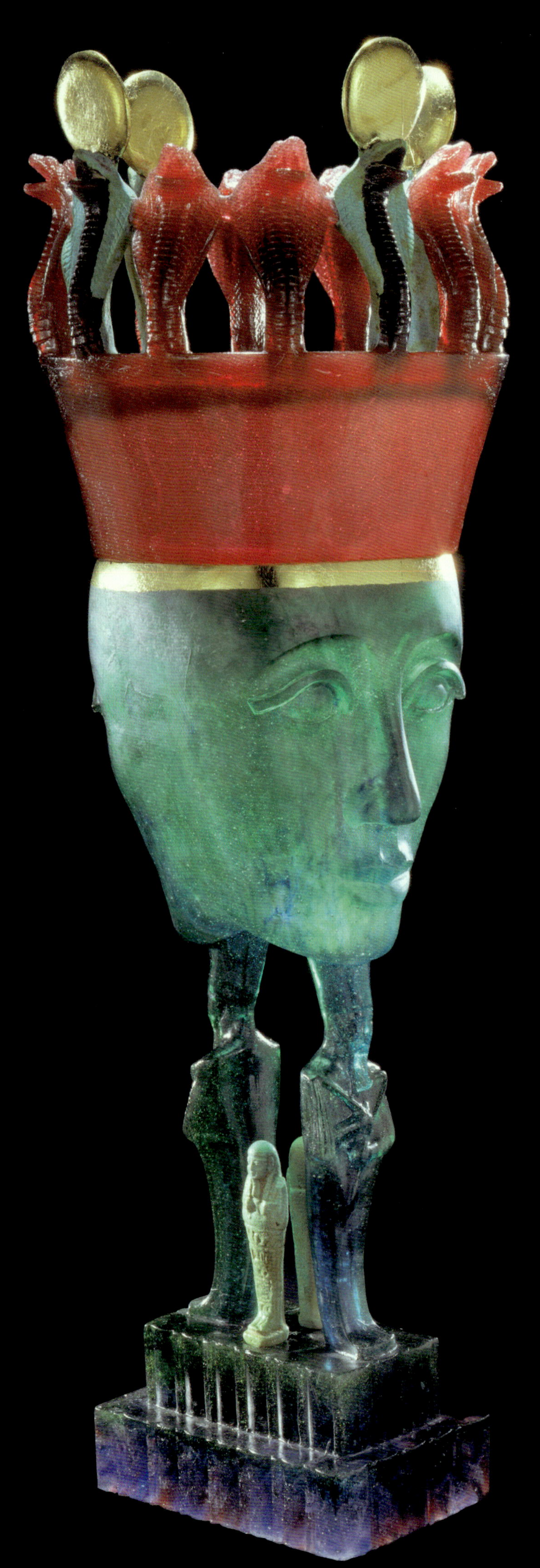

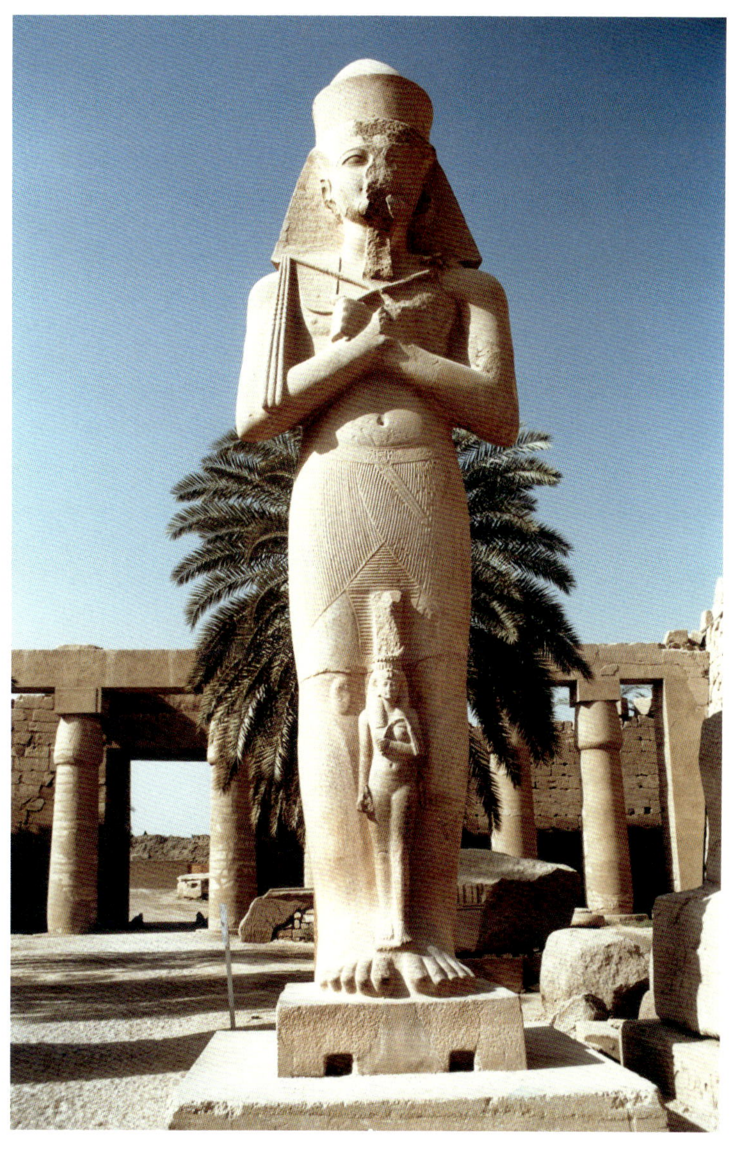

Colossal statue, Luxor, Egypt

In *Ushabti Princess* Randal further explored the idea of mixing cultures, as he skillfully combined components from ancient societies with contemporary techniques. He incorporated two authentic faience sculptures—small funerary figurines known as *ushabti*—from the 23rd Dynasty (circa 650 BC) into the base of his cast glass bust of an Egyptian princess. Ushabti figures were buried in tombs and were intended to serve the dead in the afterlife. When called upon, they would answer their masters, "Here I am—Ushabti."[14] The crown of *Ushabti Princess* is encircled with uraeus snakes. The uraeus, the royal serpent on the forehead of the headdress worn by pharaohs and persons of royal stature, was a protective image that would destroy all enemies by spewing fire. These upraised snakes, some with a gold disk above their heads representing the sun, are similar to the gold and lapis lazuli uraeus snakes found scattered throughout Tutankhamen's burial site. Based on style and attributes, we can assemble a life story for this princess, immortalized and reflected in Randal's glass effigy of prismatic splendor.

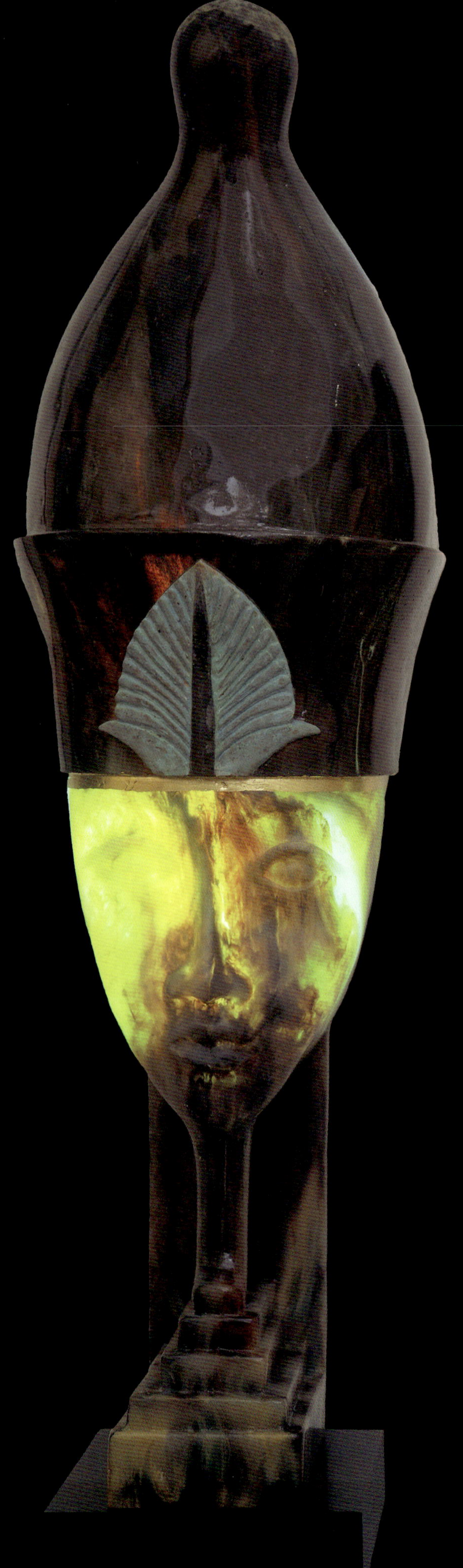

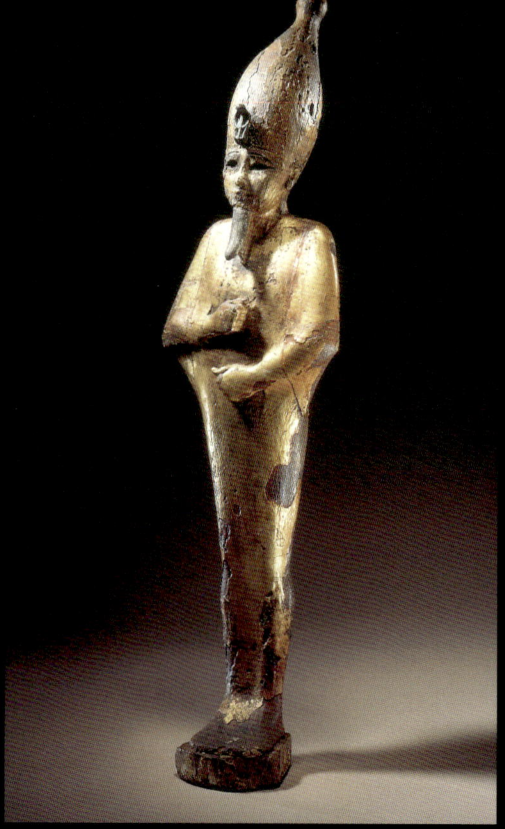

Osiris, Egypt, New Kingdom
(1550–1070 BC)

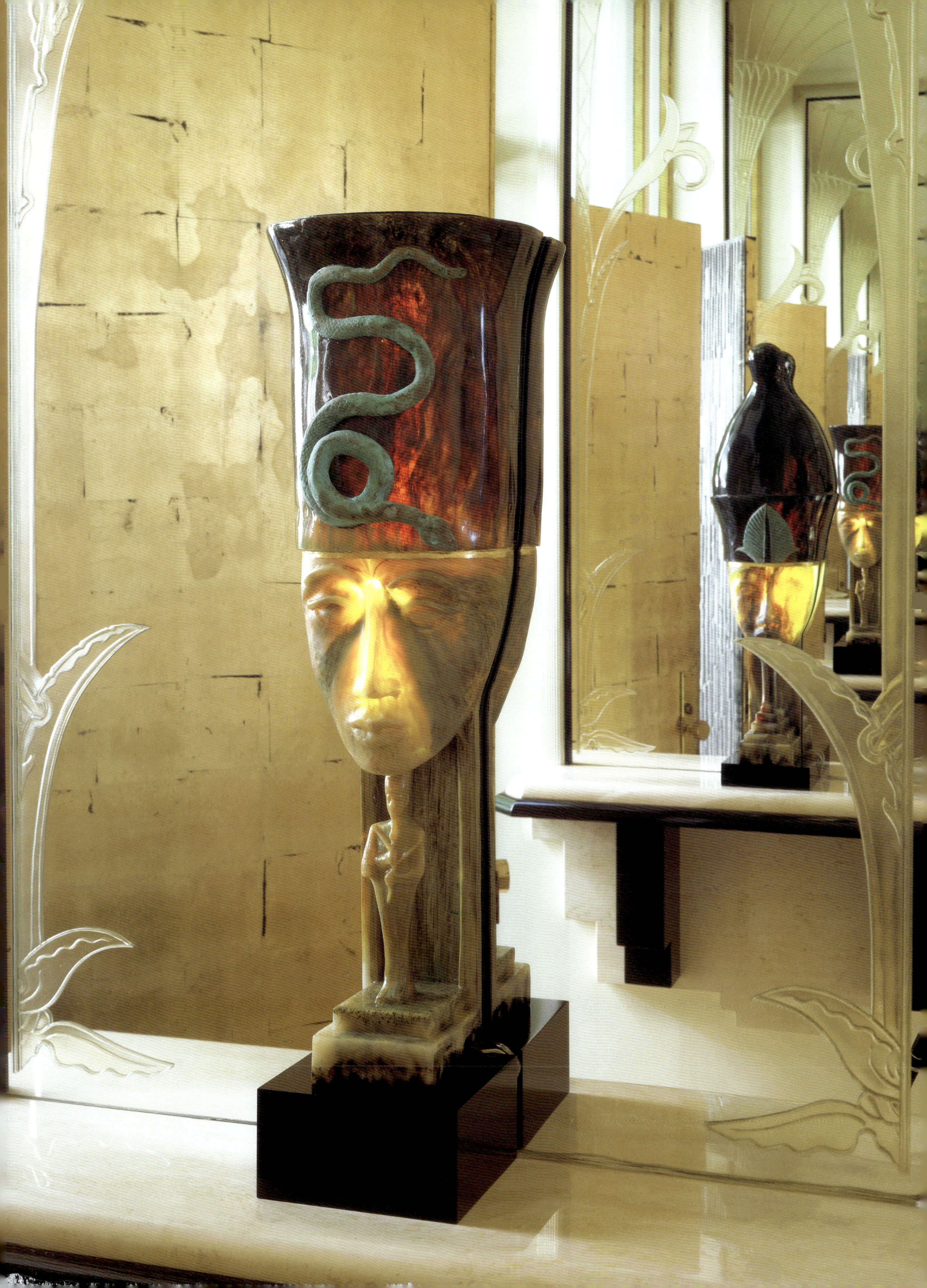

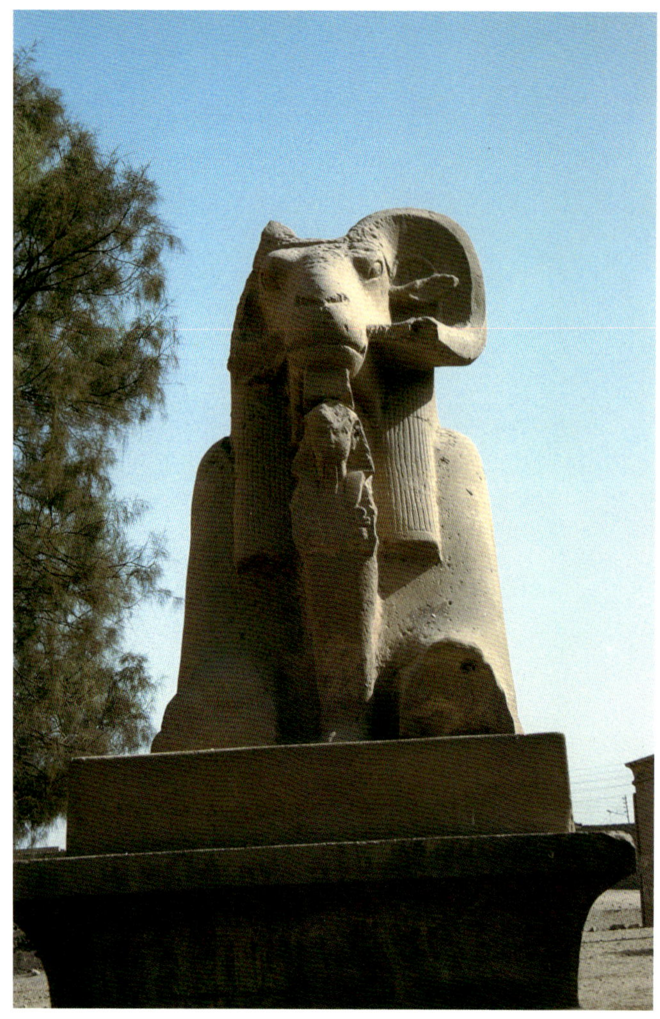

Statue of Ammun, Luxor, Egypt

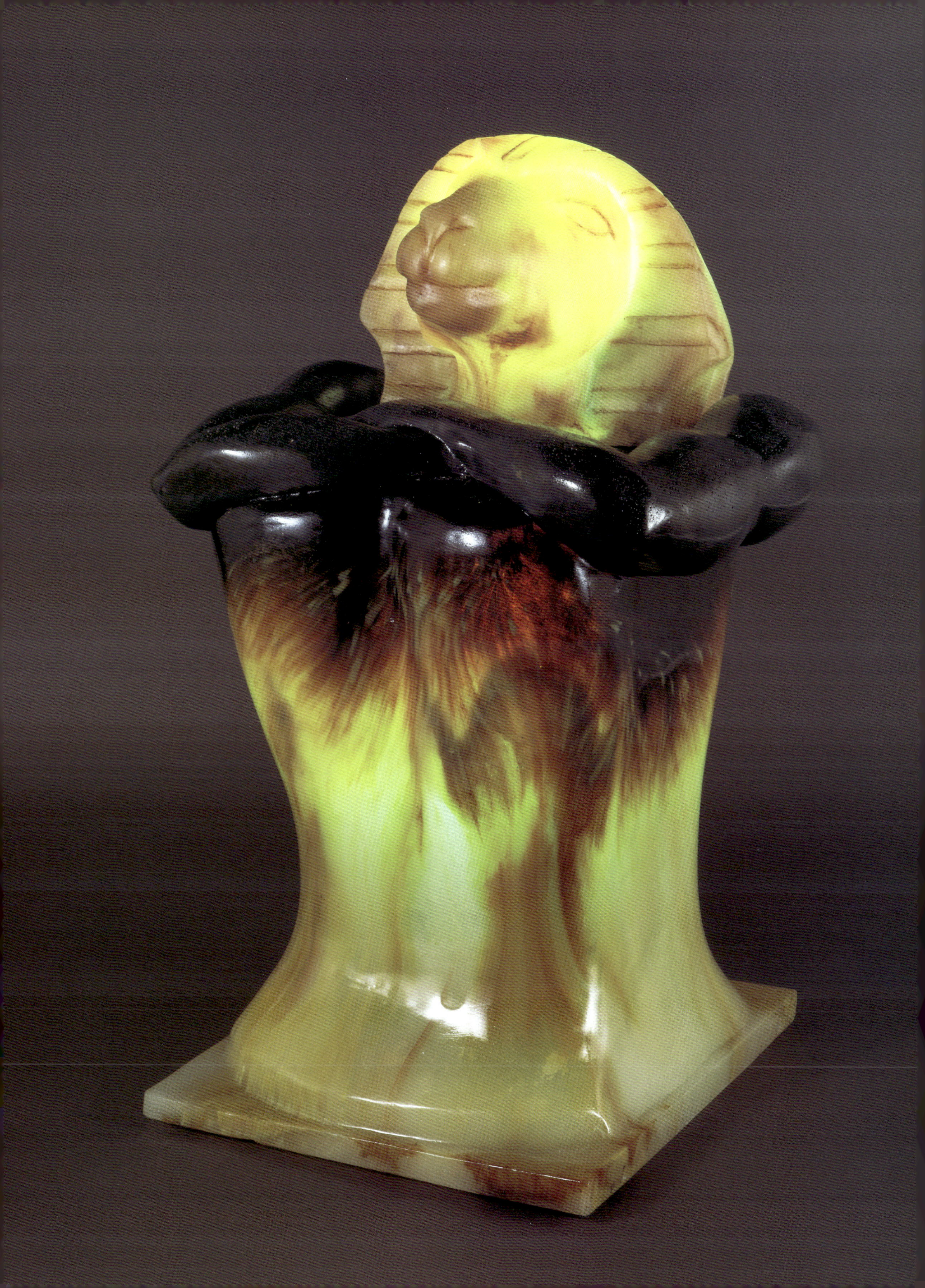

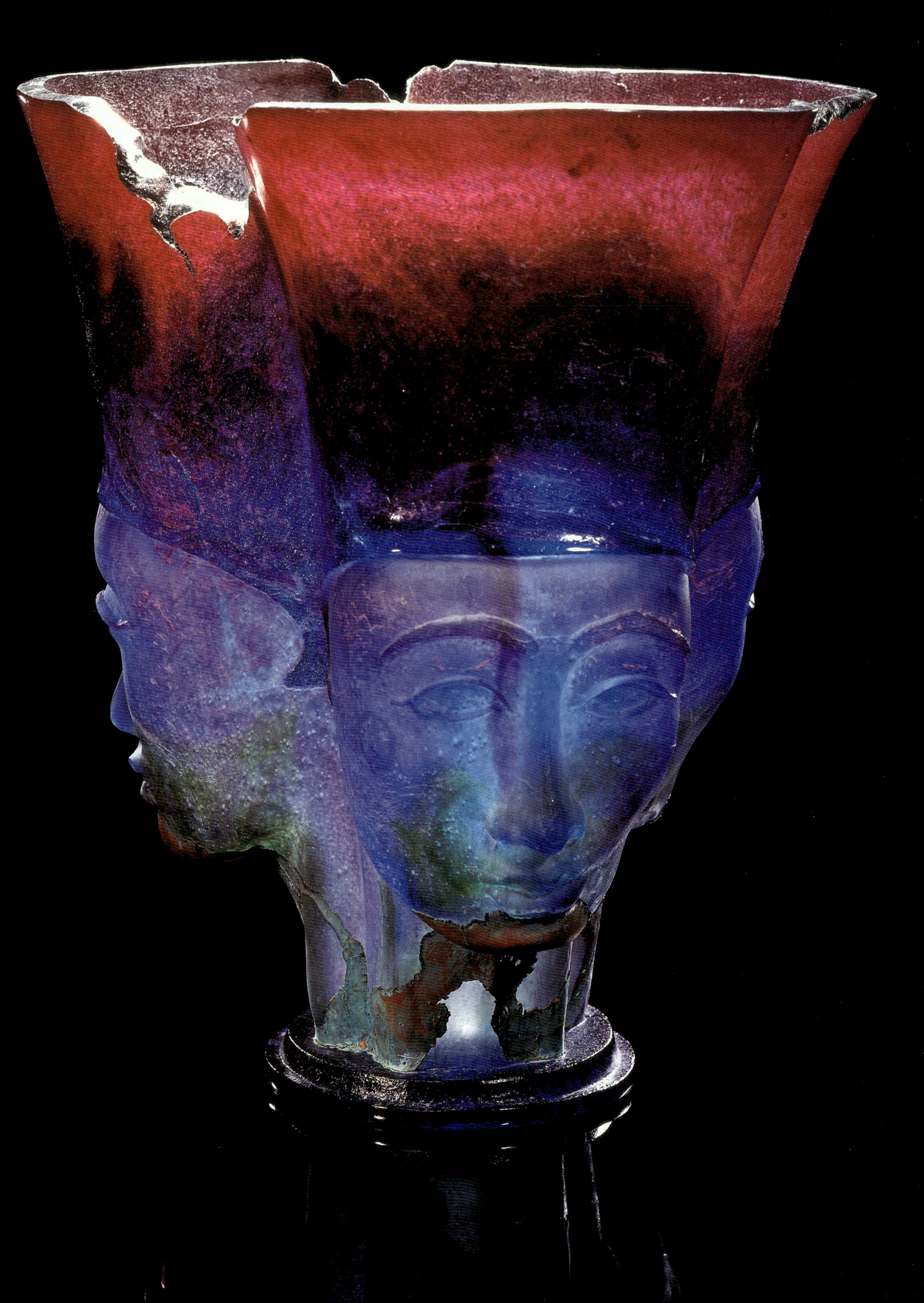

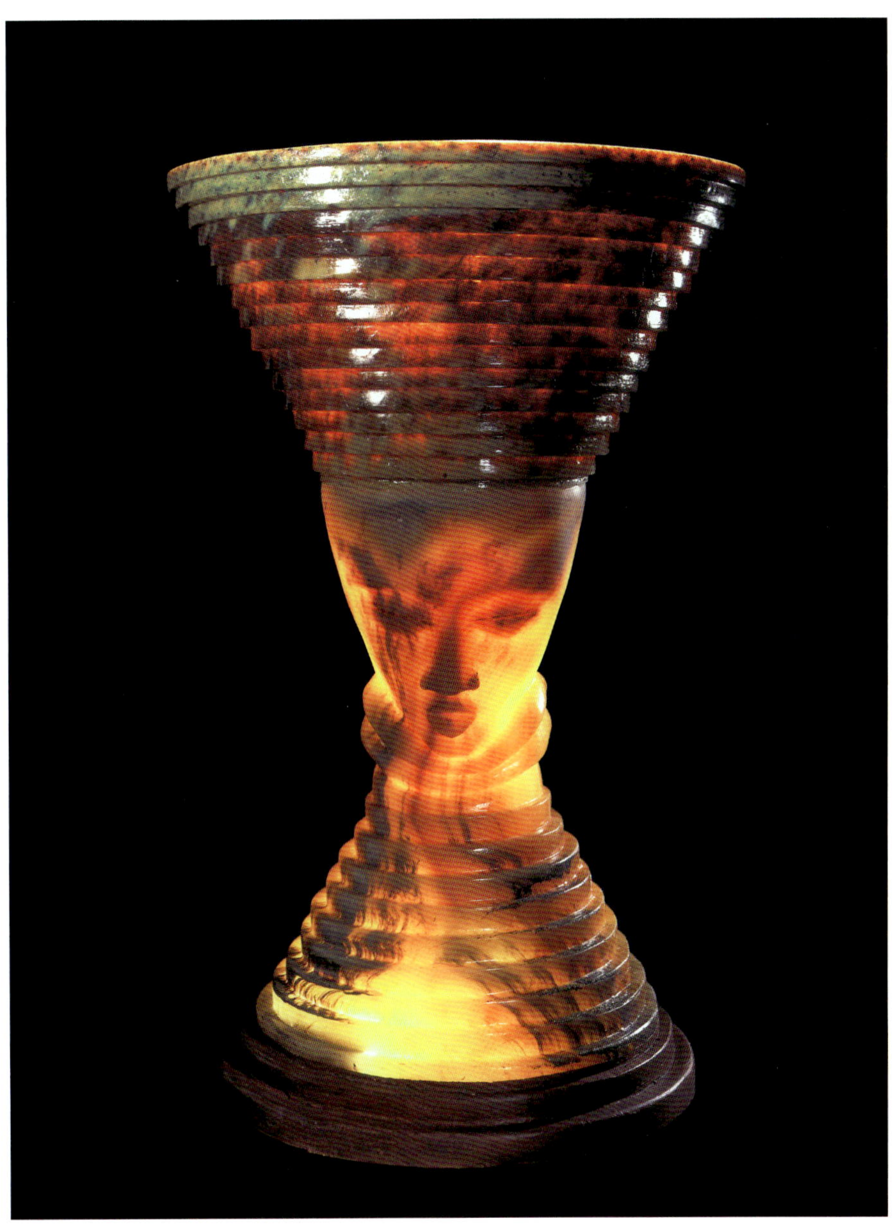

Ushabti Princess was followed by three more sculptural portrayals of powerful women. In *The Queen*, Randal undertook the challenge of making a three-sided vessel—a taxing and technically demanding process—to express three stages in the life of a beautiful Egyptian queen: first the young princess, her expression full of anticipation; next the ruler in her prime, her countenance confident and powerful; and finally the matriarch, her eyes wise and her face lined and softened by time. "This piece is about progression," Randal has commented. "It's about the journey of an idea, and of a person, from beginning to end. Progression is a quality that to me is one of the most important and defining characteristics of an artist's life or career."

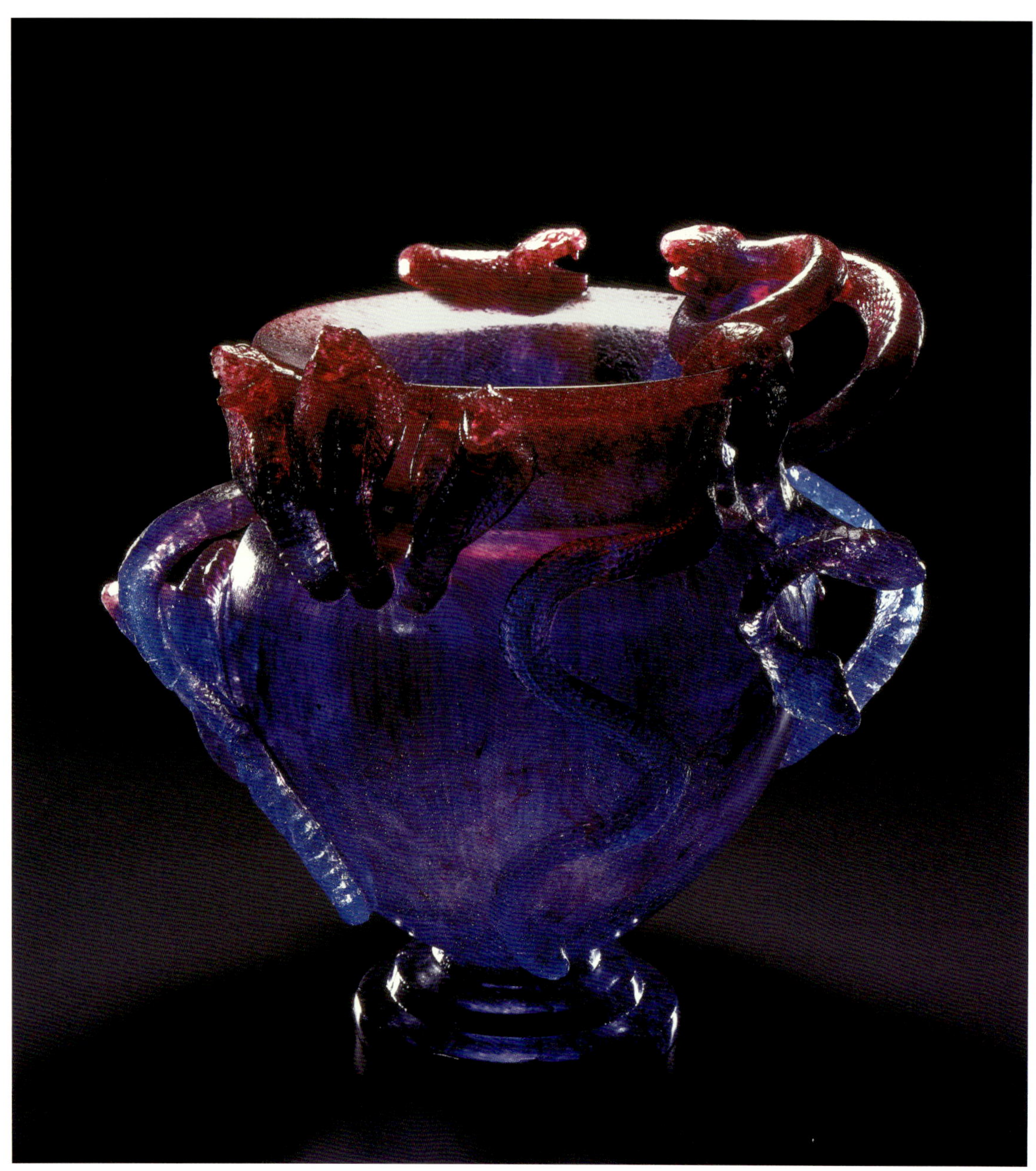

In *A Woman of Substance*, Randal portrayed the myth of the vain maiden Medusa, who was transformed into a gorgon monster with writhing live snakes in place of hair. According to legend, Medusa was so horrifying that anyone who looked her in the face was immediately turned to stone. Consequently, Randal has given her a piercing stare and has fully exposed the venomous fangs of the snakes. This piece performs a wicked trick on the viewer, who is seduced into gazing at Medusa through the spectacle of the pure and intense colors of the translucent glass.

    Medusa, 1991   A Woman of Substance, 1996

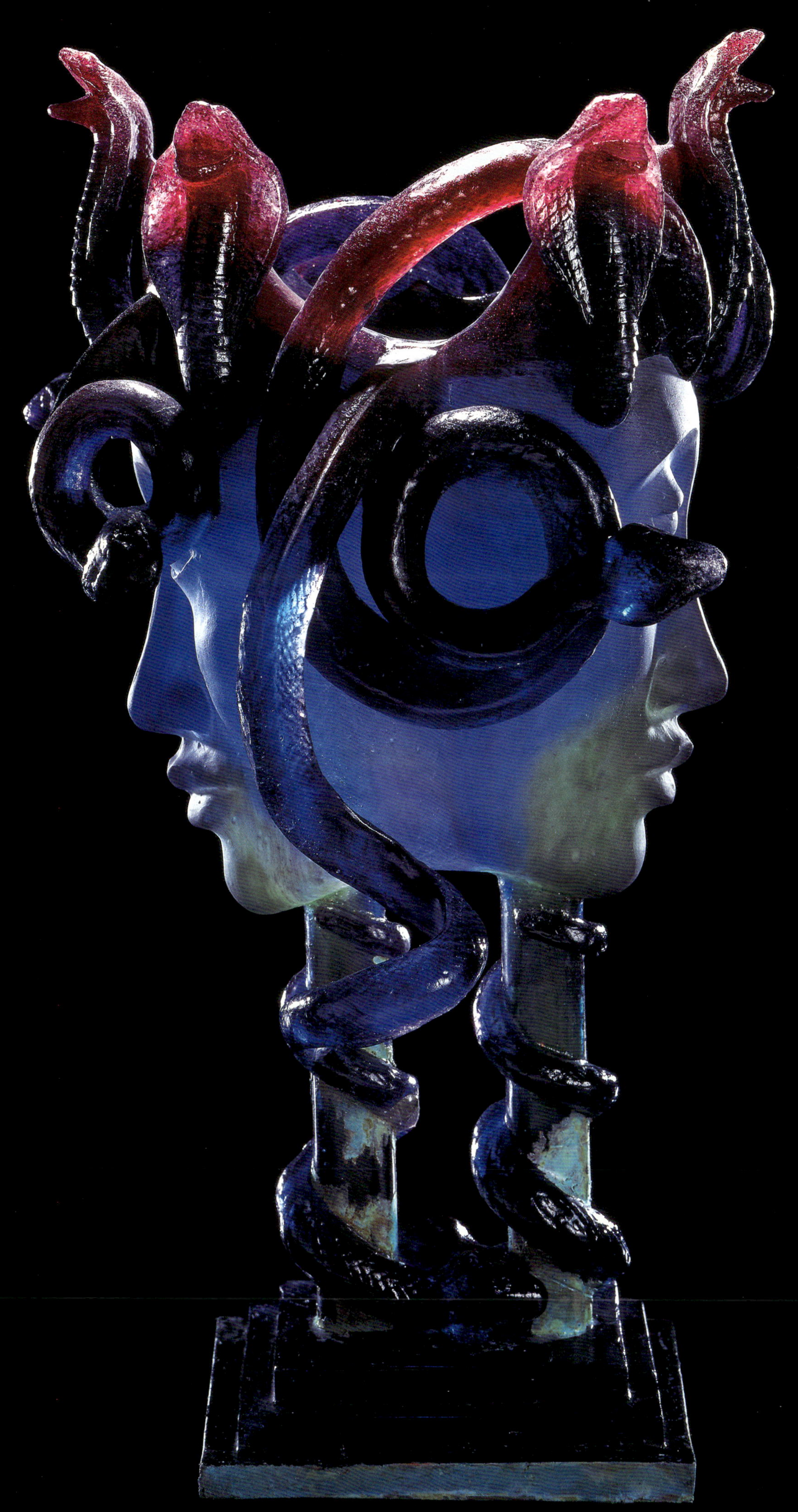

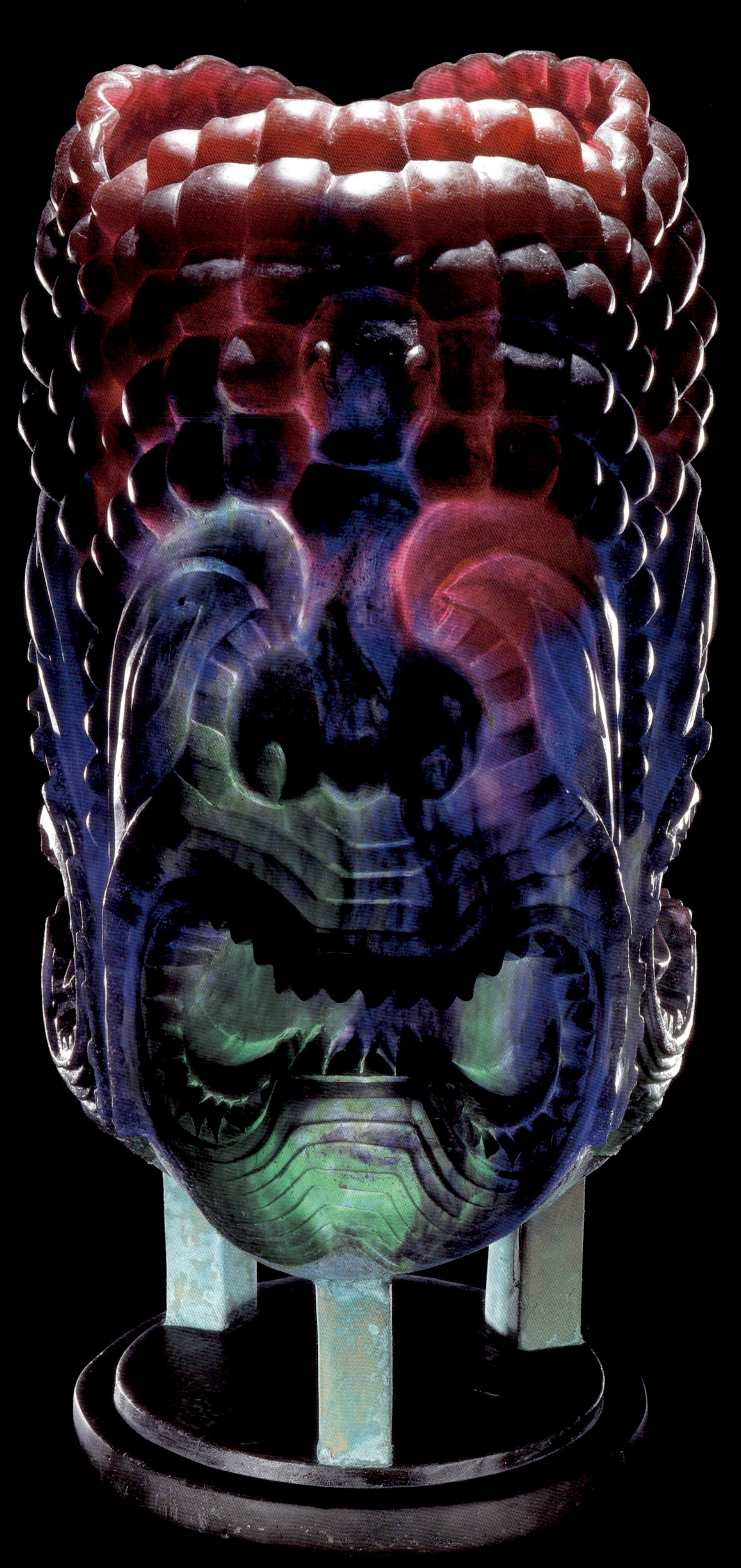

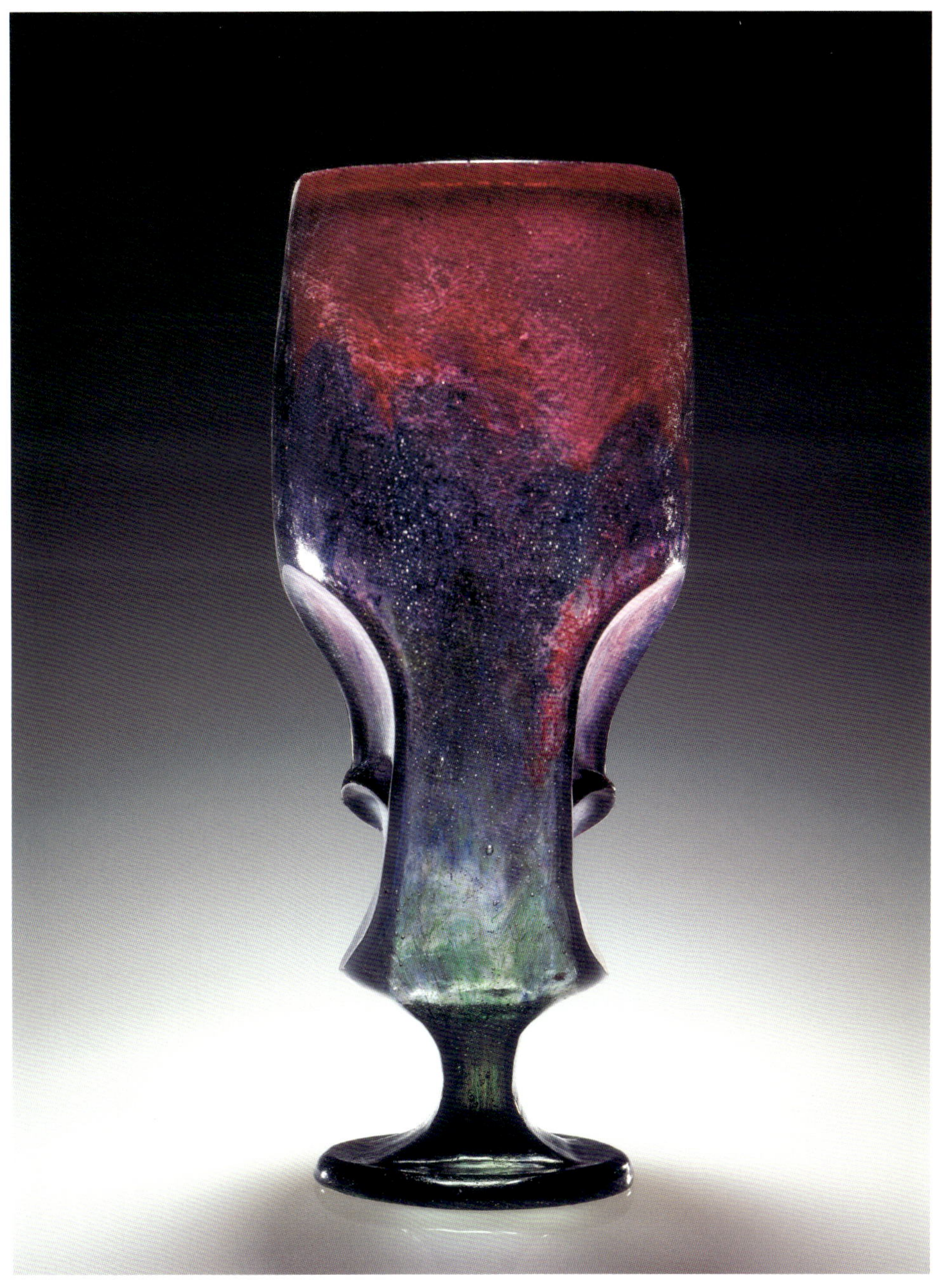

Crown of Fire (p. 89) is a regal portrait of an African beauty with a series of brass rings around her long neck. According to a tribal custom, such rings are used during the course of a girl's life to permanently stretch her neck beyond its natural proportions. The rings are removed if she is proved adulterous—a cruel fate, as the woman's weakened neck can no longer support her head, forcing her to lie prone for the remainder of her life. Here Randal addresses the diverse concepts of ideal beauty, which can vary so greatly from culture to culture. He also subtly engages us in a dialogue about the duality of life, presenting us, as it were, with both faces of reality.

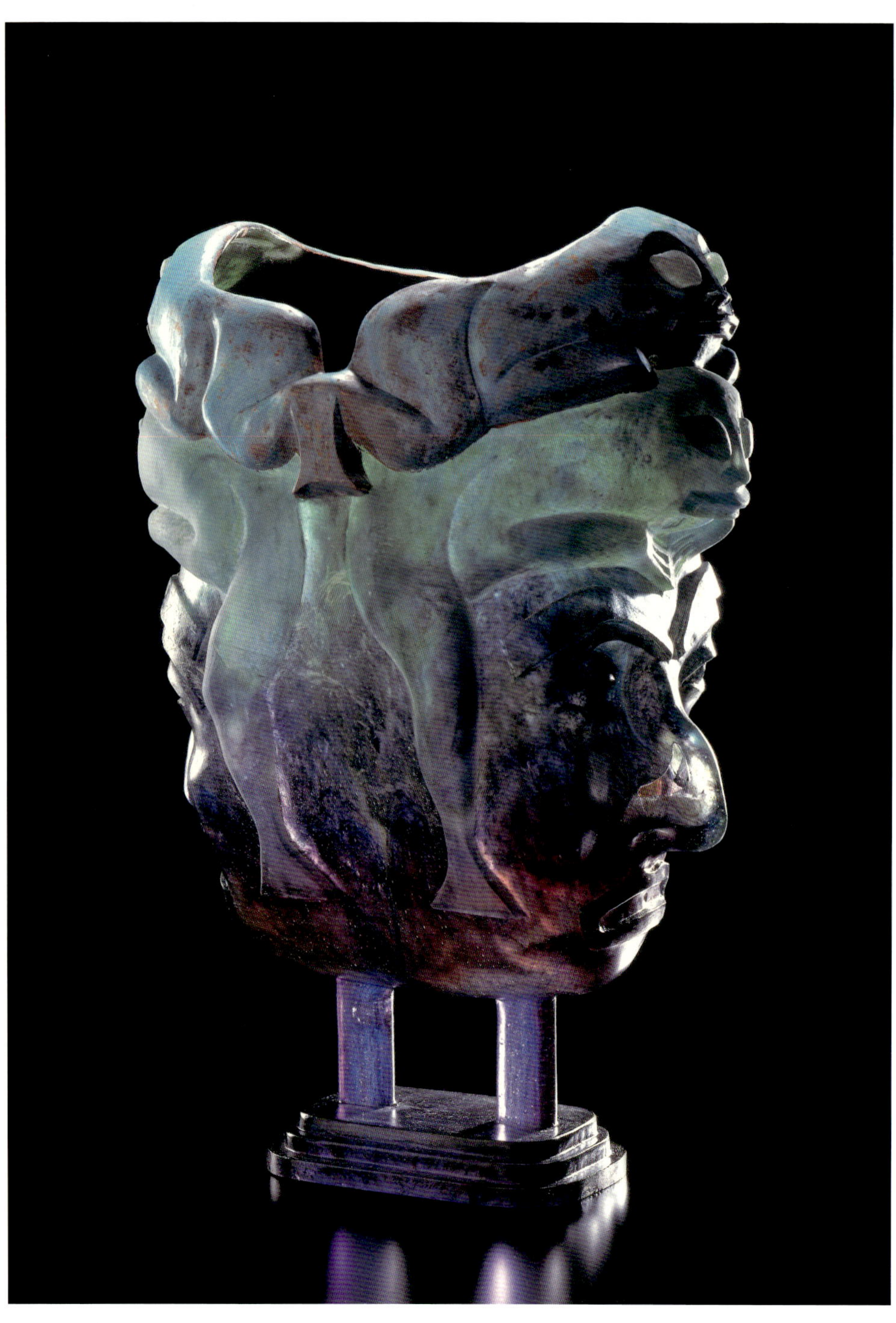

Miss Inca Jewel, 1996   Young Neptune, 2000

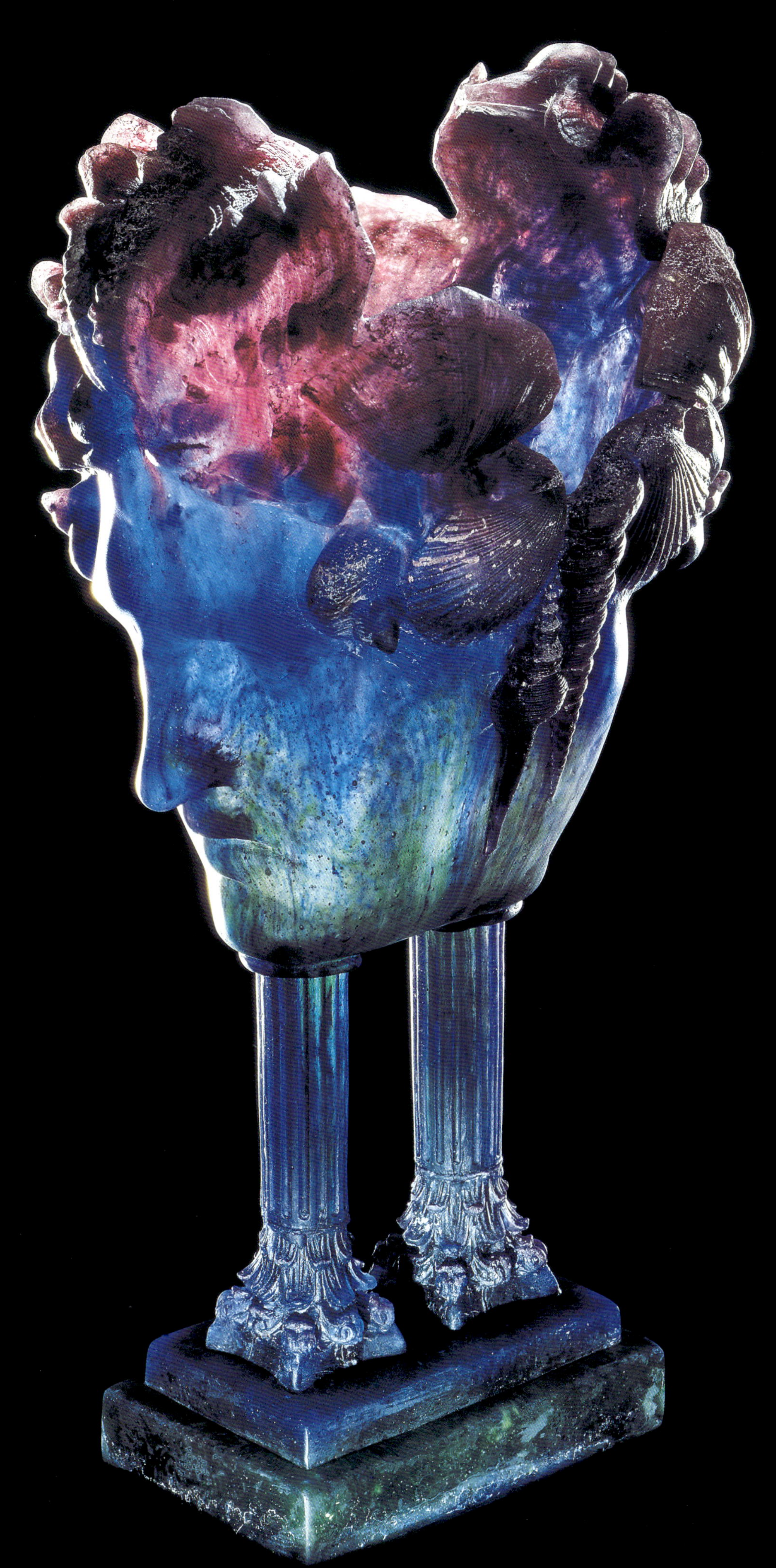

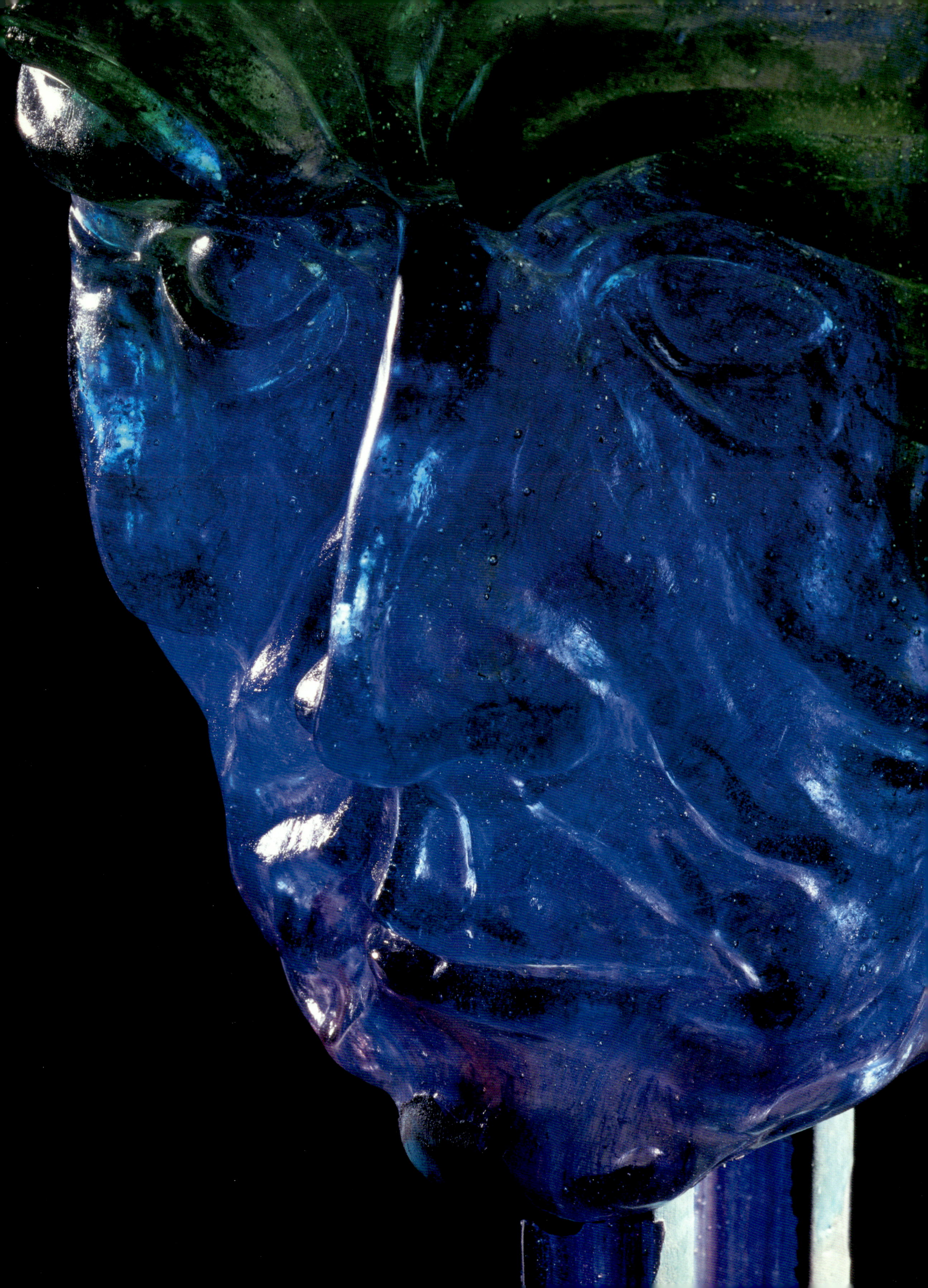

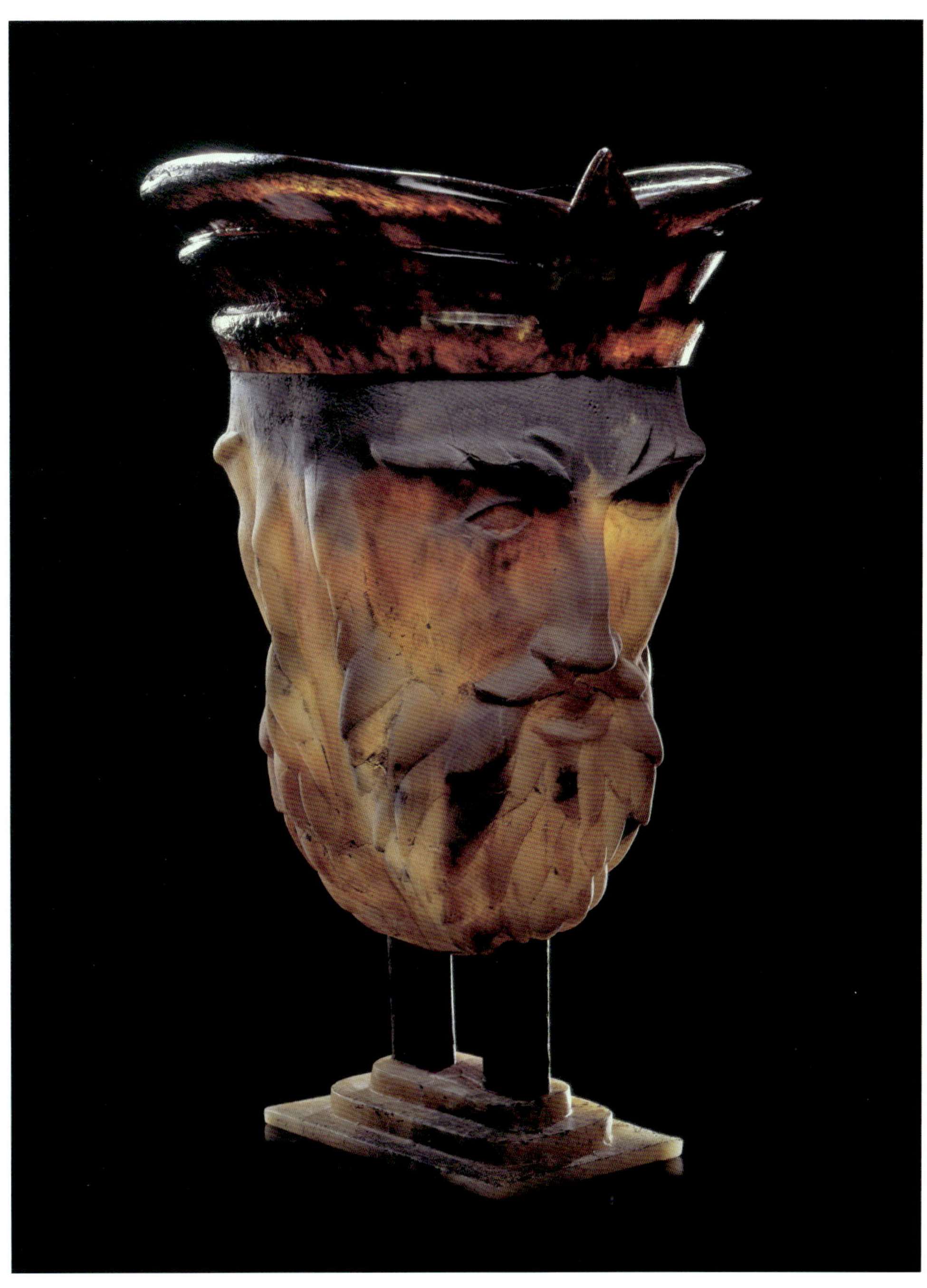

The Scholar (detail), 1998   Renaissance Man, 1997

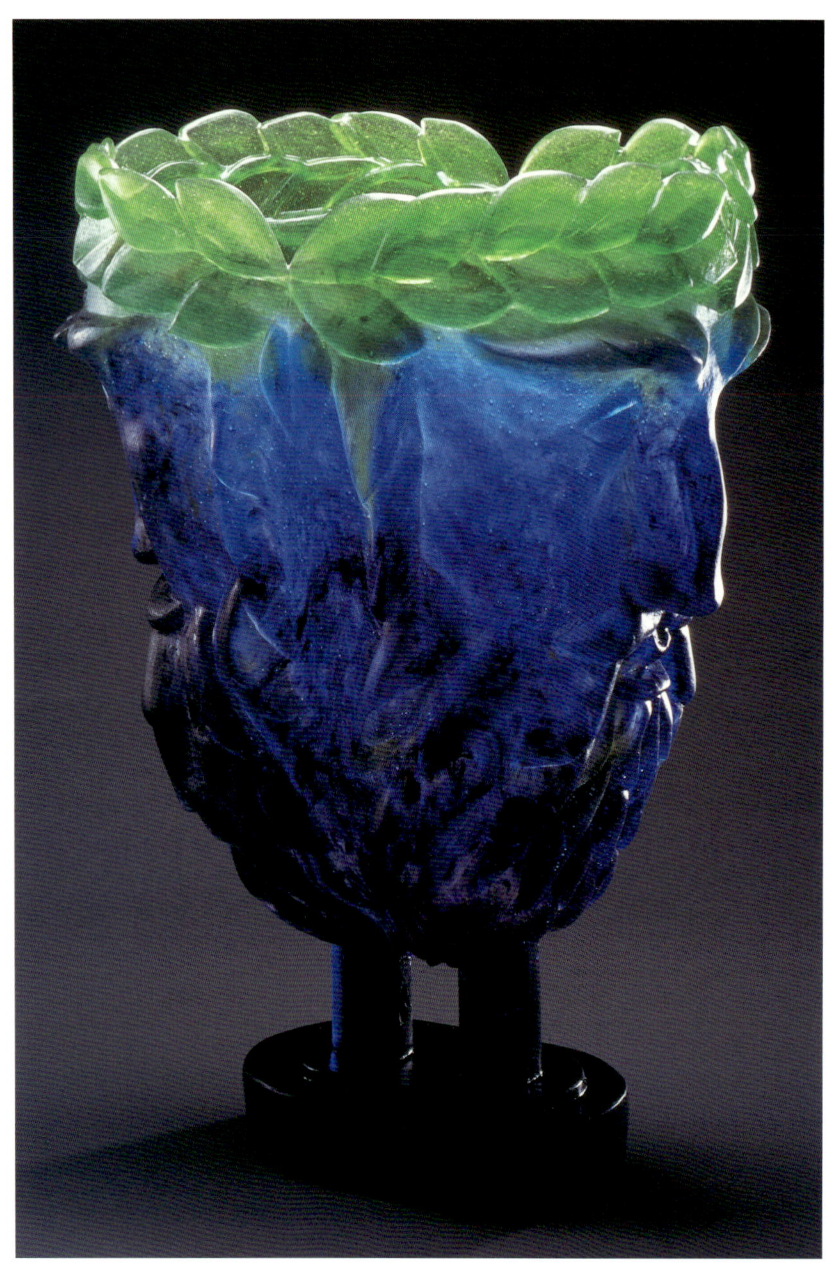

The Greek, 1996   Young Claudius, 1999

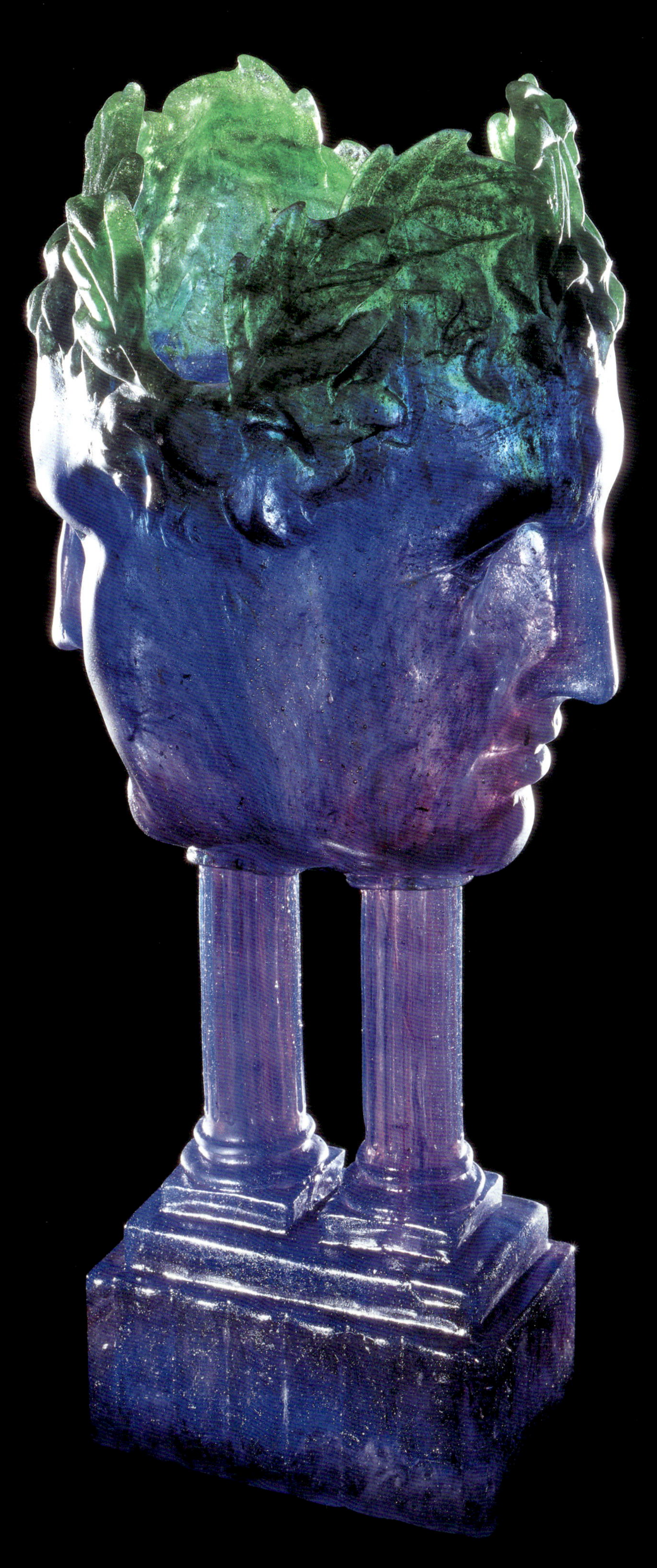

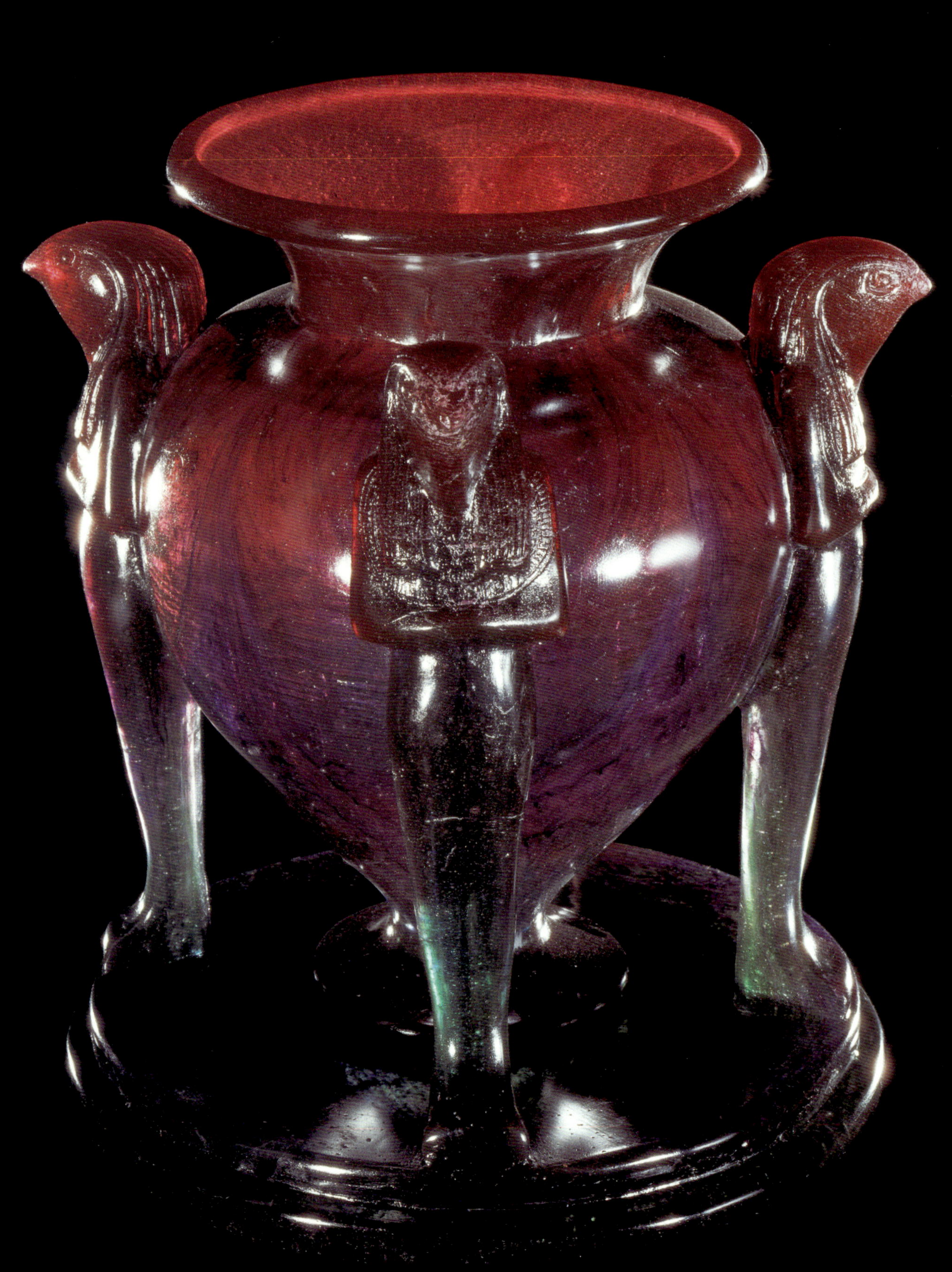

THE PTOLEMAIC SERIES

*One must always maintain one's connection
with the past and yet ceaselessly pull away from it.*

—GASTON BACHELARD

THE EFFIGY SERIES INSPIRED RANDAL TO BEGIN THE PTOLEMAIC SERIES, an almost seamless transition aesthetically. The Ptolemaic period began when the armies of Alexander the Great, king of Macedonia, conquered Egypt in 332 BC. Alexander was crowned pharaoh and was declared a god by his army and his Egyptian followers. He founded the city of Alexandria, which was to become the intellectual center of his vast domain.

Alexander's conquests ushered forth a new period in the arts, the Hellenistic era, in which the character of Greek art influenced the various cultures of the conquered nations. The Greek ideal of beauty in this period incorporated a greater sense of realism and emotionalism, wherein people were depicted with individualized features and expressions. This was a great advancement over traditional Egyptian stylization, characterized by an inexpressive stiffness.[15]

Alexander paid homage to Egyptian religious practices—honoring the pantheon of mythological gods and adopting traditional secular customs—as a way of mediating his rule. When he died in 323 BC, this strategy was continued by Ptolemy, a general in the Macedonian army who proclaimed himself king and inaugurated the period that bears his name.

In his new series Randal reshaped the myths of Ptolemaic Egypt to create offering vessels adorned with their honored deities. In *Four Gods* the vessel is encircled with sculptural figures of Montu, the patron of martial arts and warfare and the symbol of strength and masculine virility. Montu is portrayed as a hawk-headed man, wearing plumes and a sun disk. The color of the cast glass ranges from emerald to amethyst to fiery red, as the procession of gods rises from the watery depths into an eruption of

FOUR GODS, 2000

"

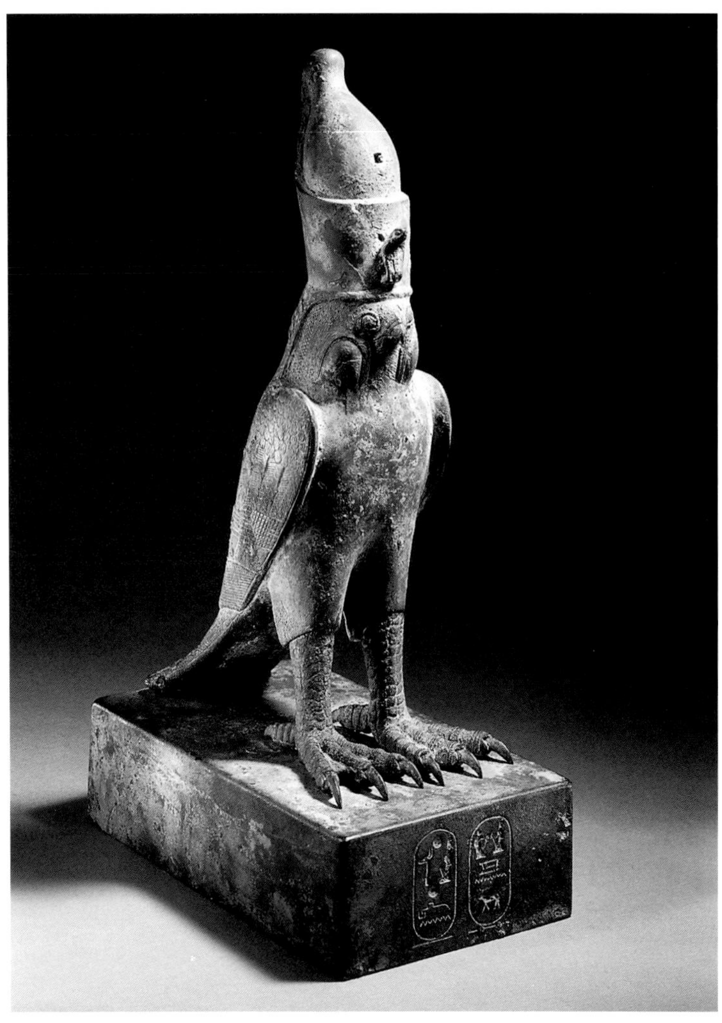

Falcon, Egypt, early Ptolemaic period (circa 300 BC)
or Roman period (30 BC–AD 395)

hot flames. The intense palette invokes Montu's warrior nature: he is wrathful and venge-
ful and poised to strike.

Ptolemaic Vessel No. 010901 venerates the god Horus, ruler of the heavens and patron of
kingship. Horus, the son of Osiris and Isis, is typically portrayed wearing the double crown
of Upper and Lower Egypt to signify his position as Lord of the Two Lands. Effigy figures of
falcons—including small cult images made of metal and clay, and monumental temple
sculptures carved from stone—were an element of Egyptian ritualistic practice for more
than four thousand years. They were worshiped as the embodiment of divine forces and
were considered the personification of the pharaoh. Randal's falcon-embellished offering
vessel, executed in hues of celadon, amethyst, and sky blue to recall the bird's airy domain,
updates this long-standing ceremonial tradition.

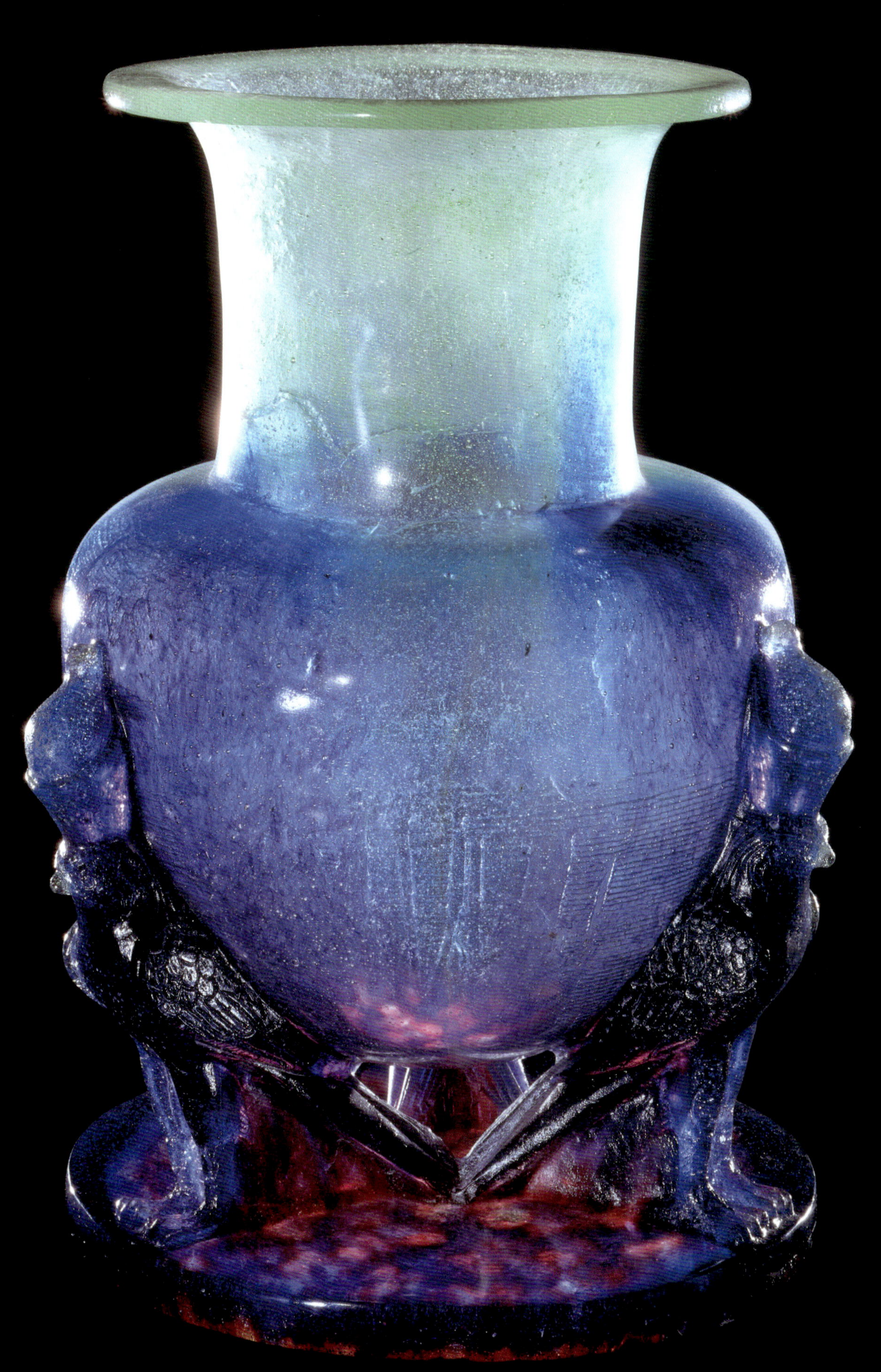

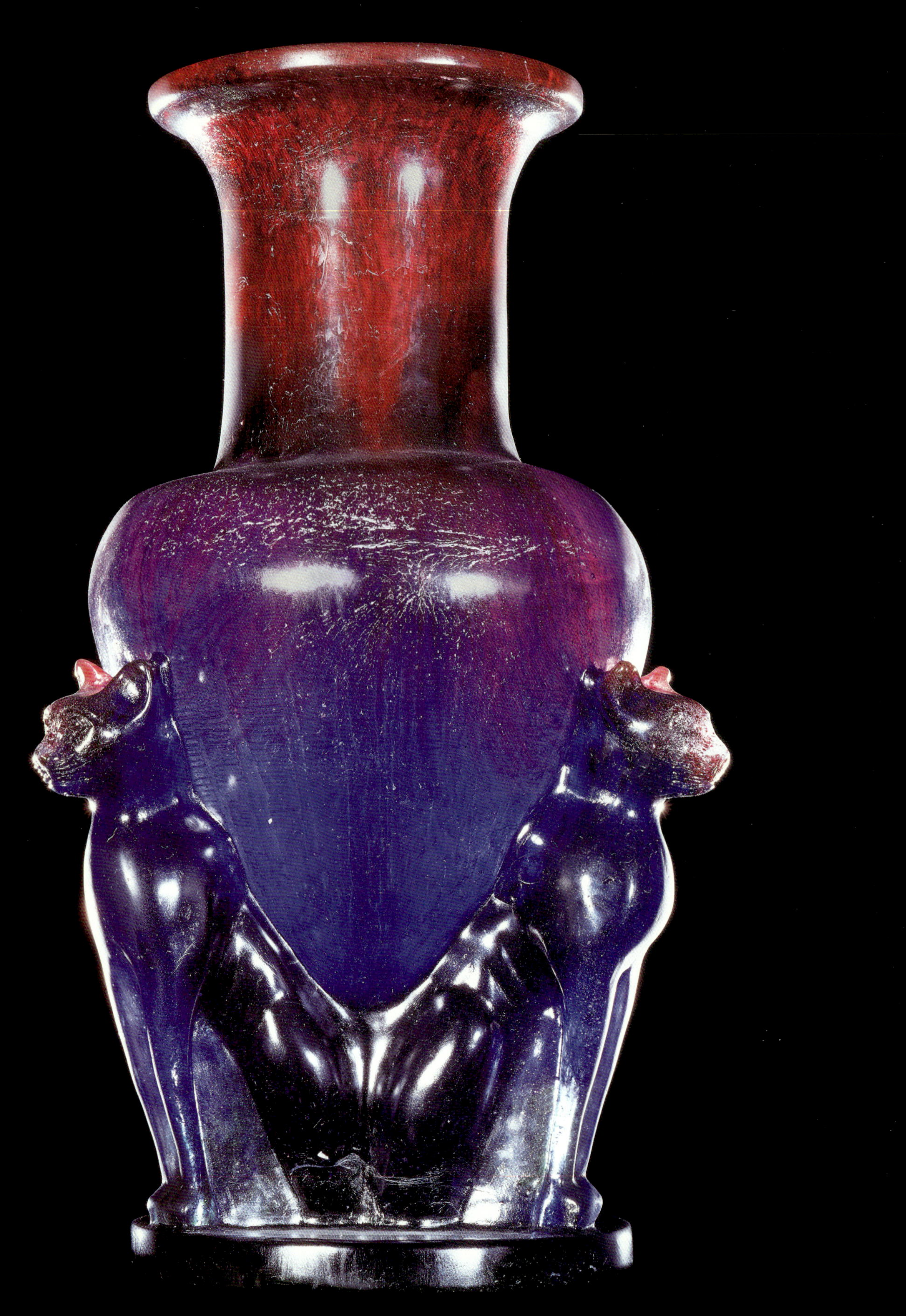

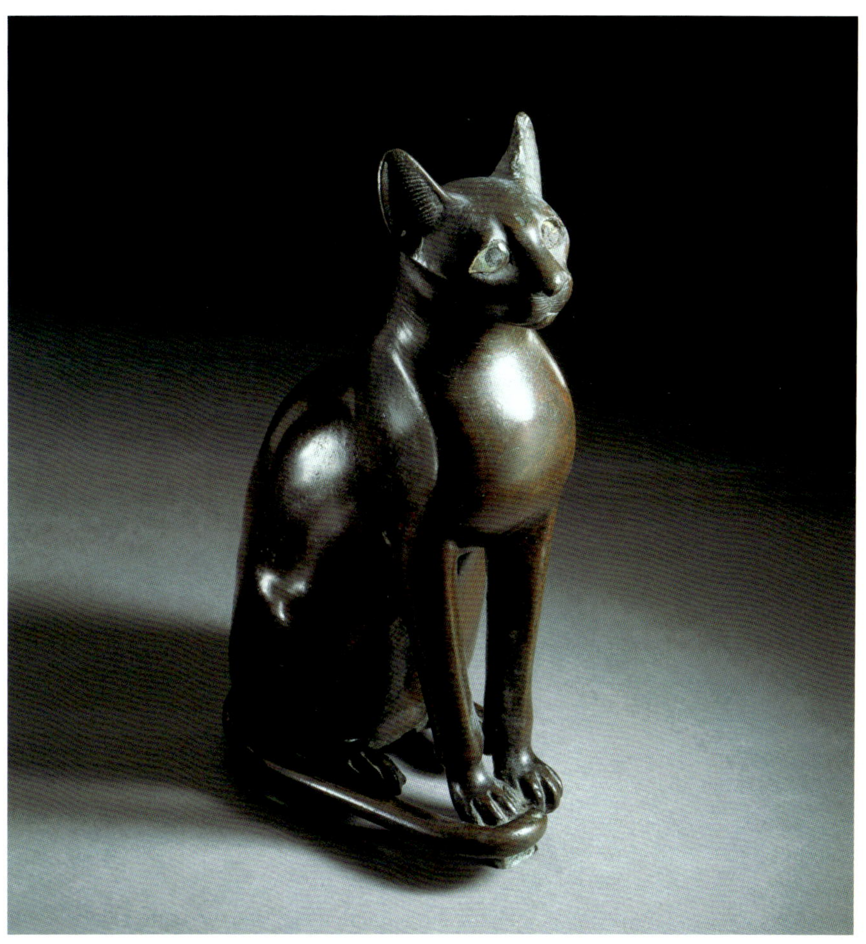

The Goddess Bastet, Egypt,
Late Period (712 – 332 BC)

Ptolemaic Vessel No. 021001 is an homage to Bastet, the Egyptian cat-goddess of the home. These exquisitely modeled felines—sitting attentively, chest upraised, back curved, in the usual Egyptian posture—are a mixture of the domesticated cat and the warlike lioness from which it descended. Cast in shimmering blue-black glass, the finely detailed figures look as if they have been carved from polished obsidian, a gemstone favored in ancient times for the mystery inherent in its reflective black surface. These deified, heraldic creatures retell their myth to a contemporary audience.

In *Ptolemaic Vessel No.* 010701 (p. 107) the god Montu appears again, supporting a shallow kylix-shaped vessel. Originally produced as a prototype for a limited edition artist's series production piece for Daum Cristal in France, it is one of Randal's favorites. The scalloped vessel supported by two statues atop a fluted capital base give this piece a distinct Art Deco feeling.

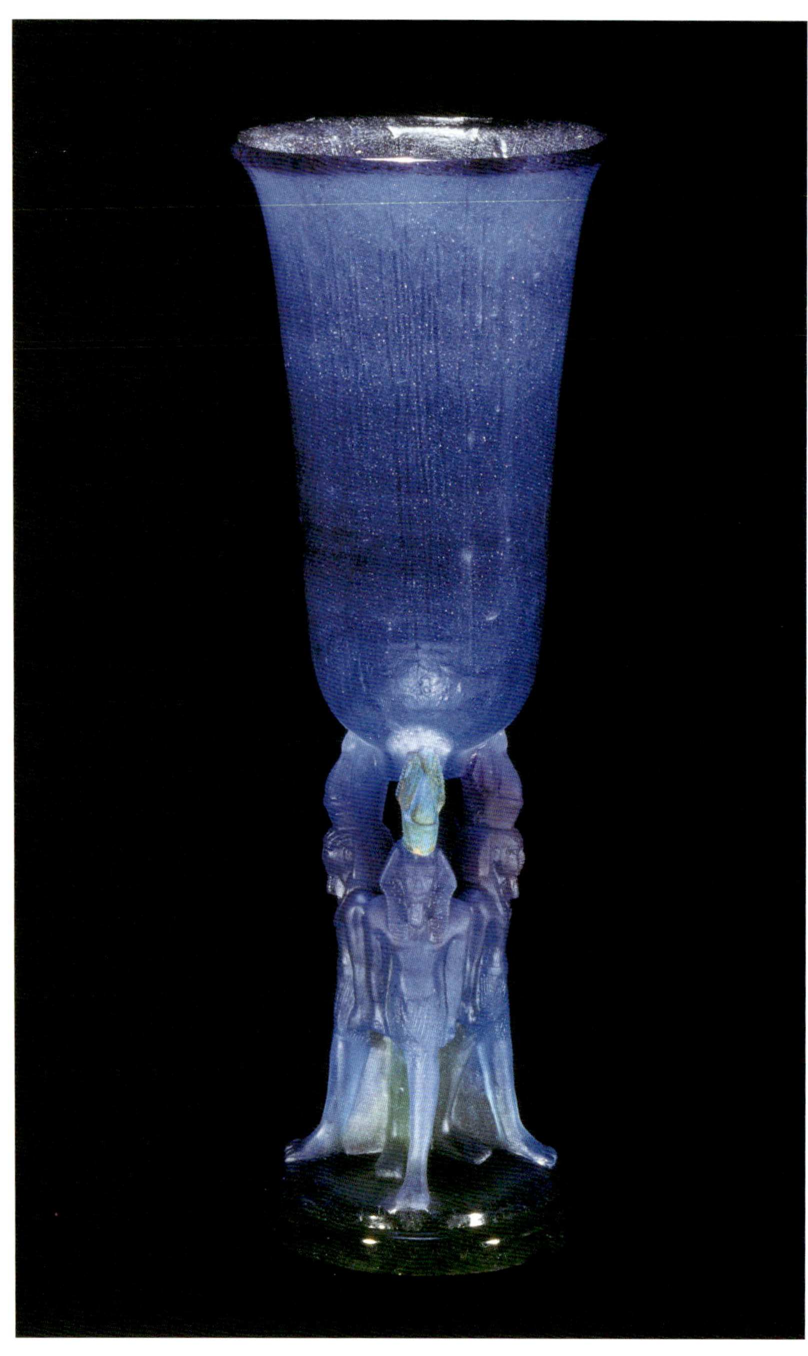

  Ptolemaic Vessel No. 020901, 2001   Ptolemaic Vessel No. 010701, 2001

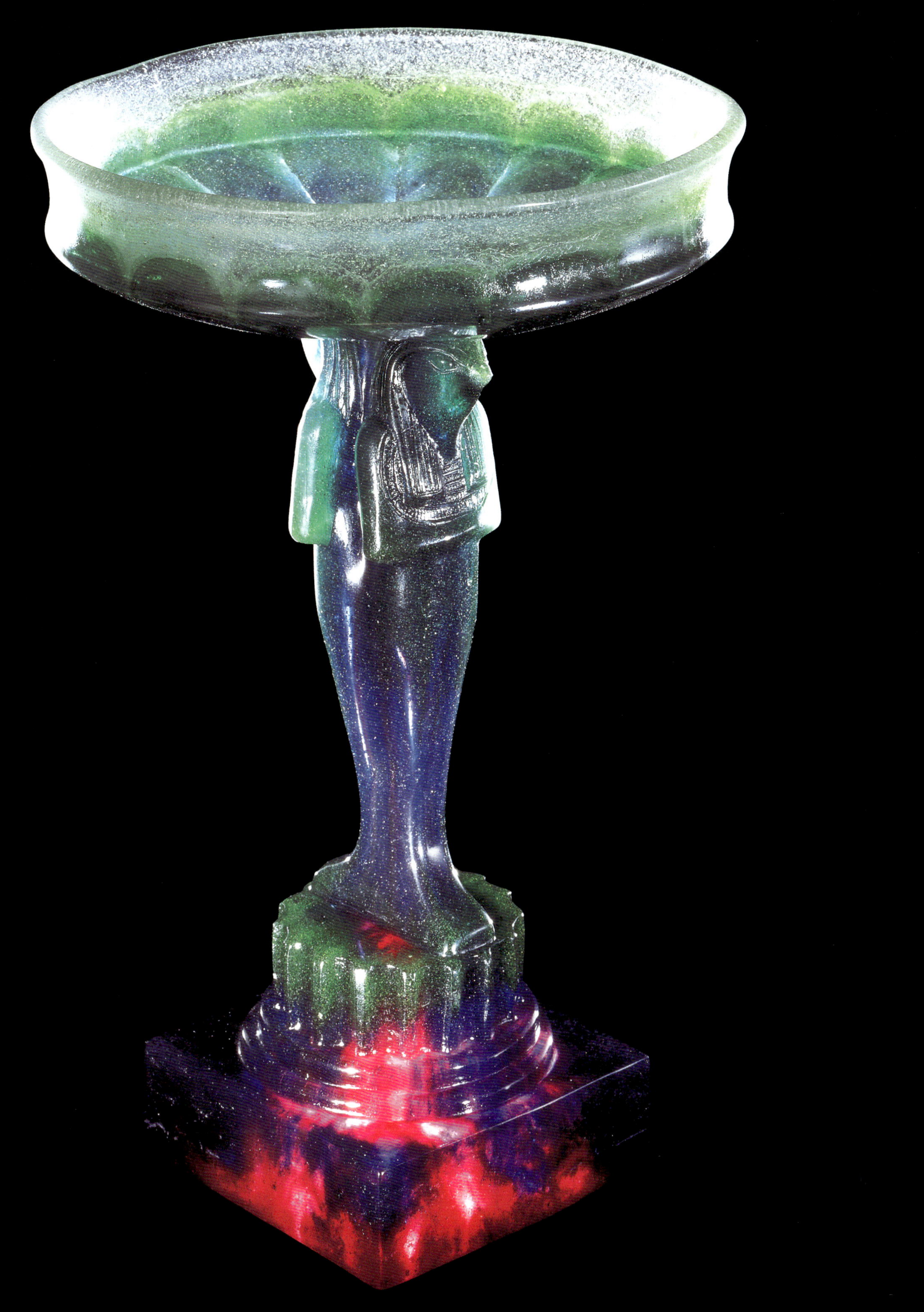

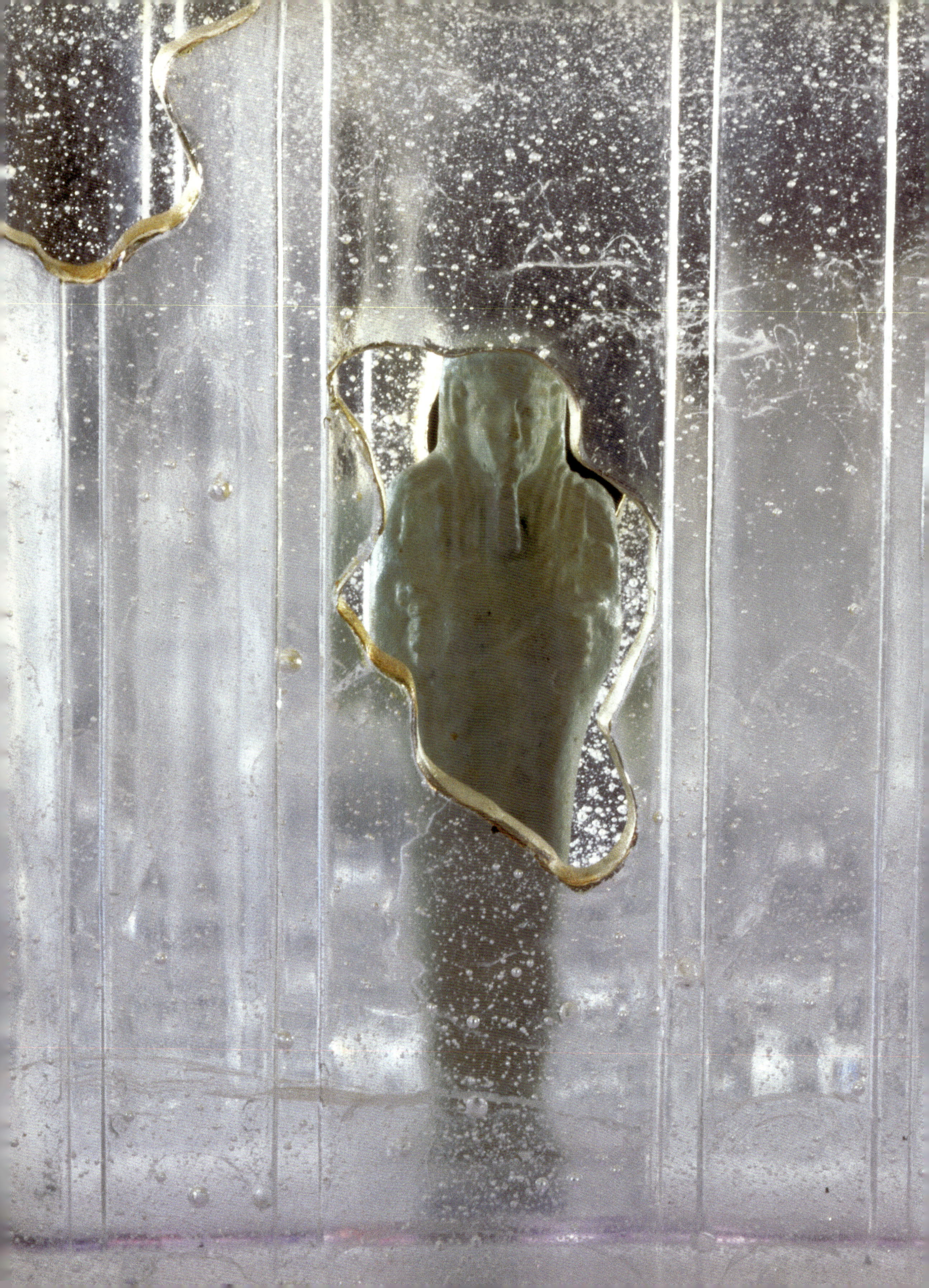

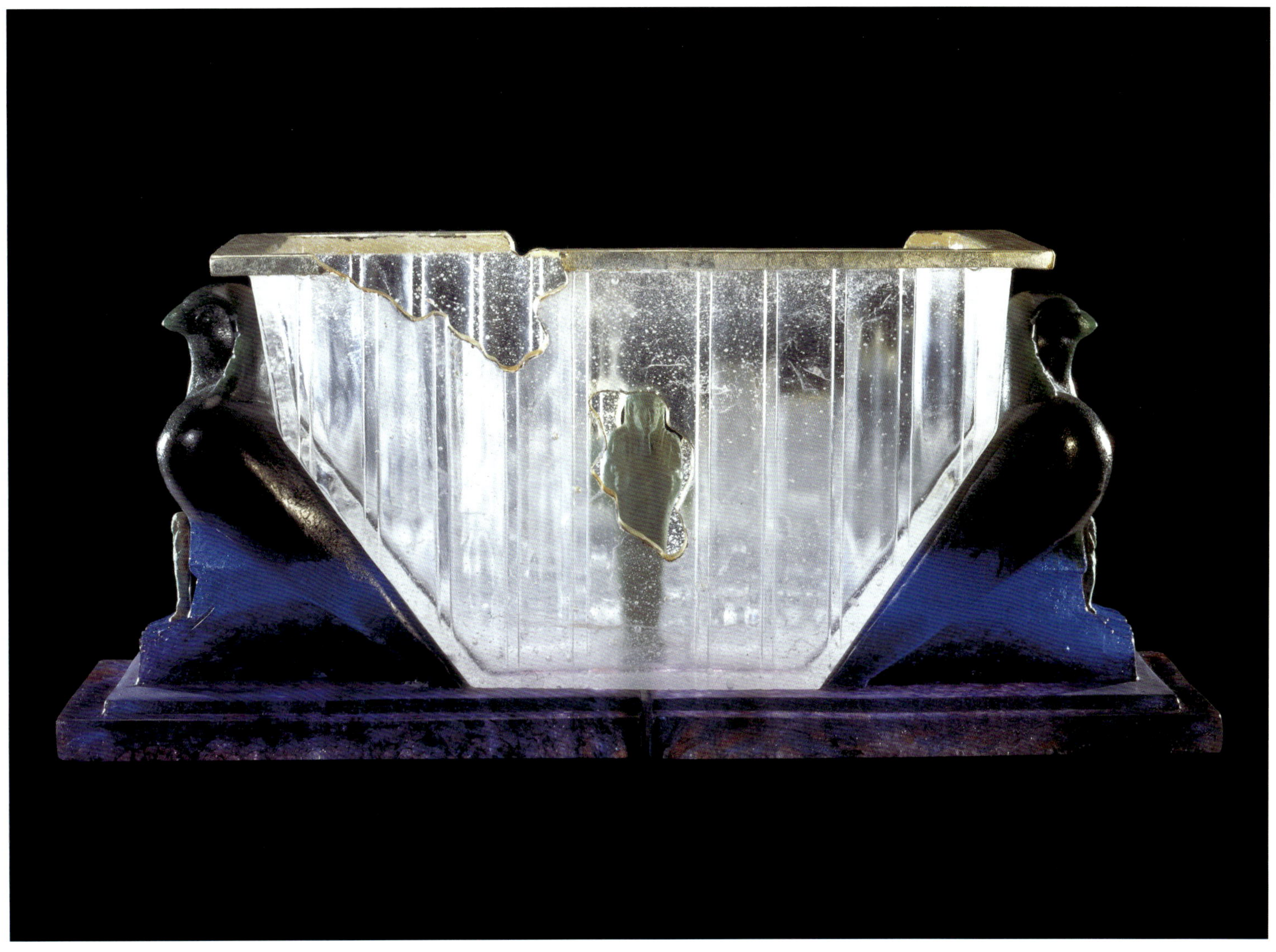

One of the most outstanding examples of the Ptolemaic Series is *Shrine of Horus*. In this piece Randal has come full circle by creating a completely sculptural object. Not based on the vessel form, it features two flanking busts of the falcon-headed Horus enshrined in a temple with fluted columns. On their backs, these figures carry the shrine, cut and worn away in places, revealing a large ancient *ushabti* in the center. Nestled between the breasts of the busts of Horus are two smaller *ushabti*. In this sculpture Randal has addressed "the concepts of life, death, and life after death, and ultimately the cycle that represents continuation and infinity."

Examining the iconography and symbology, one can fully appreciate the sculpture as a celebration of creation and regeneration. Horus was thought to be present at the coronation

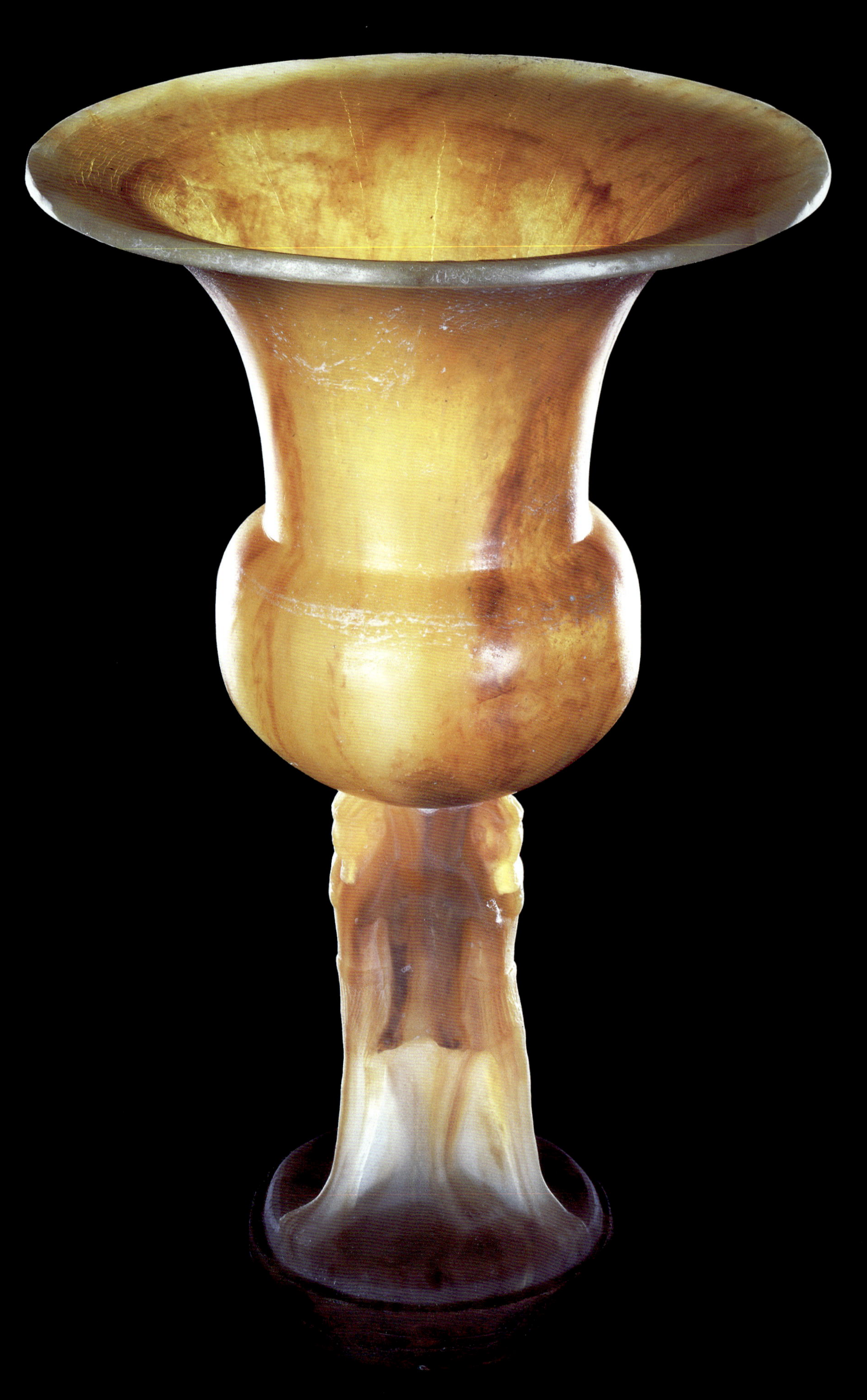

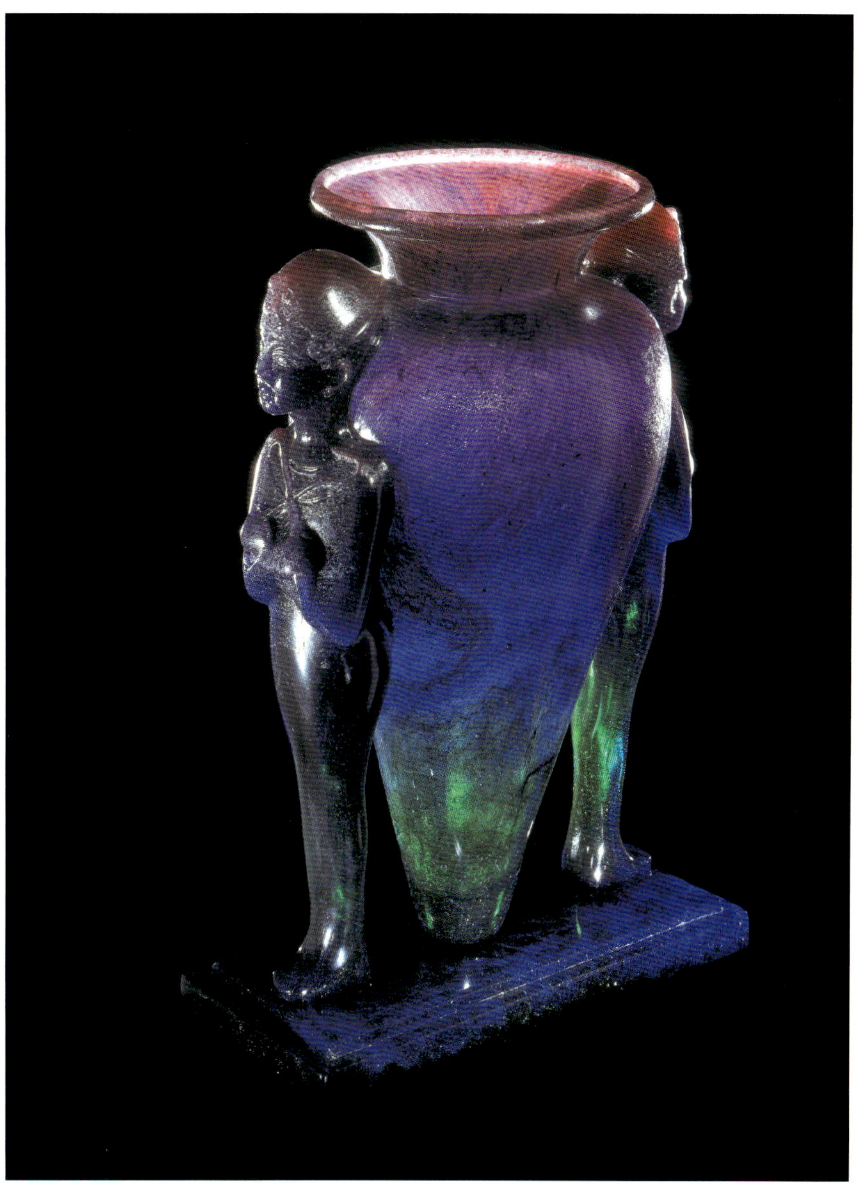

of pharaohs, and thereafter was associated with them during their rule. After their death, pharaohs were believed to be transformed into Osiris, father of Horus and god of the underworld. In this shrine Randal has cleverly implanted the clues to this timeless story of life, death, and rebirth. *Shrine of Horus* is also the perfect representation of the creative life of an artist, who moves through such a passage again and again during the perpetual process of making. Randal's muse, in drawing him onward, has led him back to his beginning.

THE PROCESS
OF LOST-WAX
PÂTE DE VERRE

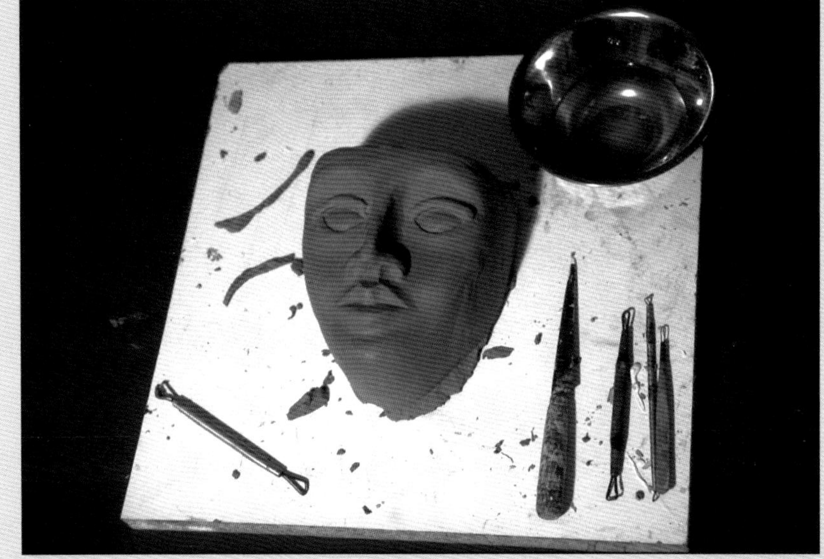

Unlike glassblowing, the technique of lost-wax *pâte de verre*
is a complicated process, involving many steps over an
extended period of time. Based on a foundation of classical
sculptural techniques, the first step is realization of the
piece in clay.

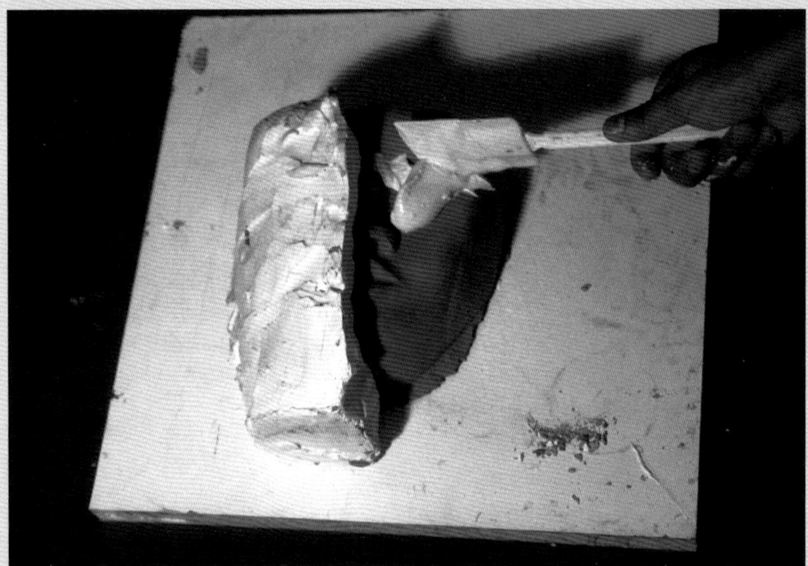

Eventually the piece will have to be made entirely of wax.
Here, a plaster mold is made of a clay face to enable the
production of wax duplicates.

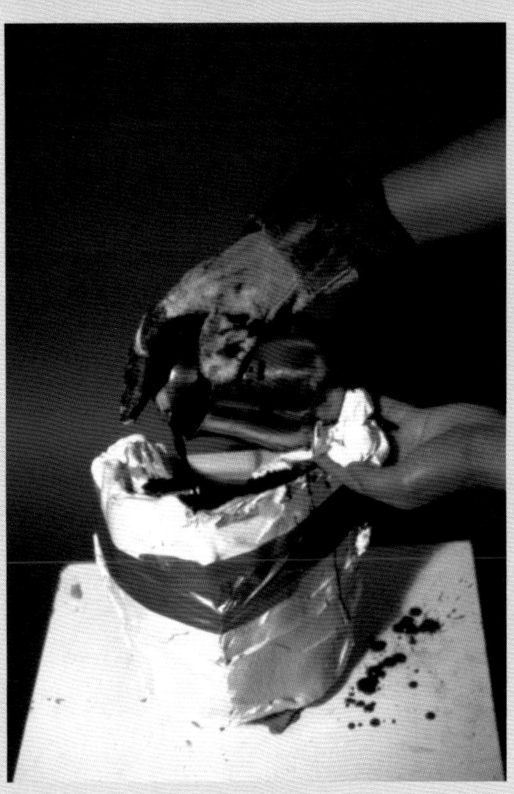

Once the mold is complete, the clay is removed and hot wax
is poured into the wet plaster mold.

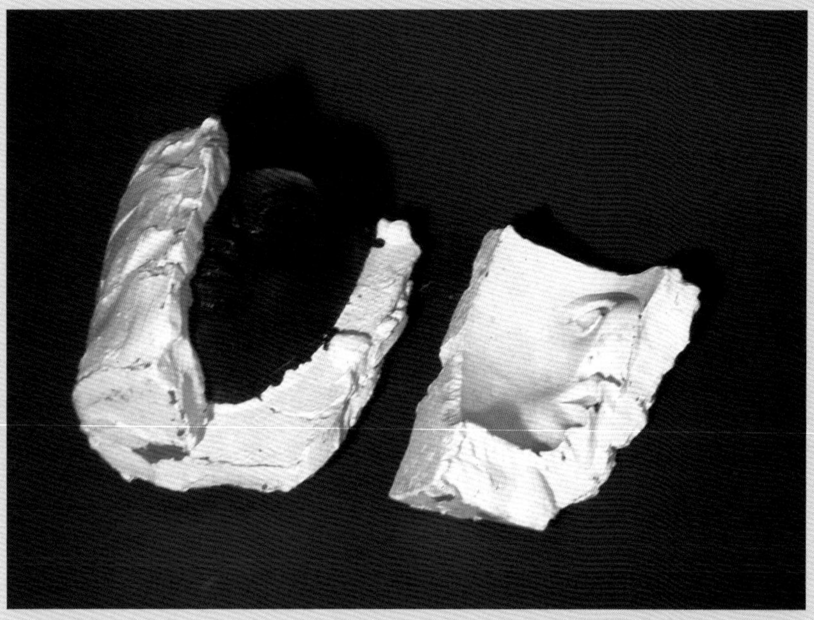

After the wax has cooled, the mold is opened and the wax can be removed. This process is repeated to produce the different wax positives that are necessary for the piece.

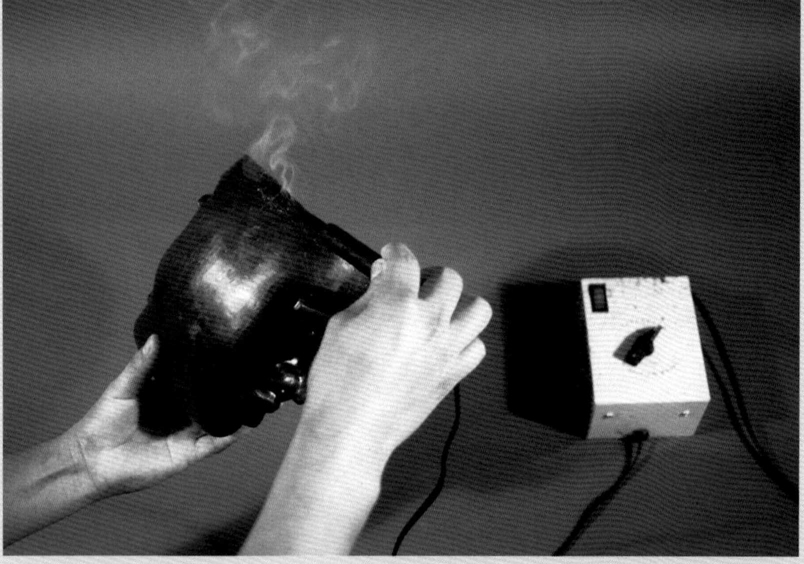

The wax pieces are slowly assembled using a jeweler's pen, a tool like a hot-tipped fountain pen.

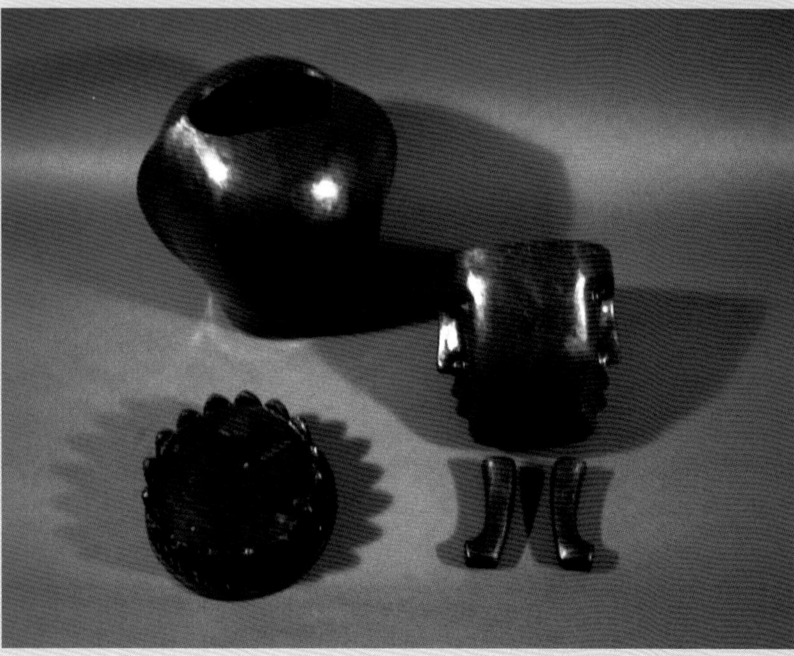

Many individual wax components are employed in assembling the final wax positive. It is not uncommon to use as many as twenty different pieces, produced from different types of molds (e.g., plaster, rubber, and so on).

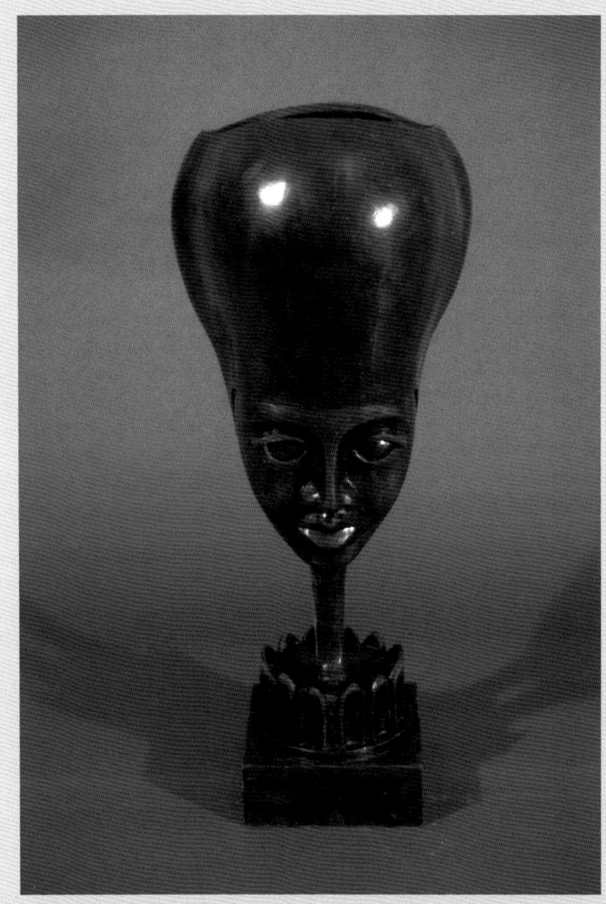

The finished wax positive is ready for casting. What you see in wax is what you will see in crystal—whether it is a nose, a scratch, or even a thumbprint.

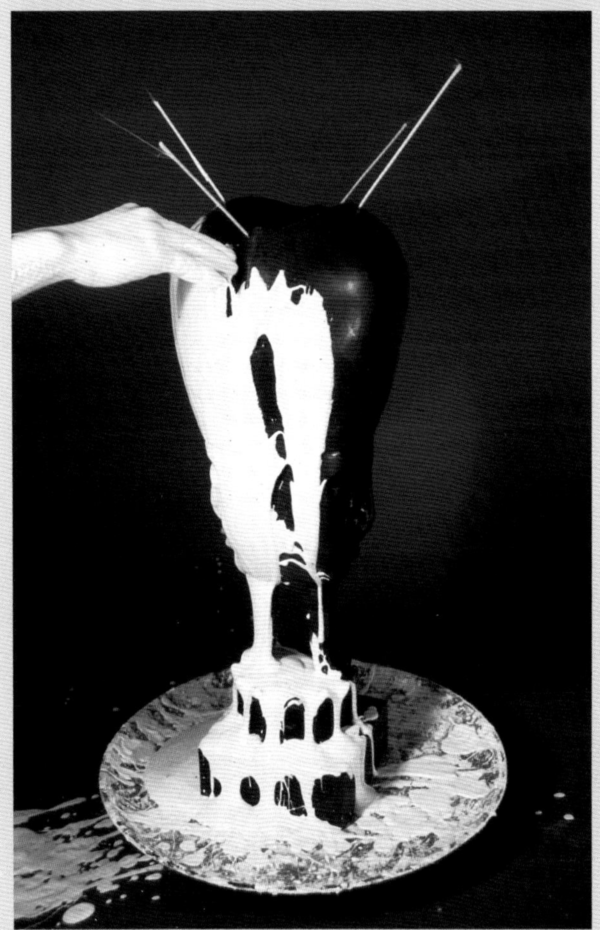

The final wax positive is encased in an investment mold using an old Italian technique called "splash coating." The mold is made of plaster, sand, ground silica, and other refractory materials. Straws are positioned throughout to create vents that will allow air and trapped gasses to escape.

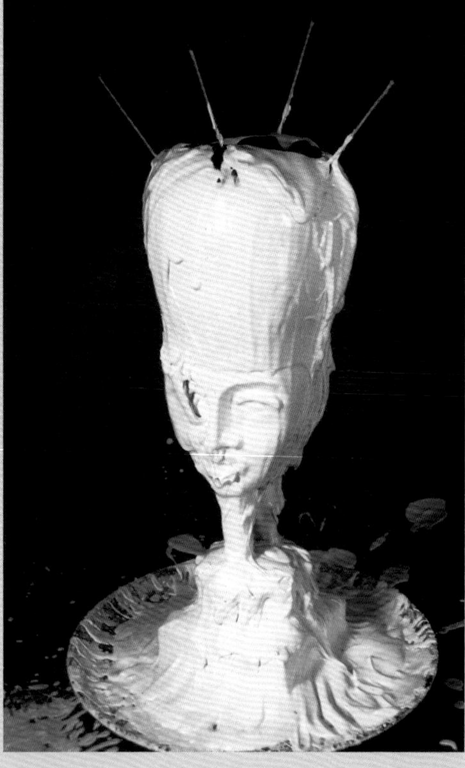

The mold is hand-built in many layers to reach the required thickness.

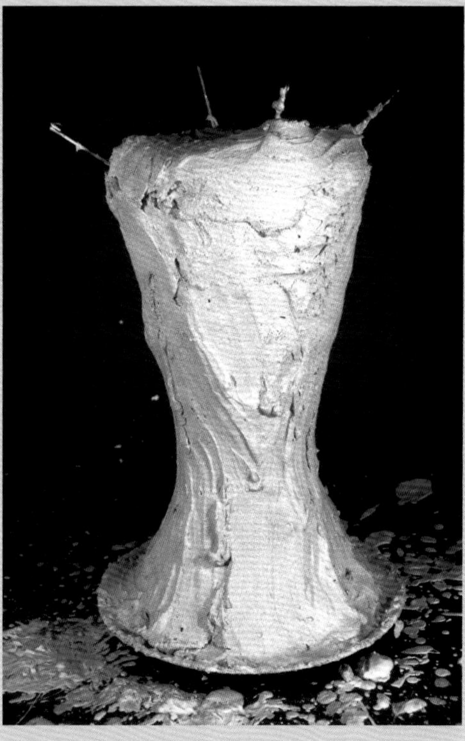

The investment mold is finished. It will be heated in order to allow all the wax to melt out, creating a negative space where the wax once was.

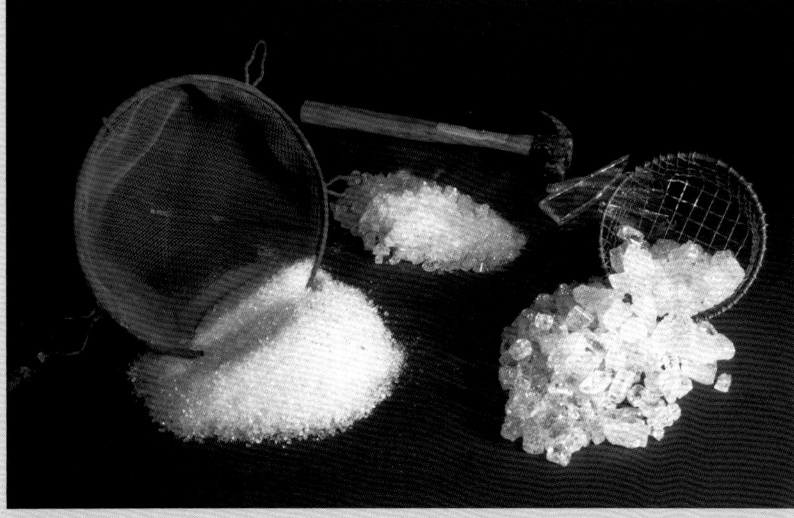

There is a common misconception that molten crystal or glass is then poured into the mold. In reality, the crystal comes in large sheets, which are crushed and sifted into different-size particles.

The mold is fired upside down in the kiln, so that the bottom of a piece is actually an opening at the top of the mold. Here crushed crystal (known as "frit") is combined with different oxides, chemicals, and coloring agents and then placed into the mold in layers. Precise color density is achieved through exact percentages, carefully weighed.

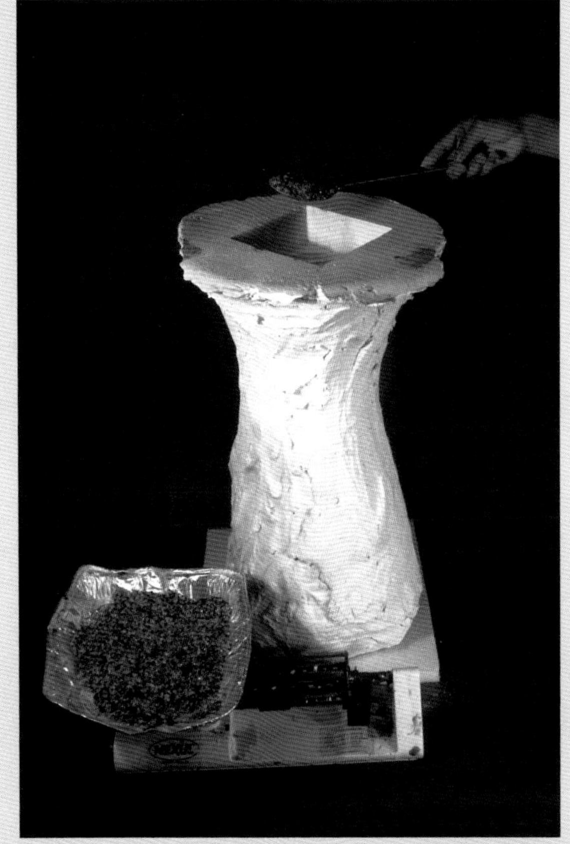

The mold is placed into the kiln and is then encased in a steel ring and packed tight with sand for support and protection. Approximately half the weight of the investment mold is water. The mold is dried slowly for several weeks and then taken to a final firing temperature of 1450° F. At this point the crystal slowly fills the mold and the air bubbles rise to the surface. As gravity pulls the crystal down, the individual layers of color will produce different effects. This process, depending on the size and the complexity of the piece, can take anywhere from twelve to thirty-six hours. The piece must now cool slowly, a process called "annealing." The kilns are controlled by computer; a piece can take anywhere between two and six weeks to cool to room temperature. The slightest temperature variation at a critical moment can cause the finished piece to crack.

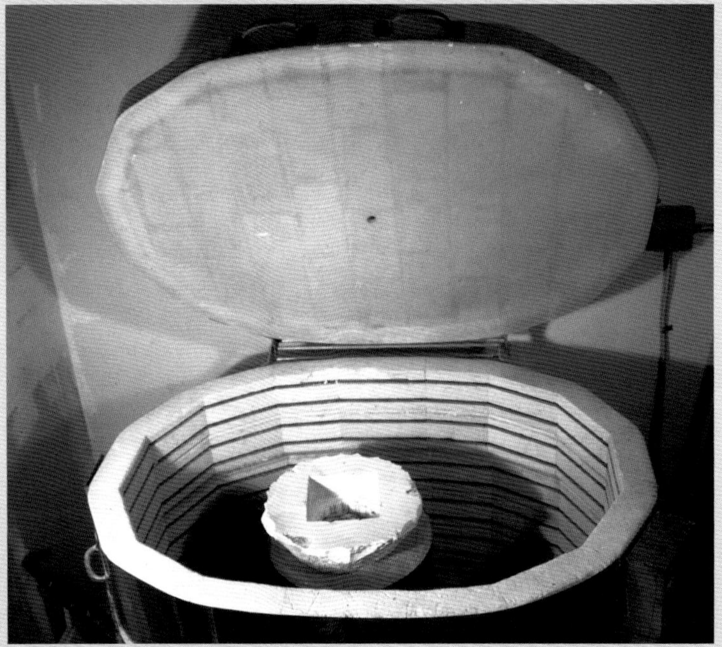

When finally cooled, the mold is carefully lifted out of the kiln using a crane.

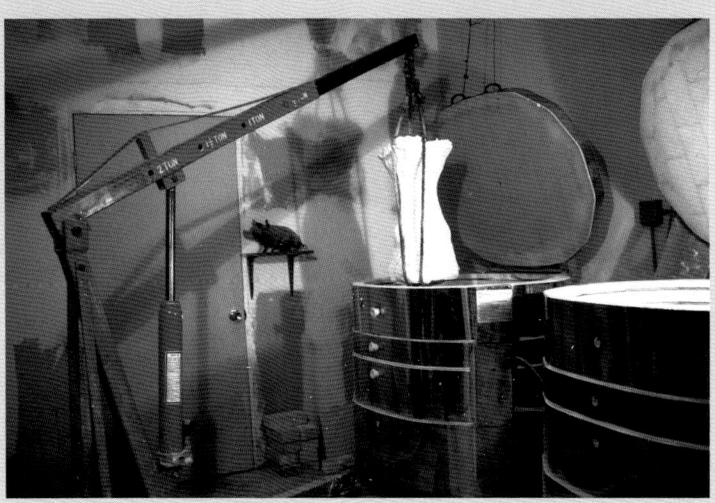

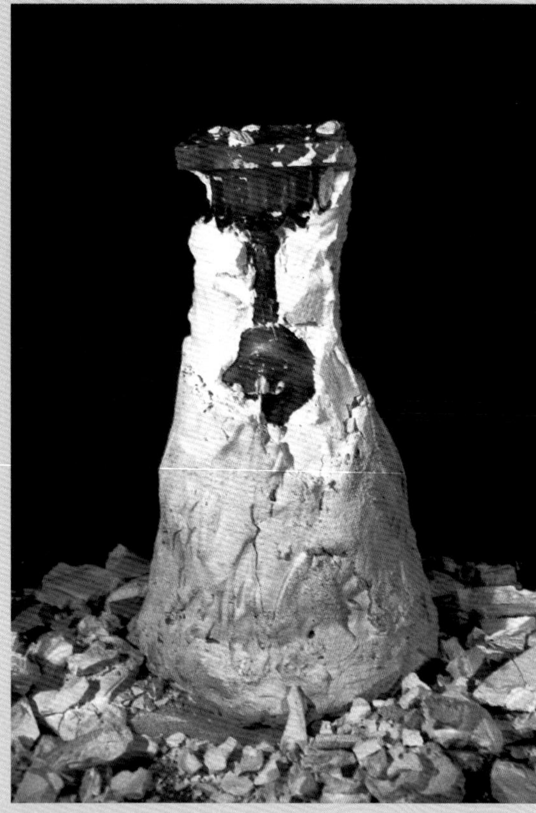

The investment mold is chipped away slowly and carefully.

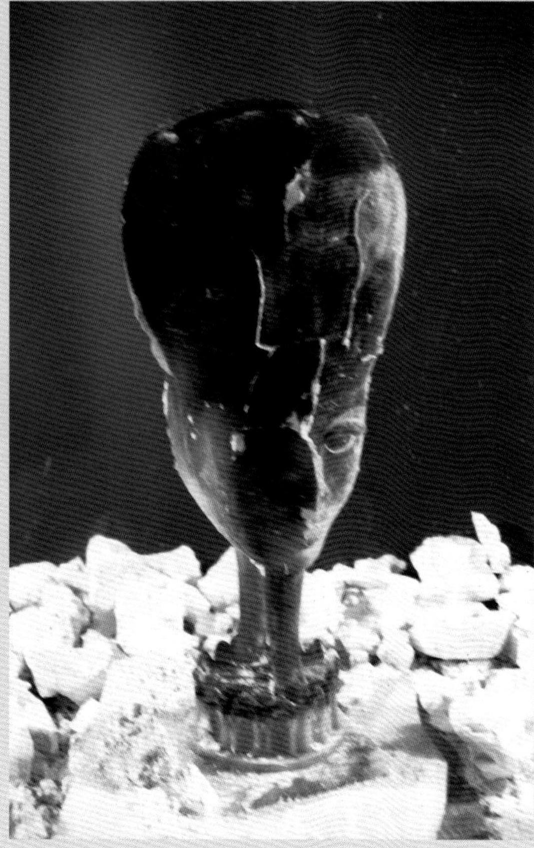

The finished casting is finally revealed. It is usually quite rough, requiring a great deal of grinding and polishing using a variety of diamond and abrasive tools. Then, through a series of acid baths (typically a combination of sulfuric and hydrofluoric acids), the final luster and translucency are revealed.

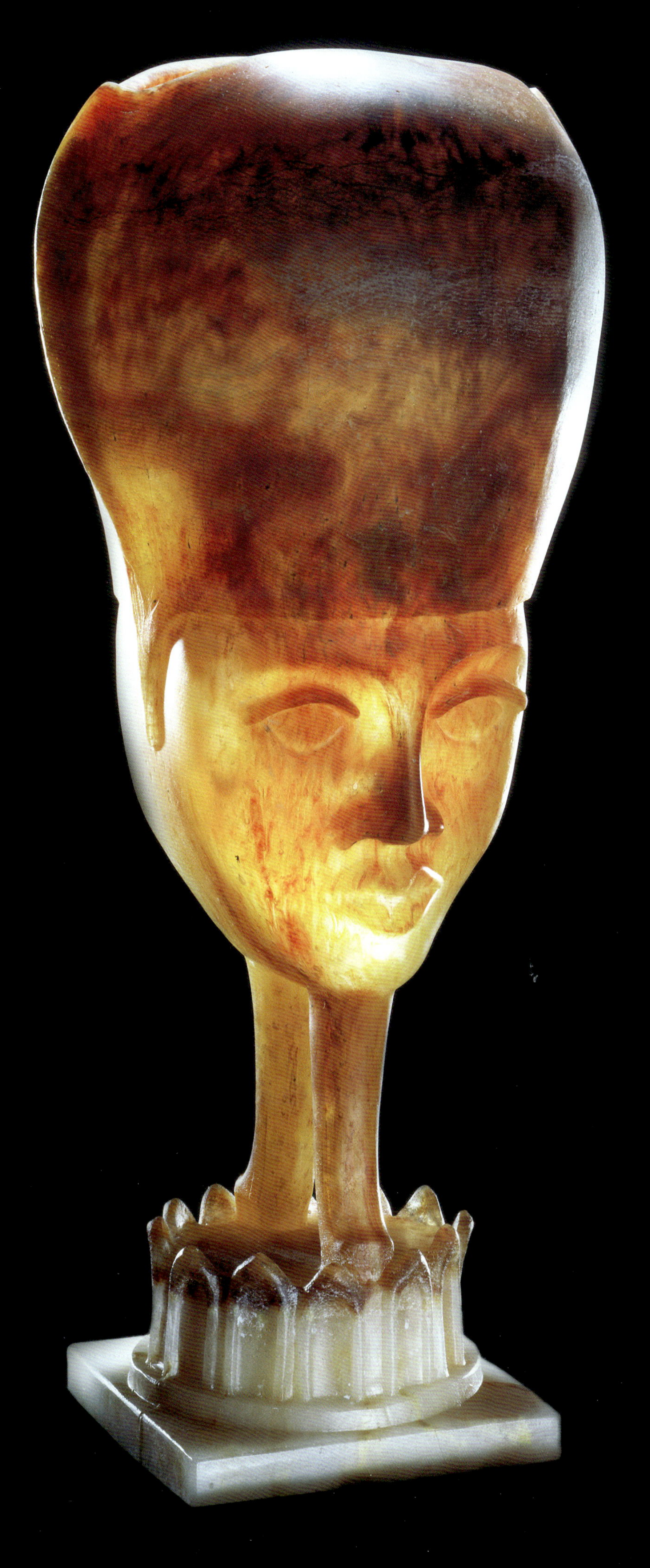

REFLECTIONS ON BEAUTY

We shall not cease from exploration
And the end of all our exploring
Will be to arrive where we started
And know the place for the first time.
—T. S. Eliot

S ETH R ANDAL IS DRAWN BOTH TO THE BEAUTY AND THE
experience of making works in glass. He is attracted to the tactility of the alchemical
processes through which pieces of glass become meditations on reflected and re-
fracted light. There is a romantic impulse underlying his visually dynamic objects,
as he believes in the innate power and efficacy of art as an embodiment of beauty.

Eighteenth-century philosophers, notably the British theoretician John Locke,
broadened the concept of Platonic beauty to include not only the pure and ideal element inherent in an object but also the pleasurable response elicited by that object. In
Locke's *Essay Concerning Human Understanding* he defines art and beauty in terms of the
experience of the perceiver, the response to beauty that could be described as "pleasure."[16]
Ipso facto, beauty connotes pleasure.

Randal attempts to create in his work the charged space that reveals and defines the beauty of an object: "Beauty, not as a thing, nor a quality of thing, but as
the charge in the space between."[17] He views this charge as analogous to the spark
of electricity jumping a gap between wires, or the stimulated synapses of human
neurons that transmit sensation—a vibrant connection between maker, object, and
spectator. He exploits this living link by creating sculptures of high valency, which
magnetize the viewer's gaze by means of their immediate sensual qualities and then
increase the viewer's interest through the depth of their engagement with historical
inspirations.

Each of Randal's elegant vessels represents a personal search for purity of form
and the meaning of beauty. His works in glass are a pilgrimage in honor of classical
ideals, taking him—and us—into realms of optical intrigue, through intricate color
fields, where personal mythologies are bestowed with the aura of majestic imagery.
Randal's objective is to bring the viewer into the circuit of shared experience, a con-
tinuous loop that begins with the primacy of creation and ends with the pleasure
of perception—a Möbius strip of beauty, and its experience, personified.

Fantasies of leaded glass, Attican Vases, Cage Cups, Effigies, and Ptolemaic
Vessels—as powerful as these series are in their formal manifestations, they inevi-
tably resolve into singular moments of divined time, where the intellect and the
senses coexist. The viewer is prompted to contemplate the origin of an idea—always
rooted in history, legend, and memory—and follow that idea as it engenders a
reshaped myth that undertakes the risks of invention and spectacle. Undeniably
beautiful, endowed with technical prowess, and infused with classic authority, these
works expand the boundaries of an ancient medium while they anchor us to the
beauty in contemporary experience.

NOTES

1. Harold Jaffe, "Introduction," in *The Age of Tiffany*, exh. cat. (New York: C. W. Post Art Gallery, 1981), unpaginated.

2. Victor Arwas, "Introduction," in *Tiffany* (New York: Rizzoli, 1980), unpaginated.

3. Chloe Zerwick, *A Short History of Glass* (Corning, NY: The Corning Museum of Glass; New York: Harry N. Abrams, 1990), 98.

4. Leslie Greene Bowman, *American Arts and Crafts: Virtue in Design* (Los Angeles: Los Angeles County Museum of Art; Boston: Little, Brown, 1990), 218.

5. Judith B. Gura, "Swedish Glass at Bard," text for the exhibition *The Brilliance of Swedish Glass* at Bard Graduate Center, at http://antiquesandthearts.com/archive/swedglas.htm.

6. "Art Nouveau: France," at http://www.groveart.com.

7. John Fleming and Hugh Honour, *The Penguin Dictionary of Decorative Arts* (New York: Viking Penguin, 1989), 612.

8. Joe Greenwald, "Ancient Greece & You—Beauty," at http://ablemedia.com/ctcweb/showcase/greenwaldgreece3.html.

9. Plotinus, *Enneads* I.6, "On Beauty," trans. Stephen MacKenna; from *Exploring Ancient World Cultures: Readings from Ancient Rome*, at http://eawc.evansville.edu/anthology/beauty.htm.

10. Ibid.

11. David Whitehouse, *Glass of the Roman Empire* (Corning, NY: The Corning Museum of Glass, 1988), 50.

12. Harold Newman, *An Illustrated Dictionary of Glass* (London: Thames and Hudson, 1977), 300.

13. Mario A. del Chiaro, *Classical Art: Sculpture* (Santa Barbara: Santa Barbara Museum of Art, 1984), 9.

14. Rose-Marie and Rainer Hagen, *Egypt: People, Gods, Pharaohs* (Cologne: Taschen, 1999), 170.

15. Del Chiaro, op. cit.

16. John Locke, *An Essay Concerning Human Understanding* (Oxford: Oxford University Press, 1975), book II, chapter 7.

17. Cole Swensen, "Some Ideas on Beauty," prepared and given at the Poetry Society of America panel on beauty in contemporary poetry, The People's Poetry Festival, New York, April 2001, at http://www.du.edu/~cswensen/beauty.html.

LIST OF ILLUSTRATIONS

BIOGRAPHY

EDUCATION

1990	Libensky Masterworks, Pilchuck Glass School, Stanwood, WA
1988–89	Massachusetts College of Art, Boston
1983–88	Parsons School of Design, New York (BA, Fine Arts)
1976–77	Royal College of Art, London
1974–75	Sir John Cass Academy of Art, London Polytechnic

PROFESSIONAL EXPERIENCE

2002–present	Trustee, Glass Alliance of Los Angeles
1999–present	Independent Designer, Daum Cristal, Paris
1990–present	Trustee, Advisory Council, Pratt Fine Arts Center, Seattle
1989	Resident Artist, Espace Verre, Montreal
1984–88	Teaching Assistant, Resident Artist, New York Experimental Glass Workshop

SOLO EXHIBITIONS

2002	Riley Hawk Galleries, Columbus, OH
2001	Imago Galleries, Palm Desert, CA
2000	Doug Macon Fine Arts, Atlanta
1999	Imago Galleries, Palm Desert, CA
1997	Leo Kaplan Modern, New York
1995	Leo Kaplan Modern, New York
1993	Habatat Gallery, Boca Raton, FL
	Leo Kaplan Modern, New York
1991	The Art Institute of Chicago, Chicago
	Kurland/Summers Gallery, Los Angeles
	Leo Kaplan Modern, New York
1988	Tennyson Gallery, Provincetown, MA
1983	Glen Smith Gallery, San Francisco

SELECTED GROUP EXHIBITIONS

1999	*Clearly Inspired*, Tampa Museum of Art
1997	*Calido*, Tucson Museum of Art, AZ
1996	*Holding the Past*, Seattle Art Museum
1993	*Contemporary Glass*, Museum of Art, Ft. Lauderdale, FL
	Maximizing the Minimum: Small Glass Sculpture, Museum of American Glass, Millville, NJ
1992	*Archives of American Art*, Smithsonian Institution, Washington, D.C.
1990	*International Exhibition of Glass*, Kanazawa, Japan
1989	*Capital Glass Invitational* (first-place award), Bethesda, MD

PUBLIC COLLECTIONS

American Museum of Glass, Millville, NJ
The Corning Museum of Glass, Corning, NY
GlasMuseum, Ebeltoft, Denmark
Los Angeles County Museum of Art
Ritz-Carlton Hotel, Atlanta
Seattle Art Museum
Tacoma Art Museum

BIBLIOGRAPHY

PERIODICALS

Neus Glass, 1990; "Corning New Review No. 11," 152.

American Craft Magazine, 1991; "Portfolio," 57–58.

Glass Art Magazine, 1991; "Choice Glass," 34.

Neus Glass, 1991; "Corning New Review No. 12," 87.

Southwest Art Magazine, 1991; "4th Dimension," 42.

American Craft Magazine, August 1992; 69–70.

Neus Glass, 1992; "Corning New Review No. 13," 89.

Santa Fe Weekly Arts & Entertainment Magazine, 1992; "Pasatiempo," 36.

Glass Art Magazine, March 1994; 2, 42, 48.

Glass Art Magazine, May 1994; cover, 2, 11.

Art News Magazine, January 1995; "Glass Art," by Matthew Kangas.

Alaska Airlines Magazine, July 1995; "Fine Art," 15.

Classic Home Magazine, summer 1995; "Endeavors Profile," 46–47.

American Style Magazine, winter 1998; 41.

Power & Motoryacht, 1998; "Megayachts," by Diane Byrne, 44–45.

Palm Springs Life, October 1999; "Gallery Scene," 68.

American Craft Magazine, October 2000; "Gallery," 114.

Art and Antiques, March 2002; 84–85.

CATALOGUES

International Exhibition of Glass Kanazawa, 1990; 171.

Christie's New York, *Masterworks of Contemporary Glass*, 1991; 30.

Habatat Galleries, *19th Annual International Glass Invitational*, 1991.

Bullseye Glass, *Contemporary Kilnformed Glass*, 1992.

Habatat Galleries, *20th Annual International Glass Invitational*, 1992.

Smithsonian Institution, *Archives of American Art*, 1992.

American Museum of Glass, *Maximizing the Minimum*, 1993; 23.

Fort Lauderdale Museum of Art, *Contemporary Glass from South Florida Collections*, 1993.

Habatat Galleries, *21st Annual International Glass Invitational*, 1993.

Leo Kaplan Modern Gallery, *Seth Randal*, 1993.

Christie's New York, *Masterworks of Contemporary Glass*, 1994; 33.

Habatat Galleries, *22nd Annual International Glass Invitational*, 1994.

Seattle Art Museum, *Holding the Past*, 1996.

Tampa Museum of Art, *Clearly Inspired—Contemporary Glass and Its Origins*, 1999; 77–79.

BOOKS

Jim Kervin and Dan Fenton, *Pâte de Verre and Kiln Casting of Glass* (Livermore, CA: GlassWear Studios, 1997), cover and two unpaginated photographs.

Richard Yelle, *Glass Art from Urbanglass* (Atglen, PA: Schiffer, 2000), 208–10.

Ray Leier, Jan Peters, and Kevin Wallace, *Contemporary Glass: Color, Light and Form* (Madison, WI: Guild, 2001), 72.

ACKNOWLEDGMENTS

I would like to thank all of the collectors and art lovers, who along with their patronage and encouragement, make me strive to do better when I think I've done my best. In particular, I would like to acknowledge and honor a special group of collectors and philanthropists, who through their tireless dedication in support of the arts, pave an easier road for future generations of artists and educators: Eve and Chap Alvord, Dale and Doug Anderson, Becky and Jack Benaroya, Anne and Marvin Cohen, Susan Steinhauser and Dan Greenberg, Jon and Mary Shirley, and the many others too numerous to mention.

This book is dedicated to the ladies in my life: my mother, my aunt Joyce, Pat Rohe, Astri Reusch, Ginny Ruffner, Becky Benaroya, Eve Alvord, and Anne Cohen.

SETH RANDAL